A COMPREHENSIVE INSTRUCTION COURSE

The Guitar ADVANTAGE

99 Lessons!

by Matthew Von Doran

To access video visit:
www.halleonard.com/mylibrary

Enter Code
3330-5822-7712-8845

ISBN: 978-1-5400-1529-7

HAL•LEONARD®

Visit Hal Leonard Online at
www.halleonard.com

Contact us:
Hal Leonard
7777 West Bluemound Road
Milwaukee, WI 53213
Email: info@halleonard.com

In Europe, contact:
Hal Leonard Europe Limited
42 Wigmore Street
Marylebone, London, W1U 2RN
Email: info@halleonardeurope.com

In Australia, contact:
Hal Leonard Australia Pty. Ltd.
4 Lentara Court
Cheltenham, Victoria, 3192 Australia
Email: info@halleonard.com.au

Table of Contents

5 **Lesson 1** Learn the parts of the guitar

6 **Lesson 2** Learn how everything is numbered

7 **Lesson 3** Learn to tune the guitar

9 **Lesson 4** Learn your first chord on the guitar: C major

11 **Lesson 5** Learn two new chords: A minor & D major

12 **Lesson 6** Learn two new chords: G major & A major

13 **Lesson 7** Learn about basic strumming technique with Preparatory Strumming Exercise #1

14 **Lesson 8** Learn three new chords: E major, E minor & E dominant 7th

15 **Lesson 9** Develop technique with "Lift & Replace"

16 **Lesson 10** Learn two new chords: D minor & A dominant 7th

17 **Lesson 11** Learn how to transition from one chord to another

19 **Lesson 12** Learn two more chord transitions

20 **Lesson 13** Learn even more chord transitions

21 **Lesson 14** Learn about basic strumming technique with Preparatory Strumming Exercise #2

22 **Lesson 15** Learn to play barre chords: F major, F minor & G minor

23 **Lesson 16** Learn how to play certain chords with different fingerings

24 **Lesson 17** Learn yet another chord transition

25 **Lesson 18** Learn how to play chord transitions in time

27 **Lesson 19** Learn about music notation for chord progressions

28 **Lesson 20** Learn a chord progression

29 **Lesson 21** Learn another chord progression

30 **Lesson 22** Learn a chord progression where chords last for only two beats

31 **Lesson 23** Learn a chord progression with four different chords in it

32 **Lesson 24** Learn the basics of strumming technique: tempo

33 **Lesson 25** Learn the basics of strumming technique: dynamics

34 **Lesson 26** Learn the basics of strumming technique: foot tapping & accents

36 **Lesson 27** Learn your first strum pattern

37 **Lesson 28** Learn another strum pattern

38 **Lesson 29** Learn yet another strum pattern

39 **Lesson 30** Learn two more strum patterns

40 **Lesson 31** Learn about strumming accuracy

41 **Lesson 32** Learn yet even two more strum patterns

42 **Lesson 33** Learn to put it all together: chord progressions & strumming patterns

43 **Lesson 34** Learn some more chord progressions & strumming patterns

44 **Lesson 35** Learn the note names on the 6th string
45 **Lesson 36** Be introduced to 16th-note strumming
46 **Lesson 37** Learn two 16th-note strum patterns
47 **Lesson 38** Learn two more 16th-note strum patterns
48 **Lesson 39** Learn how to combine 16th-note strum patterns with chord progressions
49 **Lesson 40** Learn how to create your own chord progressions & strumming patterns
50 **Lesson 41** Learn the note names on the 5th string (and a little bit of music theory)
52 **Lesson 42** Be introduced to fingerpicking
53 **Lesson 43** Learn some fingerpicking patterns
54 **Lesson 44** Learn some fingerpicking string set variations
55 **Lesson 45** Learn to fingerpick a chord progression
56 **Lesson 46** Learn a chord progression fingerpicking variation
58 **Lesson 47** Learn how to create longer fingerpicking patterns
59 **Lesson 48** Confidently know the fret numbers
60 **Lesson 49** Learn some more dominant 7th chords
61 **Lesson 50** Learn to play two chord progressions that use dominant 7th chords
62 **Lesson 51** Learn to play a full barre chord: major
63 **Lesson 52** Learn to play two more barre chords: minor & dominant 7th
65 **Lesson 53** Start to develop right hand picking technique: picking one note at a time
66 **Lesson 54** Learn the "Percussive Muted Strum"
68 **Lesson 55** Learn another major barre chord
69 **Lesson 56** Learn another minor & dominant 7th barre chord
71 **Lesson 57** Learn some more music theory: sharps & flats
74 **Lesson 58** Learn how to identify barre chords
78 **Lesson 59** Learn how to use barre chords in chord progressions
81 **Lesson 60** Learn Right Hand Picking Exercise #1
83 **Lesson 61** Learn Right Hand Picking Exercises #2 & #3
85 **Lesson 62** Learn the Pseudo-Chromatic Exercise
87 **Lesson 63** Learn the note names on the 4th, 3rd, 2nd & 1st strings
89 **Lesson 64** Learn to play hammer-ons
91 **Lesson 65** Learn to play pull-offs
93 **Lesson 66** Learn about slash chords
95 **Lesson 67** Learn the Minor Pentatonic Scale Pattern #1
97 **Lesson 68** Learn the Minor Pentatonic Scale Pattern #2
98 **Lesson 69** Learn the Minor Pentatonic Scale Pattern #3
99 **Lesson 70** Learn the Minor Pentatonic Scale Pattern #4
100 **Lesson 71** Learn the Minor Pentatonic Scale Pattern #5
101 **Lesson 72** Learn about tonic shapes

105 **Lesson 73** Learn to play hammer-ons & pull-offs with groups of three fingers
107 **Lesson 74** Learn how to play power chords
109 **Lesson 75** Learn how to play slides
111 **Lesson 76** Learn how to combine hammer-ons & pull-offs
113 **Lesson 77** Learn how to bend strings
122 **Lesson 78** Learn how to use hammer-ons & pull-offs with the Minor Pentatonic Scale Patterns (as well as explore some new fingerings)
127 **Lesson 79** Learn how to transpose scales with Transposition Drill #1
133 **Lesson 80** Learn about vibrato
134 **Lesson 81** Learn to play a blues rhythm riff
137 **Lesson 82** Learn to play a riff based on Minor Pentatonic Scale Pattern #1
139 **Lesson 83** Learn to play a riff based on Minor Pentatonic Scale Pattern #2
140 **Lesson 84** Learn to play a riff based on Minor Pentatonic Scale Pattern #3
142 **Lesson 85** Learn to play a riff based on Minor Pentatonic Scale Pattern #4
143 **Lesson 86** Learn to play a riff based on Minor Pentatonic Scale Pattern #5
145 **Lesson 87** Learn to play a jazz chord progression
146 **Lesson 88** Learn to play a jazz-blues chord progression
148 **Lesson 89** Learn Major Scale Pattern #1
150 **Lesson 90** Learn Major Scale Pattern #2
151 **Lesson 91** Learn Major Scale Pattern #3
152 **Lesson 92** Learn Major Scale Pattern #4
153 **Lesson 93** Learn Major Scale Pattern #5
154 **Lesson 94** Learn Transposition Drill #2
158 **Lesson 95** Learn to play a riff based on Major Scale Pattern #1
160 **Lesson 96** Learn to play a riff based on Major Scale Pattern #2
161 **Lesson 97** Learn to play a riff based on Major Scale Pattern #3
162 **Lesson 98** Learn to play a riff based on Major Scale Pattern #4
163 **Lesson 99** Learn to play a riff based on Major Scale Pattern #5

164 **Appendix**
- 164 The Basic Chord Vocabulary
- 166 Scale Vocabulary
- 170 Note Names on the Fretboard
- 171 Concordance
- 173 Index

176 **Biography**

Lesson 1

Learn the parts of the guitar

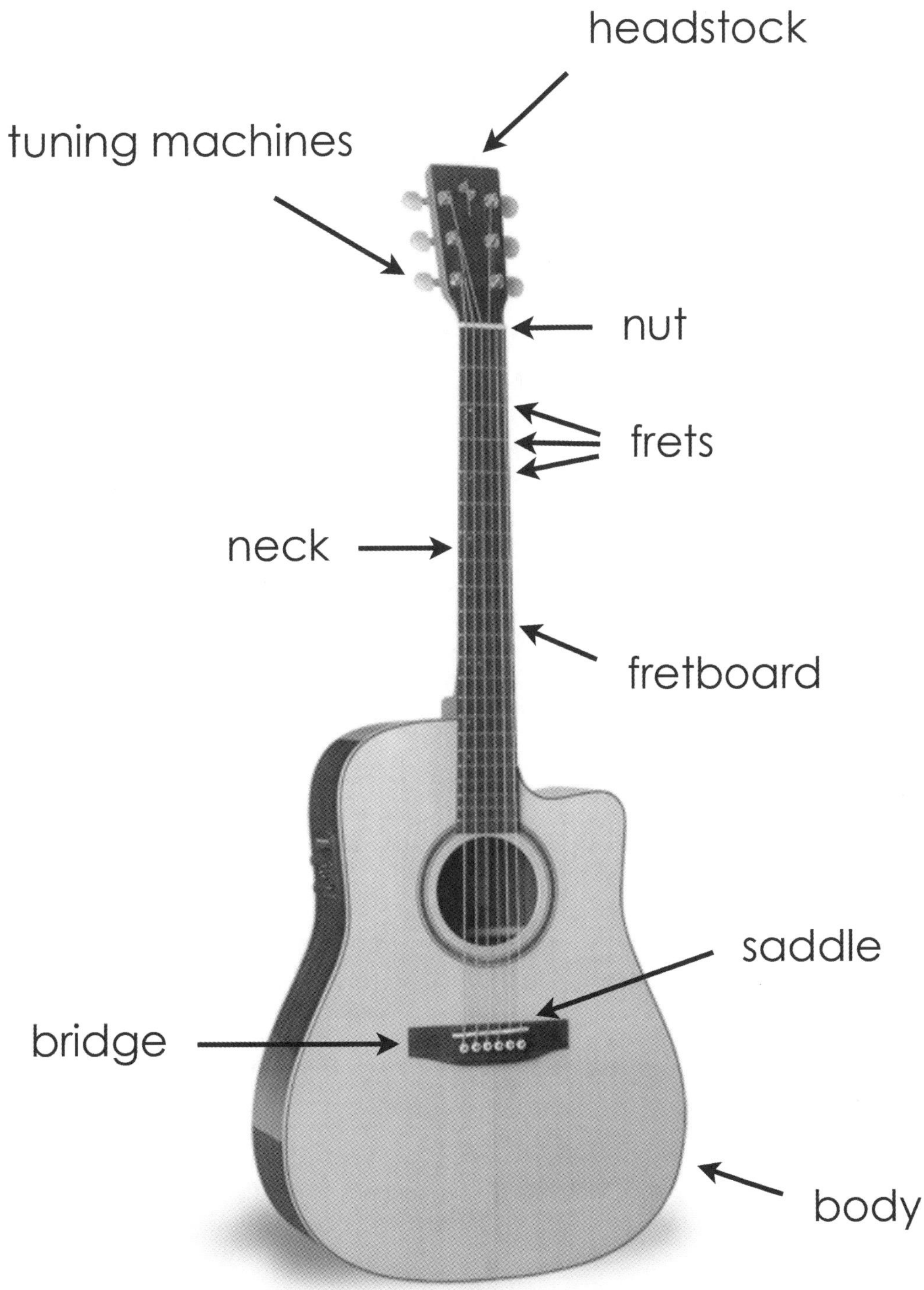

Lesson

2 Learn how everything is numbered

Strings:

1 2 3 4 5 6 *thinnest* string to *thickest* string

Frets:

nut I II III IV V etc. all the way up to the end of the fretboard

Roman numerals are commonly used for fret numbers

The dots on the fretboard (and on the side of the fretboard) are usually at these frets:

III V VII IX XII XV

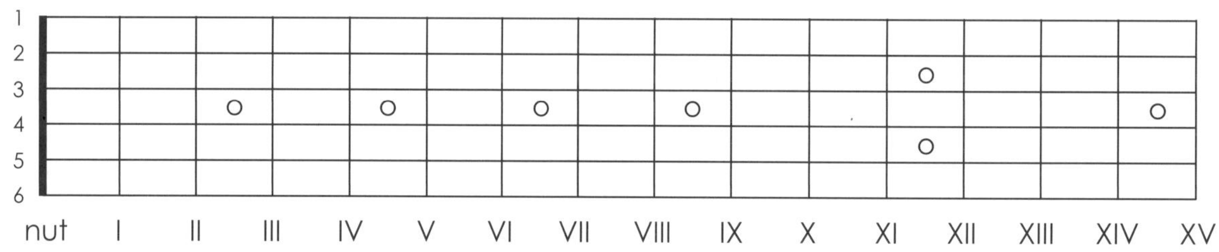

An **open string** refers to playing a string without putting a finger down on the fretboard. The **open string** notes are at the **nut**.

Fingers:

index = **1** middle = **2** ring = **3** pinky = **4**

Learn to tune the guitar

In the beginning, it's best to use an electronic tuner. There are many different kinds of tuners available. They are usually quite affordable. The tuner will come with instructions on how to use it, or you can find instructions on the manufacturer's website. Some guitars actually come with a built-in electronic tuner.

You can also learn to tune by ear. As a beginner, your ears are just starting to learn how to recognize notes so it isn't realistic to expect to be able to tune your guitar in this way. I recommend getting an electronic tuner in the beginning and then you can learn to tune by ear later.

But let's take a look at how to tune by ear now, just so you know...

Start with the 6th string tuned to the note E. It's the string that's closest to your face.

Open 6th String = E

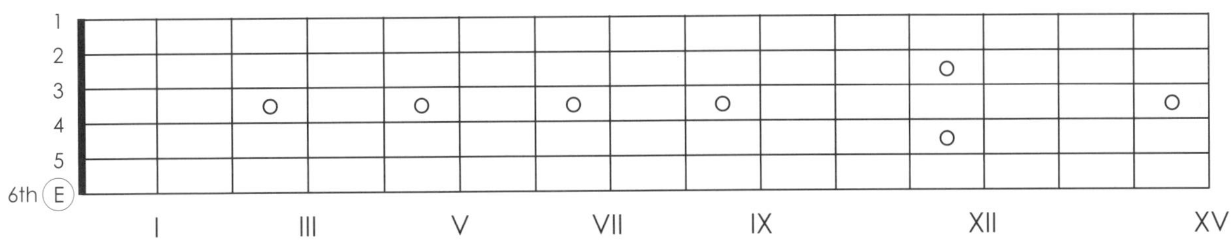

Tune the 5th string open A to the A on the 6th string, 5th fret

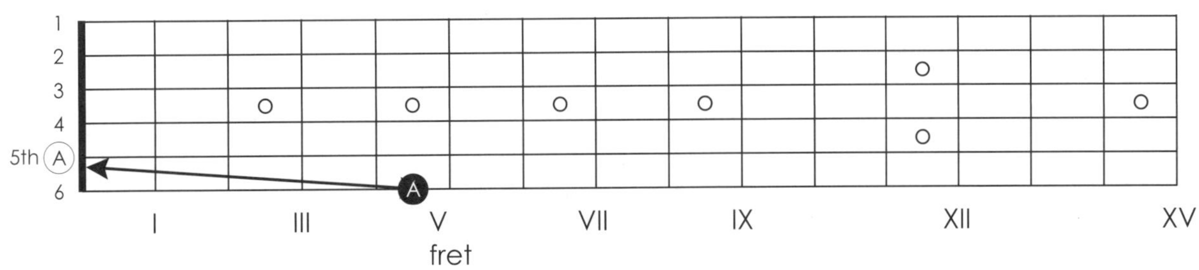

Remember, the term **open string** refers to playing a string without putting a finger down on the fretboard. The string is vibrating from the nut to the saddle.

Tune the 4th string open D to the D on the 5th string, 5th fret

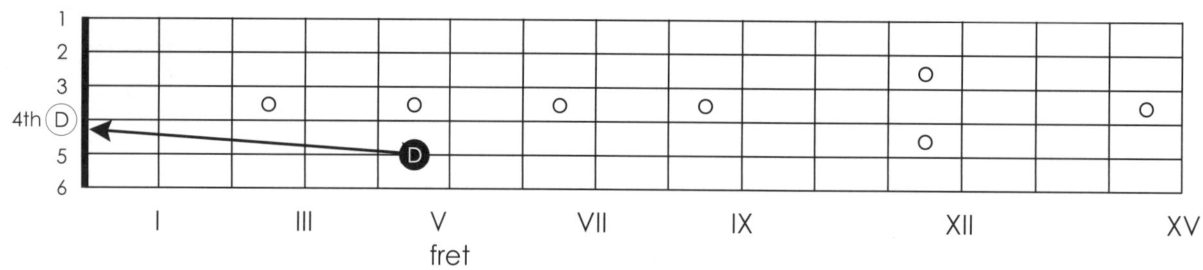

Tune the 3rd string open G to the G on the 4th string, 5th fret

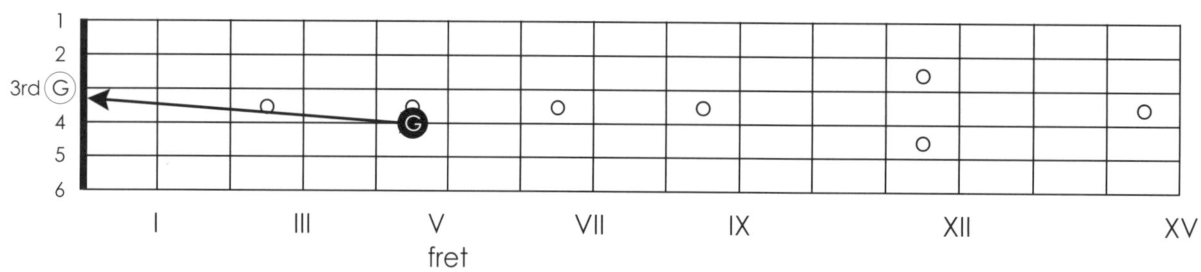

Tune the 2nd string open B to the B on the 3rd string, 4th fret

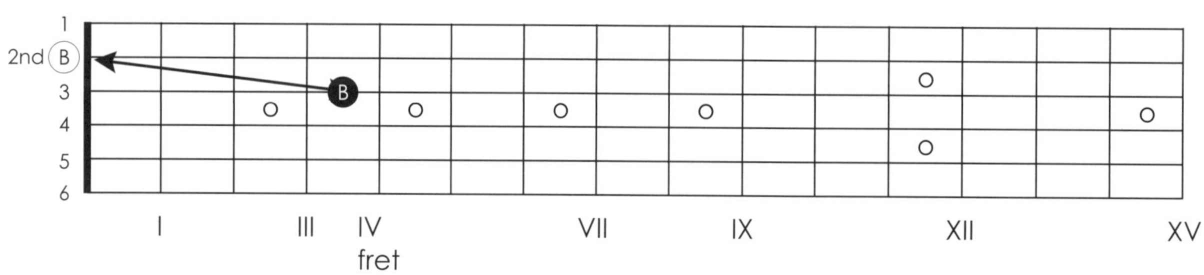

Tune the 1st string open E to the E on the 2nd string, 5th fret

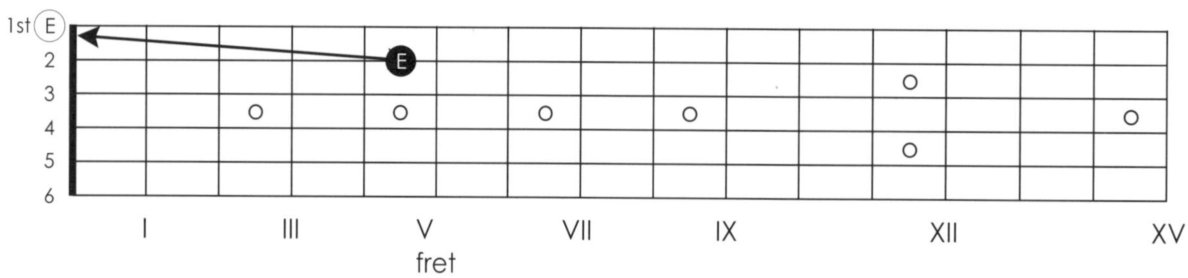

Lesson 4

Learn your first chord on the guitar: C major

The C major chord is quite often the first chord everyone learns to play. It is very common in music and a good place to start.

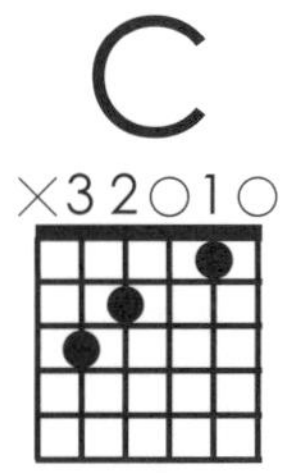

chord diagram

This chord diagram provides the information that you need to create the chord on the guitar with your hand.

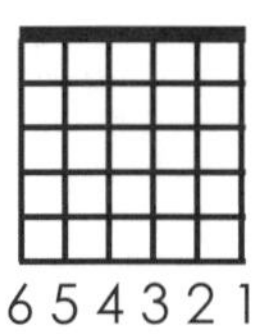

string numbers

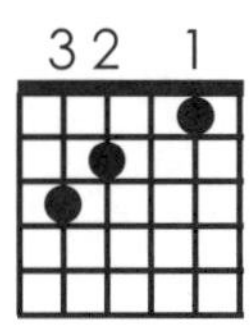

finger numbers

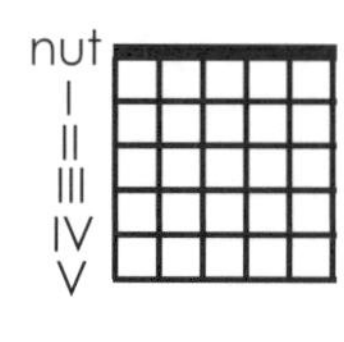

fret numbers

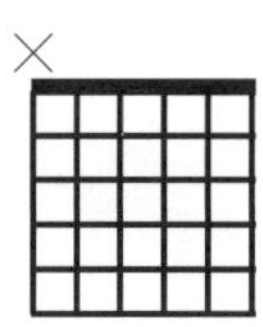

× = don't play

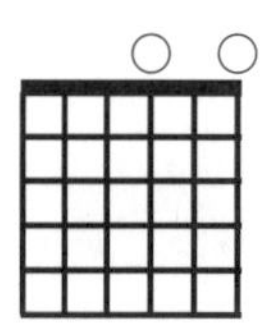

○ = open string

The best approach to learning a chord is to read the chord diagram from left to right, *one string at a time*. It's all about placing the correct finger on the correct string at the correct fret.

As you build the chord with your fingers, don't press down right away—just keep them there on the strings. Then, when you go to strum the chord with your right hand using the pick, that's when you press down on the strings with your fingertips.

So, from left to right, the C major chord goes like this:

- *6th string: don't play*
- *5th string: 3rd finger on the 3rd fret*
- *4th string: 2nd finger on the 2nd fret*
- *3rd string: open*
- *2nd string: 1st finger on the 1st fret*
- *1st string: open*

Before you strum the chord, make sure:

- *Your thumb is behind the neck*
- *Your fingers are arched*
- *Your fingertips are snug behind the frets*

Now press down on the strings with your fingertips and strum through the chord:

- *One string at a time*
- *Strum the correct amount of strings*
  (with the C major chord, you'll start your strum at the 5th string)

Listen for each note ringing out clearly.

- *Make adjustments, if necessary*

Lesson

5

Learn two new chords: A minor & D major

Remember to read the diagram carefully from left to right, one string at a time, and ask:

- *What string?*
- *What finger?*
- *What fret?*

These three pieces of information will enable you to place your fingers accurately every time.

Before you strum the chord, always make sure:

- *Your thumb is behind the neck.*
- *Your fingers are arched.*
- *Your fingertips are snug behind the frets.*

Lesson 6

Learn two new chords: G major & A major

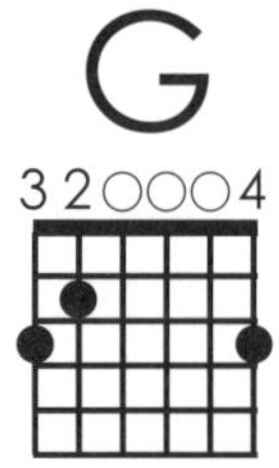

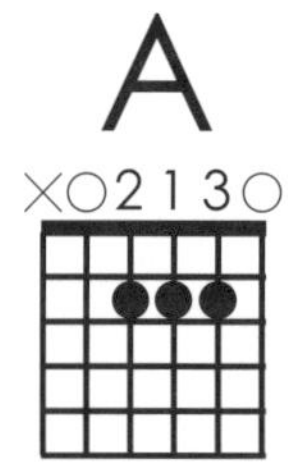

If the strings don't ring clearly when you strum, make adjustments with your left hand:

- *Is your thumb is behind the neck?*
- *Are your fingers arched?*
- *Are your fingertips snug behind the frets?*

Quite often, the reason why a string isn't sounding clearly (it makes a "thump" or "buzz" when you pick it) is that the back of another finger is touching it. Make sure you have clearance between the strings and the backs of the fingers on the other strings.

Sometimes, just a slight adjustment will make a huge difference.

Lesson 7

Learn about basic strumming technique with Preparatory Strumming Exercise # 1

This exercise is extremely basic. It is designed to "teach" the strumming motion to your arm. By doing this for at least three to five minutes a day, you will be prepared for the upcoming lessons on strumming technique.

This kind of exercise is what we'll call an "accelerator." It helps you achieve more results in a shorter period of time.

Procedure:

- Grab the neck and strings with the left hand so that the strings are muted.
- Hold the pick in your right hand and strum the strings in an up and down motion.
- Strive for a smooth, continuous even motion.
- Make sure your pick strums all six strings during both the down and the up strums.

Lesson 8

Learn three new chords: E major, E minor & E dominant 7th

There are three chord "families": major, minor and dominant 7th (more about this later).

These three chords all have six strings in them.

Can you see how they have notes in common?

E

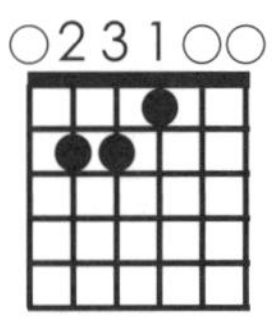

Em

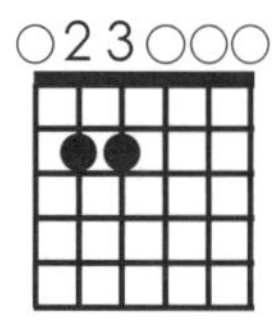

E7

In all three chords, the 2nd finger is on the 5th string at the 2nd fret.

The 6th, 2nd and 1st strings are open in all three chords.

Lesson 9

Develop technique with "Lift & Replace"

This is a simple practice that will teach your fingers to land simultaneously on the fretboard.

You've been building your chords one note, one string, at a time. This is a great way to begin, however, this approach is very different from how you will do it when you play chords in songs.

When you transition from one chord to the next in music, you must get to the next chord quickly and accurately. Most importantly, you must have the fingers land *simultaneously*!

This exercise will help you develop that skill.

Procedure:

- Grab any one of the chords you've learned so far.
- Slowly lift your fingertips off the fretboard while maintaining the shape of the chord. Lift them up just a little bit, about a quarter of an inch.
- Place your fingertips back on the strings, making sure to place them *simultaneously*.
- Repeat this three or four times with the same chord.
- Do this procedure with *all* the chords you learn.

Lesson 10

Learn two new chords: D minor & A dominant 7th

Here are two more chords for you to learn.

Dm

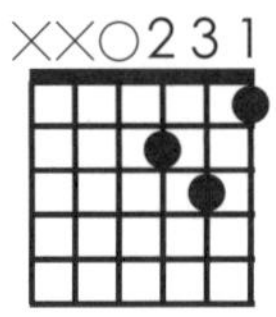

A7

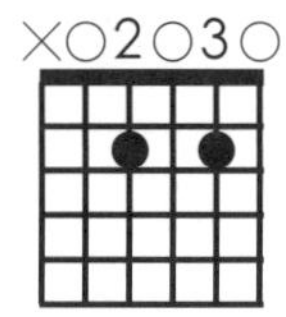

This would be a good time to review the process on how to finger chords accurately and cleanly.

Grab the chord one note at a time:

- *What string?*
- *What finger?*
- *What fret?*

Refer to this technique list and make adjustments, if necessary:

- *Thumb behind neck*
- *Arch fingers*
- *Fingertips snug behind frets*

Strum through chord:

- *Make sure you strum the correct number of strings*
- *Strum one string at a time so you can hear each note*

Make adjustments, if necessary:

- *Refer to the technique list*

Learn how to transition from one chord to another

We will start with these two chords, C major and A minor.

To transition between the two chords, you will only have to move the 3rd finger.

Make sure to keep the 1st and 2nd fingers right where they are.

Strum the C chord once, then pick up the 3rd finger and place it on the 3rd string at the 2nd fret. This action creates the Am chord.

Now strum the A minor (Am) chord once.

Pick up and place the 3rd finger back on the 5th string at the 3rd fret. You have returned to the C major chord.

Continue to go back and forth between the two chords for a few minutes. Strum each chord only once. Do all of this *slowly and calmly*.

The 1st and 2nd fingers are called **common fingers**.

common finger = same finger
same string
same fret

Now let's learn another chord transition using A minor and E major.

Am

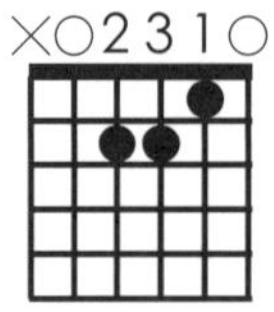

E

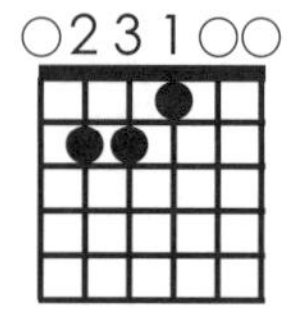

These two chords have a **similar shape**. The fingers are in the same basic configuration although on different strings. The brain loves to see similarities in shapes. This will help you learn and memorize chords.

Important!

Make sure you place your fingertips *simultaneously*! This is fundamental to making smooth chord transitions.

Also, pay attention to the fact that A minor has five strings and E major has six strings, so make sure you strum the correct number of strings.

Again, just casually go back and forth between these two chords, one strum each, for a few minutes (*or longer*). Remember: the more you do it, the quicker your guitar playing skills will develop.

Lesson 12

Learn two more chord transitions

Remember, the goal here is to strive for placing your fingers on the strings simultaneously!

This is what the "Lift & Replace" exercise in Lesson 9 prepared you for.

With G major and C major, you have a **similar shape** with the 3rd and 2nd fingers in each chord. Just pick those two fingers up as a single shape and move them over a set of strings. Meanwhile, the 1st and 4th fingers go where they need to go as you move from one chord to the other.

G

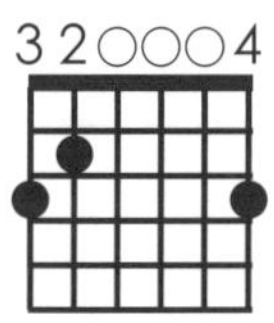

C

With the D minor and A7 transition, we have a new finger movement we'll call a **guide finger**. Keep your 3rd finger down on the string as you slide the finger from the 3rd fret to the 2nd fret (but don't push down too hard as you slide).

guide finger = same finger
same string
different fret

Dm

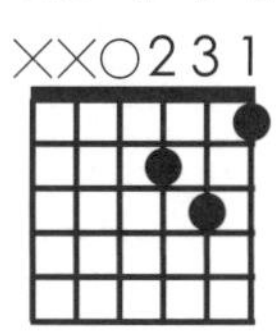

A7

Lesson 13

Learn even more chord transitions

Remember to look for **similar shapes**, **common fingers** and **guide fingers** when going from one chord to the next. Sometimes they are hidden within the movements of the fingers.

Here, with E major and A major, there is a guide finger on the 3rd string. Keep the 1st finger down on the 3rd string as you transition from E to A and from A to E.

E

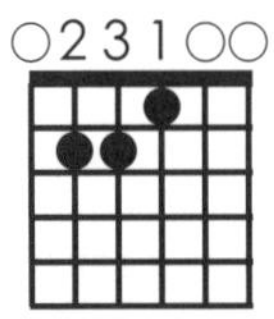

A

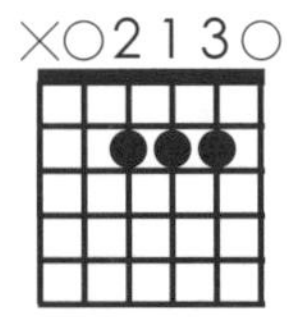

With A major and D major, you have a common finger and a guide finger. Can you find where they are?

A

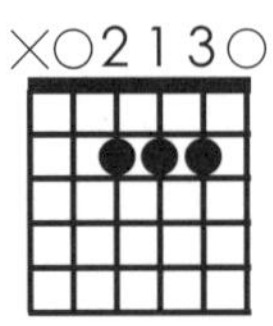

D

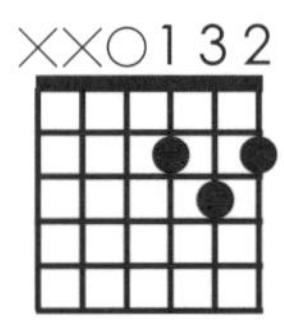

The 1st finger is a common finger and the 3rd finger is a guide finger.

Learn about basic strumming technique with Preparatory Strumming Exercise #2

Lesson **14**

This exercise is an extension of the Preparatory Strumming Exercise #1. The only difference is that you will be holding a chord instead of muting the strings.

You will now learn how it feels to strum the strings as they ring out, just like you experience when you strum chords while playing a song.

Procedure:

- Grab an E major chord with the left hand.
- Hold the pick in your right hand and strum the strings in an up and down motion
- Strive for a smooth, continuous *even* motion.
- Make sure your pick strums all six strings during both the down and up strums.

Again, do this for at least three to five minutes a day. The more you practice,the quicker your musical skills will develop.

Lesson 15

Learn to play barre chords: F major, F minor & G minor

These three new chords will introduce you to the technique of barring. This is where you hold down two or more strings with the same finger at the same fret. Chords that use the barring technique are called **barre chords**.

Roll your first finger to the left to give yourself better leverage as you hold down the two, or the three, strings.

Whenever you learn new chords, practice by forming the chord shape one note at a time and getting all the strings to ring out clearly. Then take your hand off the guitar and shake it out a little. Next, carefully reform the chord again.

Do all of this a few times and then move on to the next chord shape. Eventually your fingers will get the idea of how to grab each chord accurately and quickly.

Learn how to play certain chords with different fingerings

Lesson 16

It is a good thing to know more than one way to finger some of these chords you are learning. These alternate fingerings will help you transition between other chords in a smooth and efficient manner.

When you practice the G major, E minor and A dominant 7th chords, practice each chord with both fingerings so that you can use whichever fingering works best depending on what chord you're going to, or what chord you're coming from.

G

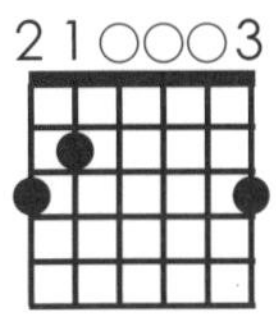

Em

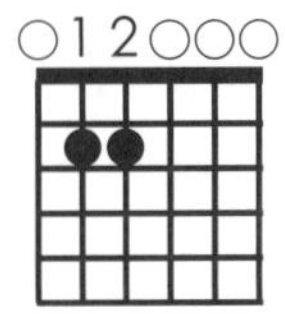

A7

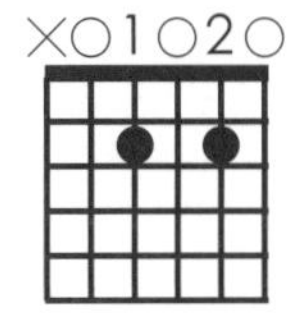

Lesson 17

Learn yet another chord transition

This chord transition uses the chords from Lesson 16. It is good to apply a new fingering right after you learn it.

Once again, focus on *simultaneous* finger placement as you move deliberately from the E minor back to the G major.

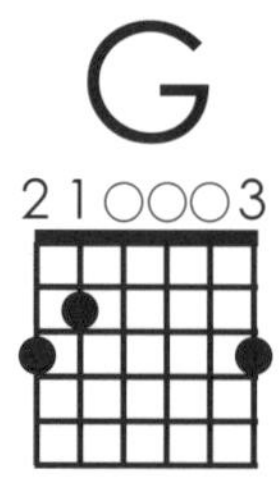

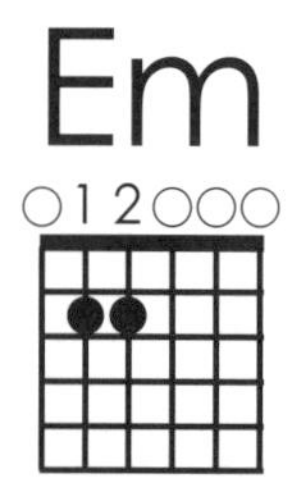

I bet you discovered the common 1st finger on the 5th string, didn't you?

This is a good time to address how sometimes your fingers are side by side and cramped together, making it challenging to keep your fingertips snug behind the fret. The main thing is to do the best you can to get the fingertip as close to the fret as possible. You'll know if you are too far away from the fret because the string will start to make a rattling noise as it vibrates against the fret.

Lesson

Learn how to play chord transitions in time

18

This will be our first experience of dealing with rhythm. It is a very important aspect of music.

You might not realize this yet, but you already possess a strong sense of time and this lesson will be the start of your development of a connection with your own inner rhythm.

Procedure:

- Strum each chord four times, using all down strums.
- Focus on keeping the strums evenly spaced. Go slowly at first.
- Loop the chord combination back and forth repeatedly for a few minutes with each chord combination.

Important!

If you can't make the chord transition and maintain the rhythm, go back to doing one strum each chord for a while. This will increase your ability to move from one chord to the next in a smooth and accurate manner. Then, go back to doing four strums per chord and see if you can maintain the tempo (the rate of speed of your down strums) without any pauses between the chords.

Your chord technique sometimes develops in phases so it will help to be patient with the process.

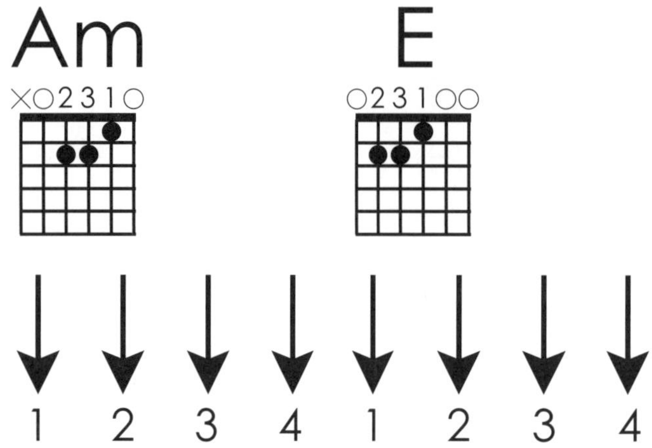
Am
×○231○
E
○231○○
1 2 3 4 1 2 3 4

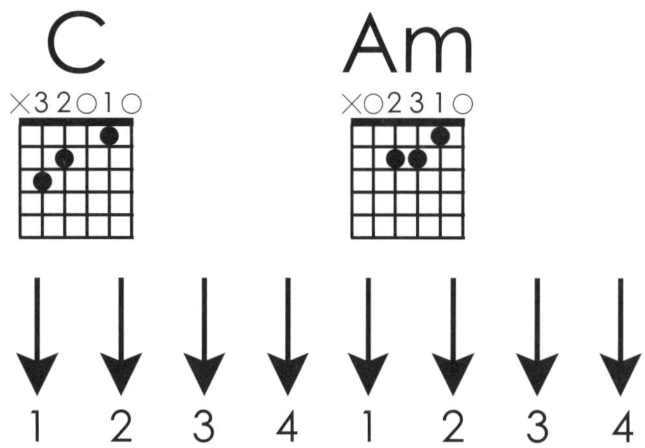
C
×32○1○
Am
×○231○
1 2 3 4 1 2 3 4

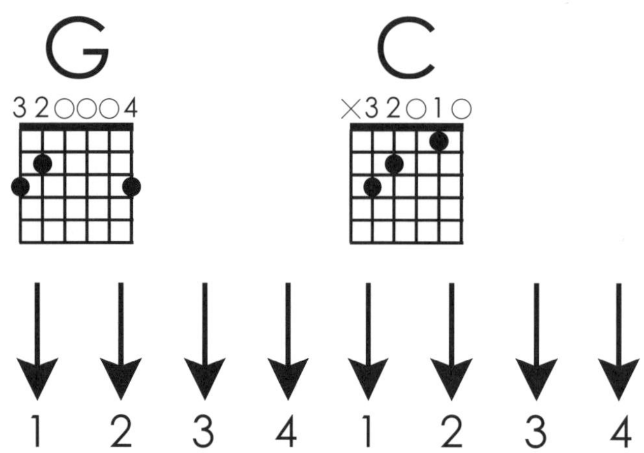
G
32○○○4
C
×32○1○
1 2 3 4 1 2 3 4

Lesson
19

Learn about music notation for chord progressions

This is how chord progressions are commonly notated in the world of music. Becoming familiar with these symbols now will help you learn songs quickly and easily.

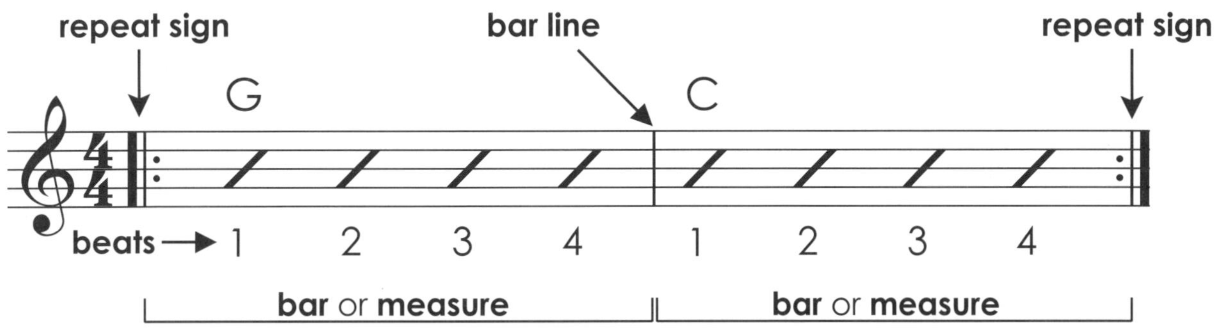

Note: Although it might look like it, the hash marks (diagonal lines) are not indicating strumming. They are there to help you visually keep track of the **beats** as you read the music. The beat is the "pulse" of the music. You feel this pulse when you connect to the rhythm of music.

Treble Clef

This symbol is at the beginning of a line of music notation.

Its true meaning is not necessary for you to know yet. Right now, you can just say it looks cool!

Time Signature

The top number tells you how many beats are in the bar.

The bottom number is something you won't need to deal with for now—we'll get to it later.

Lesson 20

Learn a chord progression

Here is what a chord progression looks like using notation:

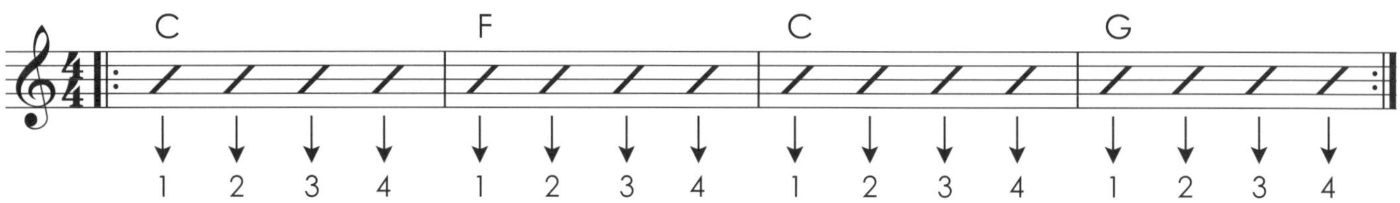

Strum each chord with four down strums. The down arrows are strum indicators and are not usually there below the chord progression notation. They are written here so that you can see what your strumming hand is doing.

But, remember, those hash marks are *not* strum indicators. They are there to help your eyes keep track of the beats in the bar and to let you know how many beats each chord receives.

For your convenience, here are the chords needed for this progression. At this point, it is realistic to find that you are starting to memorize the chords and their names.

C

F

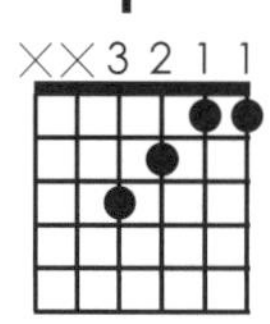

G

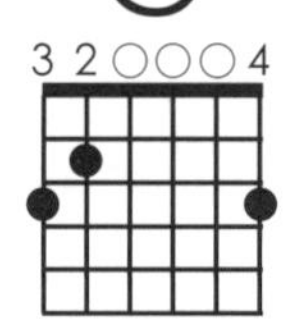

Learn another chord progression

Lesson 21

Learning these short chord progression exercises is preparing you for what you will be doing when you start to play complete songs.

This is an excellent way to learn any new skill in life: break it down into smaller goals so that your mind can focus on the details. Then put it all back together to see the big picture.

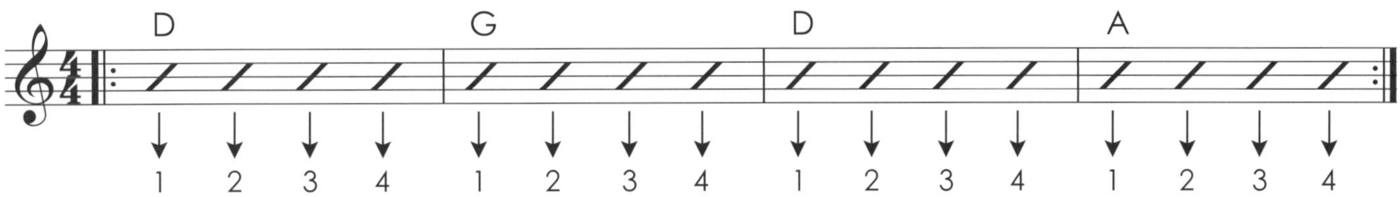

It's good to start with going through the chords one strum each, out of time, for a few minutes. This teaches the chord transitions to your left hand. Then move on to doing the four strums with each chord, in time.

Also, counting aloud with your strumming will help you develop a conscious awareness of time and rhythm.

Notice that the G major fingering is the 2-1-3 fingering.

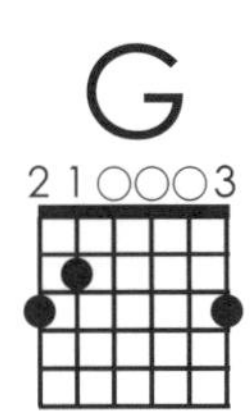

Lesson 22

Learn a chord progression where chords last for only two beats

This chord progression uses the same chords as in Lesson 20. However, they are in a different order and some of the chords last for only two beats instead of four.

These kinds of details are what you will be encountering on your path to learning guitar and playing songs.

Make sure you are using the 3–2–4 fingering for the G major chord.

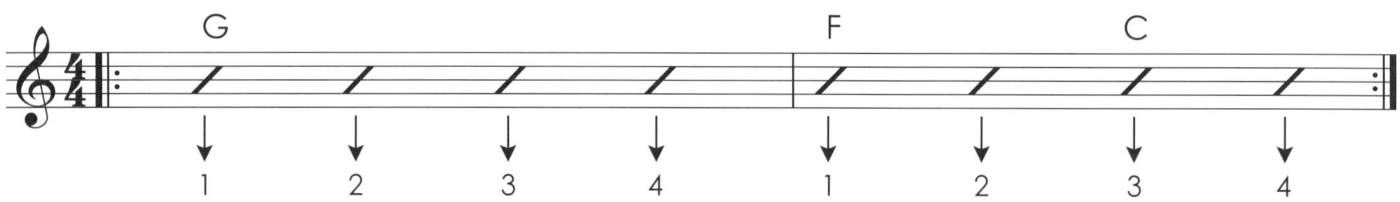

Focus on making smooth transitions between the chords. After you can go from one chord to the next with just one strum each at a casual pace, start to play the progression “in time”, meaning that you are keeping a consistent beat as you strum G major for four strums and F major and C major for two strums each.

Learn a chord progression with four different chords in it

There are some chords you will commonly see together in chord progressions that have been popular for a good long time. This progression goes back a few hundred years and you might also recognize it as being in a few modern pop or rock songs.

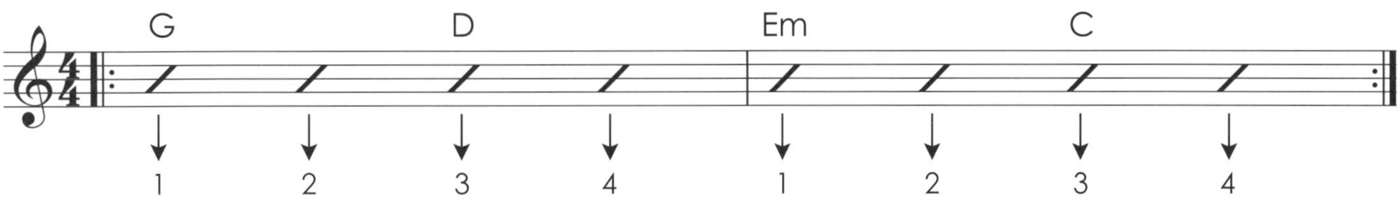

Remember to look for efficient fingering movements. Here you have a common finger (the 2nd finger) between the E minor and the C major chords. This is why you want to use the 1–2 fingering for the E minor. Also, you have the similar shape between the G major and the C major.

Another thing to be aware of is strumming accuracy with your right hand. Notice that each chord has a certain amount of strings in it and you need to pay attention to where you start your down strum as you transition between the chords in the chord progression.

Lesson

24 Learn the basics of strumming technique: tempo

As you know, some music is fast, some music is slow and some music is anywhere in between. This lesson will allow you to experience what it is like to strum at various tempos.

tempo = the rate of speed of the music

While holding an E major chord, spend a few minutes strumming at different tempos. Pay attention to your right arm, wrist and hand as you continuously strum the chord in a steady up and down motion.

Remember to make sure you are strumming all six strings on both the down and the up strum. *Keep the arm and wrist relaxed.*

Count aloud as you strum: "1 & 2 & 3 & 4 &". This will really help you develop your sense of rhythm and enable you to learn the strum patterns of songs quickly.

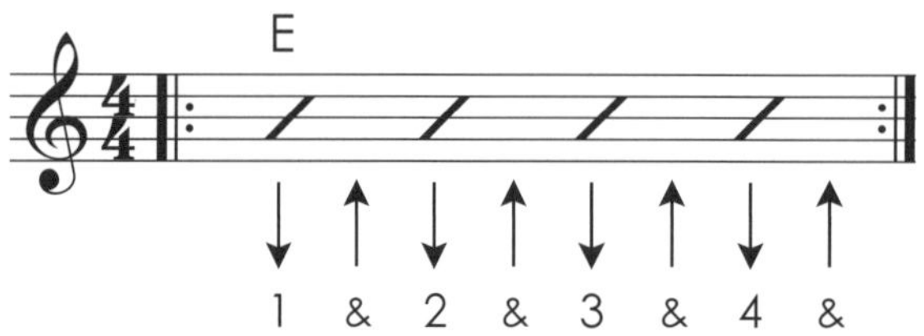

As you play, be aware of the fact that you are in control of how fast or slow you strum. Let your arm and your body learn what it *feels* like to move at different tempos.

It is good to cultivate an explorative mindset, meaning that you want to experience the different aspects of the musicianship skills you are developing right now. Spend some time experimenting with strumming at various tempos.

Lesson 25

Learn the basics of strumming technique: dynamics

When you strum, you want to be able to control the volume of your strums. It's about changing from loud to soft and soft to loud, and every volume in between. This range of volume refers to one of the more expressive qualities of music: **dynamics**. It allows the music to "breathe."

dynamics = volume = the range of loud to soft

Like you did with tempo, experiment with different volumes of strumming. Explore the range of loud to soft so that you see what that *feels* like. Each practice session, spend a few minutes strumming at soft, medium and loud levels of volume.

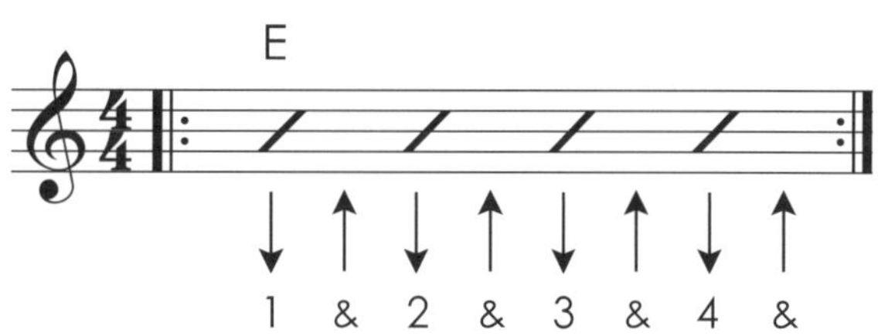

How hard you strum is the dominant factor in the resulting volume, but another way to control your dynamics is with your pick grip.

- When you grip the pick *tightly*, the volume *increases*.
- When you grip the pick *loosely*, the volume *decreases*.

So experiment with that as well.

As you learn to play any instrument, your awareness changes and expands so that when you listen to music performances, either live or recorded, you will hear at a deeper level. You will hear more details.

The next time you are listening to music, see what you notice about **tempo** and **dynamics**.

Lesson 26

Learn the basics of strumming technique: foot tapping & accents

Tapping your foot while you play is a good way to maintain a steady beat. In the beginning, it might feel like it's another thing to keep track of while you are developing all of your playing skills, but you will find that foot tapping will quickly become a subconscious movement for you and that it will help you play consistently.

Tap your foot only on the beats: 1 2 3 4

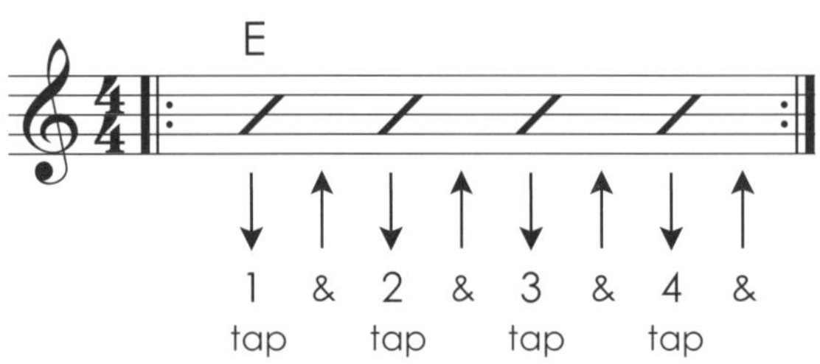

Now let's take a look at accents.

Accents are a part of dynamics in music. They add interest to the rhythm.

accent = > = slightly louder

We'll put an accent on beat 1. This will be a simple way to start learning how to use dynamics in your playing.

After you get used to the accent, add the counting aloud and the foot tapping back into the experience.

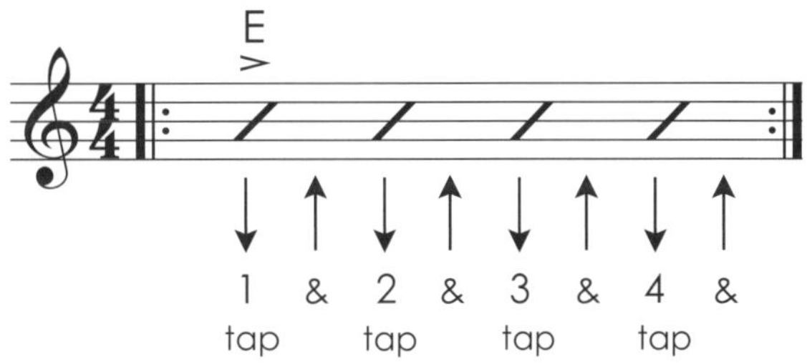

A good way to get all this strumming technique to a solid, comfortable level is to set a timer for five minutes and strum a chord consistently while you tap your foot, count aloud and accent beat one. The more you do this, the quicker your strumming technique will develop.

Accents don't always have to be on beat one—they can be on any strum, down or up. After you get comfortable with playing the accent on the first beat, spend some time experimenting with putting one in different places. Also, you can have as many accents as you like in a pattern.

One more thing...

When you listen to (and watch) guitarists playing, pay attention to their strumming dynamics. Notice how some of the strums are at various levels of loud and soft. Sometimes there is a consistent pattern to it and sometimes it just seems to randomly *flow*.

This kind of *focused listening* is really helpful to you in your growth as a musician.

Lesson

27 Learn your first strum pattern

The steady strum pattern we've been using so far is a common way to approach strumming the guitar in many songs. Yet there are many possible variations, so we will now explore how to create these variations by "taking strums out" of the basic pattern.

This will be designated by a dotted arrow. When there's a dotted arrow, simply *miss the strings* when you move your arm in that direction.

Here we have a dotted arrow on the "&" of beat 1.

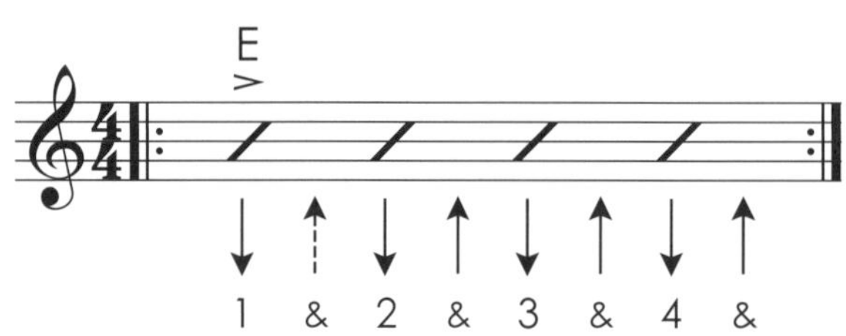

It's a good idea to start by just "walking" through the pattern with your arm. In other words, don't try to play it in tempo, just move your arm in the direction of the arrows, one after another. Either you hit the strings or you don't, depending on if it's a solid arrow or a dotted arrow.

Once your arm (and your brain) gets the idea, then you can start playing the pattern in time. Then you can loop the pattern continuously, meaning play it over and over. That's what the **repeat signs** (double barlines and double dots) at the beginning and end are telling you to do: to repeat that bar, in this case, over and over.

When you're comfortable with all of that, you can add the other elements in one at a time: counting, foot tapping and accenting.

Learn another strum pattern

Lesson **28**

This strum pattern has a dotted arrow on the down strum on beat 3.

Here we are using a G major chord just to change things up a little. You can use any six string chord you would like for your strumming patterns (we'll talk later about what's involved with strumming four and five string chords).

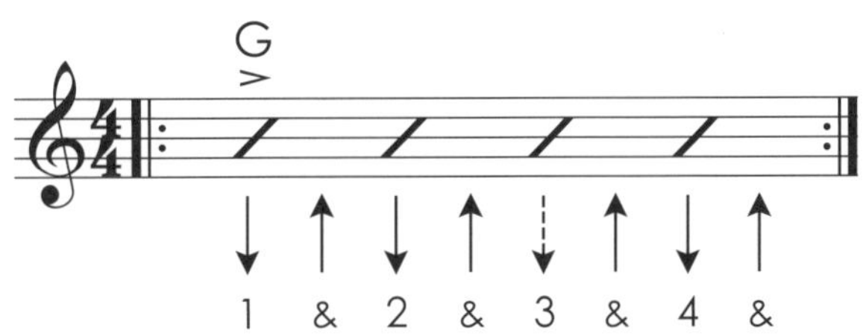

Remember to break this all down and deal with all of the particulars one at a time:

- *The arrows: solid or dotted*
- *Counting*
- *Foot tapping*
- *Accents*
- *Repeating the pattern (looping)*

Then you can put it all back together and spend as much time as you can looping the strum pattern over and over until it feels natural.

That's why using a timer is such a good idea. Try setting it for five minutes and just focus on playing the strumming pattern.

Important!

Remember to strive for a consistent steady arm motion.

Lesson 29

Learn yet another strum pattern

This strum pattern has two dotted arrows in it. There is one on the "&" of beat 1 and on beat 3.

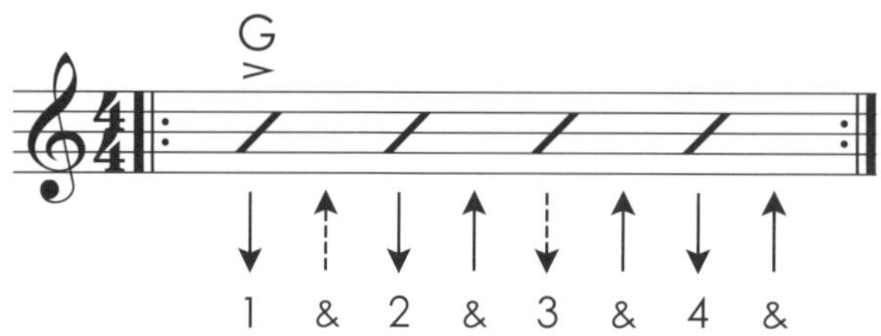

No matter how many dotted arrows are in a pattern, your arm motion should eventually look the same as it does with the very first strum pattern, where you were playing all solid arrows. This is essential to a smooth musical feel when you are strumming the guitar.

Remember to start off slowly and focus on each of the different aspects individually, then you can put it all back together and have your arm move consistently and evenly.

So now that you have a few strum patterns to work on, spend at least two or three minutes on each. Eventually your body and mind will internalize the patterns and you won't have to think so much while you play...

It will all just flow.

Lesson 30

Learn two more strum patterns

By practicing these patterns, you are laying a foundation for your rhythm guitar playing that will serve you for the rest of your musical life.

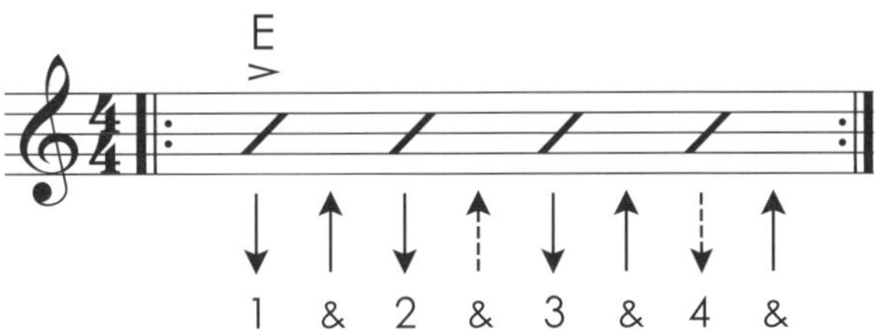

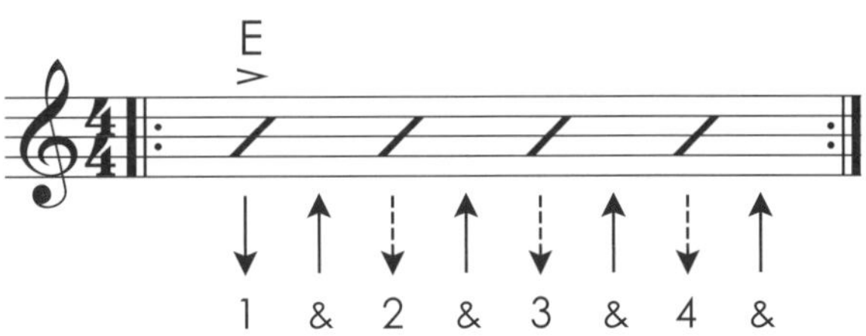

You are probably starting to realize that you can put dotted arrows almost anywhere and create a rhythmically interesting strum pattern. Perhaps after learning these two new patterns, you could explore coming up with your own strum patterns.

Lesson 31

Learn about strumming accuracy

Now that you are getting comfortable with the mechanics of strumming the strings, it is time to see what it is like to strum chords that have less than six strings in them. Chords such as C major, D major, A major or A minor only have four or five strings in them. If you haven't noticed yet, if you hit one of those "X" strings, sometimes it just sounds a little off... and sometimes it sounds pretty awful. Try strumming an F major chord with the 5th and 6th strings open and see how that sounds. Strumming accuracy is very important! Yet it is also important to maintain the flow and feel of a steady strum pattern, so trying to *not hit* the 6th or 5th string is a challenge.

One of the ways to deal with this is to mute the string that is not in the chord. For example, C major is a 5-string chord—the 6th string has an "X" on it. But if you put your thumb over the neck and touch the 6th string, it will be muted and it won't ring if you hit it with your pick. I know we've established that effective left hand guitar technique involves keeping the thumb *behind* the neck, but in this case, putting your thumb over the neck serves a purpose.

Another way of muting the unwanted 6th string in a C major chord is to move your 3rd fingertip over a bit and use it to mute the 6th string. This approach allows you to keep your thumb behind the neck for good leverage.

There is another way to keep your right hand strumming more accurate and it is more of a mental trick. In your head, imagine you are striving to only strum one less string than what is actually in the chord. For example, with a D chord, you could maybe mute the 6th string with your thumb, but what about the 5th string? Pretend it is a 3-string chord and strum freely and you will find that you will most likely hit four strings.

The reality is that for each chord there are specific approaches that are subtle, yet effective, in muting unwanted strings so that you can strum without compromising the flow and "groove" of the strum pattern. This lesson was designed to introduce you to this aspect of guitar technique. So now you can start practicing your strum patterns using any of the chords with four and five strings in them, as well as the 6-string chords, and start experimenting with these ways to achieve strum accuracy.

Lesson 32

Learn yet even two more strum patterns

So, by now you know what to do... break it down and work on the new strum pattern slowly. Then build it back up so that you are strumming the pattern smoothly and consistently with all the particulars: counting, accents, steady arm motion, etc.

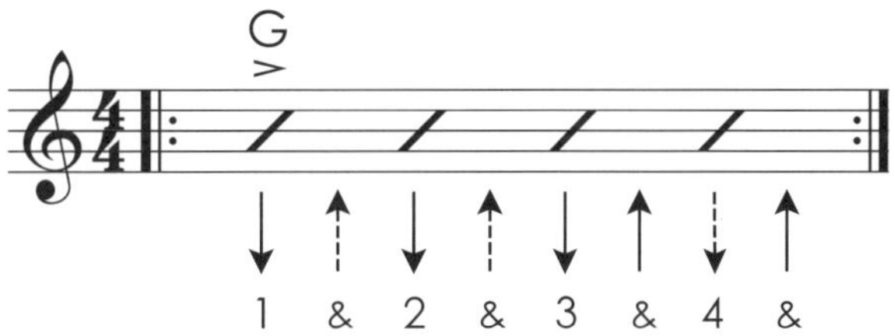

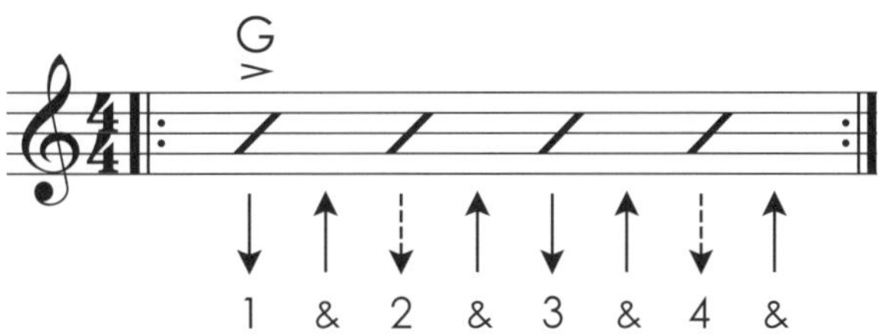

At this point, you have quite a collection of strum patterns to work on. By spending a few minutes on each, every time your practice, you will be well on your way to being a guitarist with strong rhythm technique.

Lesson 33

Learn to put it all together: chord progressions & strumming patterns

We've been focusing on each hand separately and now it is time to bring it all together in a way that represents what you will be doing a lot of as a modern guitarist: strumming chord progressions.

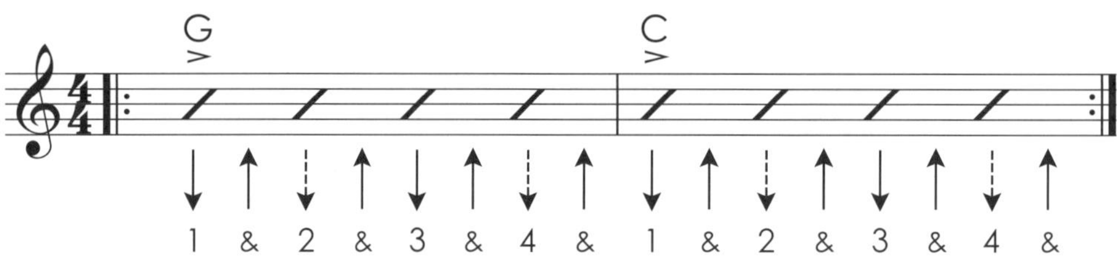

- Start by making sure you can smoothly transition between the two chords.
- Then work on just the strum pattern by itself.
- Then combine the two. Go slowly!!
- Work up to where you can maintain the chord progression for a few minutes at a time.

Important!

Pay attention to the chord transitions so that you don't pick up your fingers until the last possible moment (even when playing at a slow tempo). Otherwise, you might hit the open strings on the up strum on the "&" of beat 4.

Learn some more chord progressions & strumming patterns

Lesson

34

Once you get the idea about how strum patterns can be combined with chord progressions, you can take any of the strum patterns you've learned so far and pair them up with any of the chord progressions. Any combination of the two will work and sound musical.

That's a big part of what this has been about so far: developing a vocabulary of chords, chord combinations and strum patterns. These things are often what you'll be using the most of when you learn to play songs.

Here are a couple of examples using previous chord combinations and strum patterns.

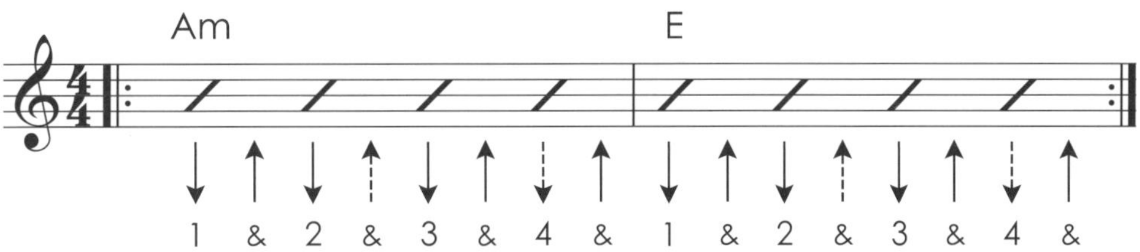

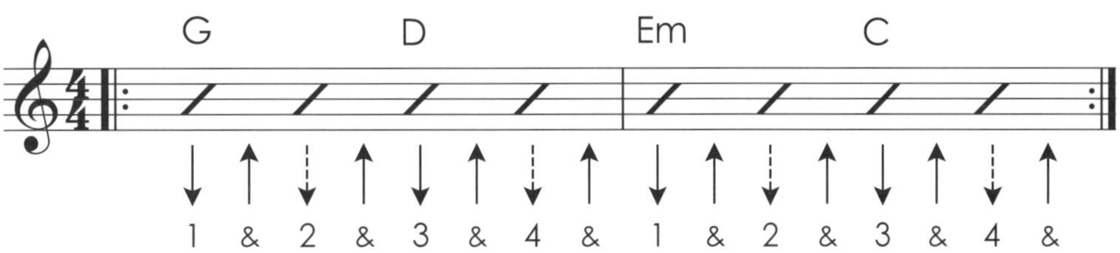

Lesson

35 Learn the note names on the 6th string

Knowing what each note on the fretboard is called is a valuable skill to develop as a guitarist. Starting to work on it now will enable you to be prepared down the road when you need it to function with barre chords, scale patterns and music theory.

This simple drill is designed to teach you the note names in an efficient and thorough manner. It works by breaking down the goal of learning the note names on the guitar fretboard to one string at a time. We shall start with the 6th string.

Here are the names of the notes on the 6th string:

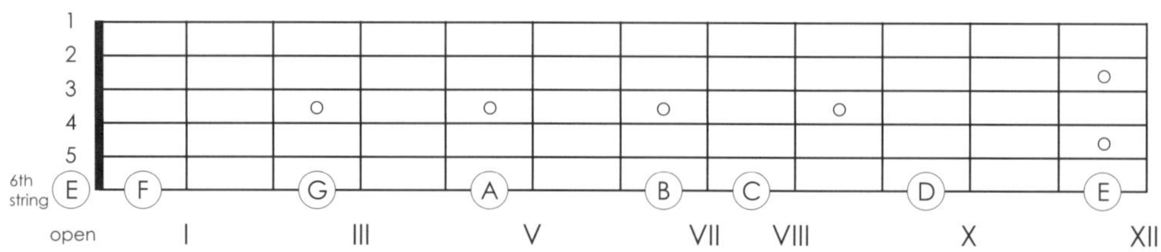

Drill:

- Choose a note name randomly: C D E F G A B
- Find that note on the 6th string and play it with your 1st finger
- Choose another note name, find it and play it (go slowly)
- Continue in this manner for at least five minutes

Important!

- Use first finger only
- Always play both E's and go to the closest E first
- For open E, put 1st finger behind nut
- Be sure you pay attention to what the fret number is for each note name

And one more thing...

Notice that E and F and B and C are one fret apart. All the other notes are two frets apart (more about this later).

Lesson **36**

Be introduced to 16th-note strumming

Now you will learn another way to approach strum patterns.

In rhythmic music theory, we have 8th notes and we have 16th notes. For now, you do not need to know the details of each except for how it works out with the down strums and the up strums per beat and per bar (or measure).

eighth notes = two strums per beat x four beats = 8 strums per bar

sixteenth notes = four strums per beat x four beats = 16 strums per bar

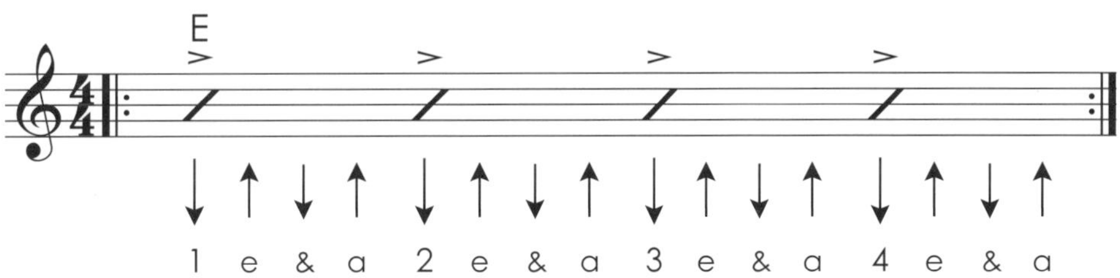

We use "e & a" along with the beat number to count aloud. This helps us keep track of the 16th-note rhythm for each beat.

Make sure you tap your foot only on beats 1, 2, 3 and 4, not with every down strum, which is what we did for 8th-note strumming.

Also, put an accent on each beat. That will help you really feel the 16th notes.

Strum this basic 16th-note pattern for a few minutes each practice session and you will quickly internalize this new strum. You will soon be creating variations using dotted arrows, just like we did with the 8th-note strum patterns.

Lesson 37

Learn two 16th-note strum patterns

Once again we will add dotted arrows to indicate a "missed strum". This will create the rhythmic interest. Space in music is as important as the notes.

Remember to break it down like we'e been doing. There are more strums to keep track of here, so going slowly will enable you to process the information.

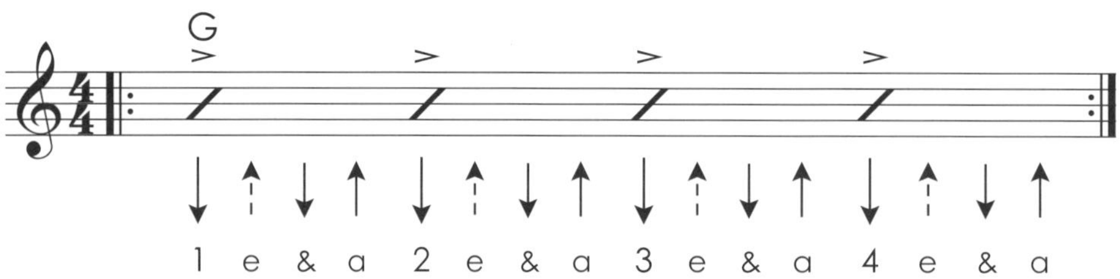

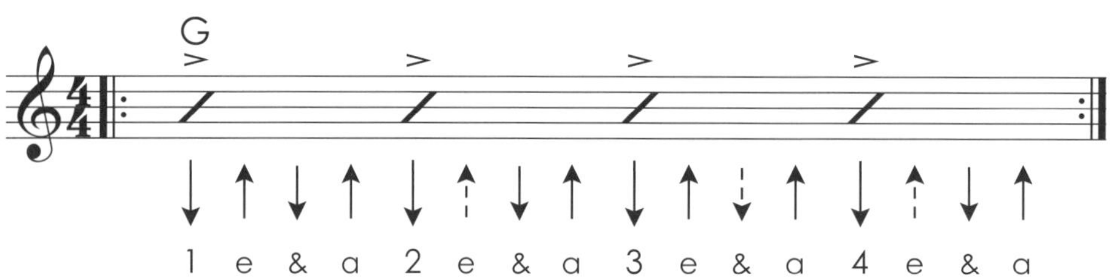

And just like with all previous strum patterns, remember to keep the arm moving in a steady motion.

When you start working on songs, you will see how common 16th-note strumming is in the world of guitar.

Lesson 38

Learn two more 16th-note strum patterns

Our goal here is not to come up with every mathematical possibility of arrows and dotted arrows. By spending time with just a few examples, your mind and body will get the idea and you will eventually be able to create strum patterns in the moment.

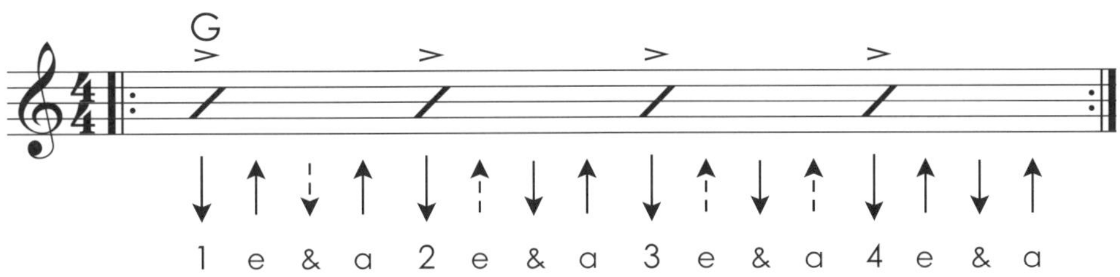

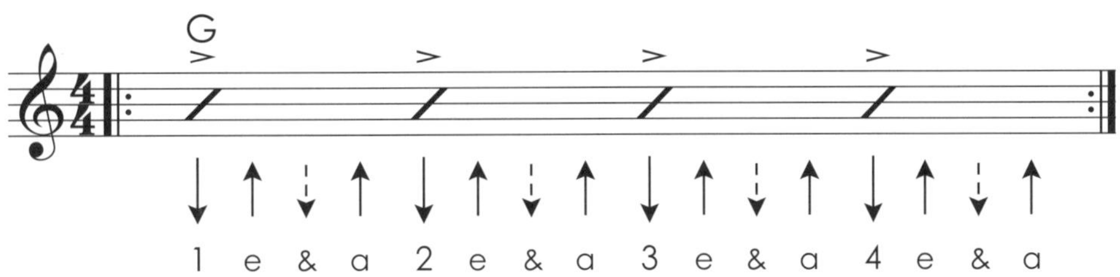

There is a point in playing a musical instrument where it becomes less about thinking and more just "feeling it" and creating freely. This is where all your efforts are leading you. Be confident that you are growing and evolving as a musician and a guitarist every time you pick it up and play.

Lesson 39

Learn how to combine 16th-note strum patterns with chord progressions

So let's use these new strum patterns with chords to create musical examples. Just like before, you can experiment with combining any 16th-note strum pattern with any chord combination.

Use these fingerings for this first one: 2–1–3 for G major and 1–2 for E minor.

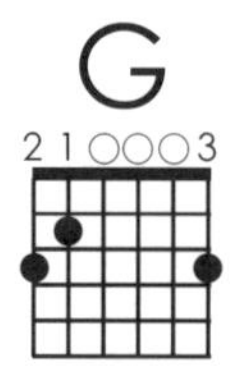

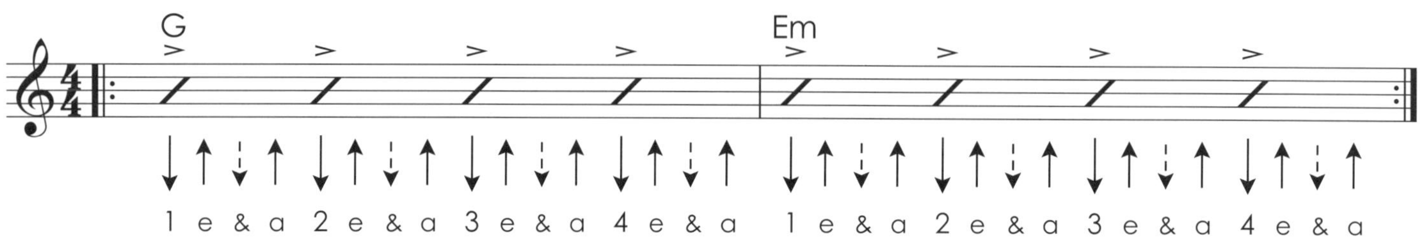

For this next one, use the "3–2–4" fingering for the G major chord.

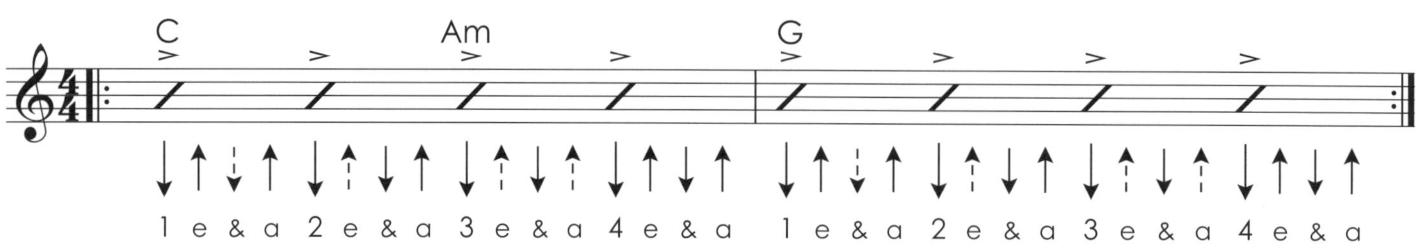

Lesson 40

Learn how to create your own chord progressions & strumming patterns

Okay, here's where you get to find the artist inside yourself. Everyone, and I mean everyone, has a creative side to themselves. It's just a matter of actualizing it, connecting with it, and discovering it.

The music you've been listening to your whole life wasn't always created by highly proficient musicians—guitarists, especially.

There is an old saying:

"It's not how *much* you know, it's what you *do with what you know*."

We have worked on enough chords and strumming techniques for you to get the idea of what is going on in simple folk, rock, pop and country music (and a few other musical styles).

Even though we haven't worked on an entire song yet, we have addressed the basic components of what a guitarist does when they write and play songs.

I encourage you to take all these chords and strum patterns and explore, create and *invent*.

You can't break anything! Do it when you're all by yourself, if you aren't comfortable at first.

This is a natural part of the process of learning to become a musician.
Have fun with it!

Just let go and play.

That's what artists do.

Lesson 41

Learn the note names on the 5th string (and a little bit of music theory)

If you feel you are confident with knowing the note names on the 6th string, then it is time to add the 5th string.

If you aren't solid with the 6th string, then spend more time with it until you can find the notes in a consistent manner "right out of the gate," which means that you don't have to warm up—you are comfortable right away.

If you start working on all the strings and their note names all at once, it will become a very jumbled mess in your brain. We've already talked about the benefits of breaking goals down into smaller goals, so taking this project of learning the notes and working on one string at a time is an excellent way to achieve success using that approach.

Here are the notes on the 5th string:

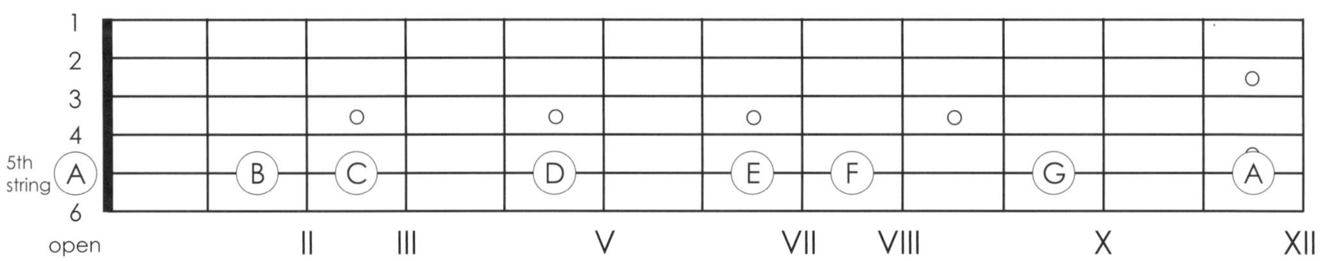

Drill:

- Choose a note name randomly: C D E F G A B
- Find that note on the 5th string and play it with your 1st finger
- Choose another note name, find it and play it (go slowly)
- Continue in this manner for at least five minutes

Here's some music theory that will help you navigate the notes on all six strings on the fretboard:

half step = 1 fret

whole step = 2 frets

E & **F**, **B** & **C** = half step apart

And all the other pairs of notes:

A & **B**, **C** & **D**, **D** & **E**, **F** & **G**, **G** & **A** = whole step apart

And here is one more term you need to know:

pitch = Refers to the highness and lowness of a note. It is often used as another word for **note**.

Lesson

42 Be introduced to fingerpicking

Fingerpicking, also known as **fingerstyle**, is a popular method of playing in many styles of guitar music. In the beginning you will just be learning the basic technique for using your fingertips to pluck the strings.

In order to work on fingerpicking, we need to be able to designate the right hand fingers individually. They each have a letter:

p = thumb **i** = index **m** = middle **a** = ring

Spend some time and get acquainted with the letters for each finger—you will need to know them to learn the fingerpicking patterns (and in case you're wondering, the letters come from the Italian words for each finger).

Start by placing each fingertip on its string...

p - 6th string **i** - 3rd string **m** - 2nd string **a** - 1st string

Now pluck each string with your fingertip in this order: **p i m a**

Here are some main considerations:

- Extend the thumb
- Leave each finger on its string until its turn to pluck
- Replace fingers simultaneously

Slowly go through this **p i m a** pattern repeatedly until you start to have control and develop finger independence.

A quick word about fingernails...

Many guitarists use their fingernails to pluck the string. I suggest that in the beginning, keep your fingernails short and pluck with the fleshy part of your fingertip.

Spend about five minutes per practice session doing this exercise. It helps to use a timer: set it for five minutes and then you can focus on just the playing and not on keeping track of how long you're doing the exercise.

Lesson

43 Learn some fingerpicking patterns

Let's develop finger independence and control by varying the order of the right hand fingers: **i**, **m** and **a**.

Here is every combination of those fingers. Each combo will start with the thumb, **p**:

p i m a
p i a m
p m i a
p m a i
p a i m
p a m i

Do each combo four times with your fingers on these groups of strings:

6 3 2 1	5 3 2 1	4 3 2 1
p = 6th string	**p** = 5th string	**p** = 4th string
i = 3rd string	**i** = 3rd string	**i** = 3rd string
m = 2nd string	**m** = 2nd string	**m** = 2nd string
a = 1st string	**a** = 1st string	**a** = 1st string

We've only changed the placement of the thumb. Soon we will change the placement of the other fingers. These exercises are designed to get you to a place where your right hand is comfortable with plucking any of the strings you want.

These groups of strings are referred to as a **string set**.

string set = the group of strings you use in any given situation

Remember the main considerations:

- Extend the thumb
- Leave each finger on its string until its turn to pluck
- Replace fingers simultaneously

Lesson

44 Learn some fingerpicking string set variations

By working with the fingerpicking combinations on different strings, your right hand will become very adept at playing all of the variations that occur in playing fingerpicking style guitar. That's essentially what all exercises are—preparation for real-life application. It is worth the time spent on such exercises to improve your technique in an accelerated manner.

You can continue to do each of the right hand combinations (from Lesson 43) four times each on the following string sets, as well as the ones we've already covered.

6 5 4 3	6 4 3 2	5 4 3 2
p = 6th string	**p** = 6th string	**p** = 5th string
i = 5th string	**i** = 4th string	**i** = 4th string
m = 4th string	**m** = 3rd string	**m** = 3rd string
a = 3rd string	**a** = 2nd string	**a** = 2nd string

It is always good to review the particulars mentioned in previous lessons.

- Extend the thumb
- Leave each finger on its string until its turn to pluck
- Replace fingers simultaneously
- Go slowly at first, without tempo, then work up to playing all the notes evenly
- You can work on these patterns using just the open strings, or you can grab a chord with the left hand to make it sound more interesting (make sure the chord string set matches your right hand string set)

Learn to fingerpick a chord progression

Now it's time to experience what it's like to use fingerpicking with a chord progression. Let's look at details concerning the chords and their string sets and how we will match them up with the right hand string sets.

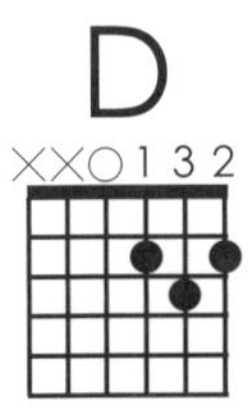

strings: 4 3 2 1
fingers: p i m a

strings: 5 3 2 1
fingers: p i m a

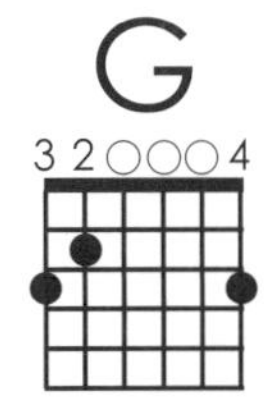

strings: 6 3 2 1
fingers: p i m a

It will most likely be obvious to you that the key to learning this is to go very slowly as you work on all the particulars. The specifics are underneath the chord progression chart here:

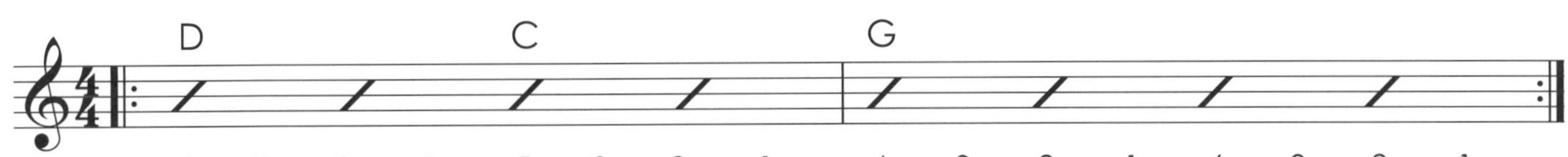

strings:	4	3	2	1	5	3	2	1	6	3	2	1	6	3	2	1
fingers:	p	i	m	a	p	i	m	a	p	i	m	a	p	i	m	a
count:	1	&	2	&	3	&	4	&	1	&	2	&	3	&	4	&

Once you spend some time with it all, your brain, fingers and ears will get the idea and you will be well on your way to being able to play this musical example, which is exactly the kind of thing you will encounter in many songs of this style.

That's what I think is so cool about the guitar: all the things we've worked on so far—chords, strumming and fingerpicking—this is all what professional players use every day. This is not the "beginning stuff" you learn before the "real stuff". You're are actually doing it now.

Lesson 46

Learn a chord progression fingerpicking variation

Here are three more examples of how one can use variations on the right hand fingerpicking patterns to give a chord progression a slightly different sound.

Ex.1

strings:	4	1	2	3	5	1	2	3	6	1	2	3	6	1	2	3
fingers:	p	a	m	i	p	a	m	i	p	a	m	i	p	a	m	i
count:	1	&	2	&	3	&	4	&	1	&	2	&	3	&	4	&

Ex.2

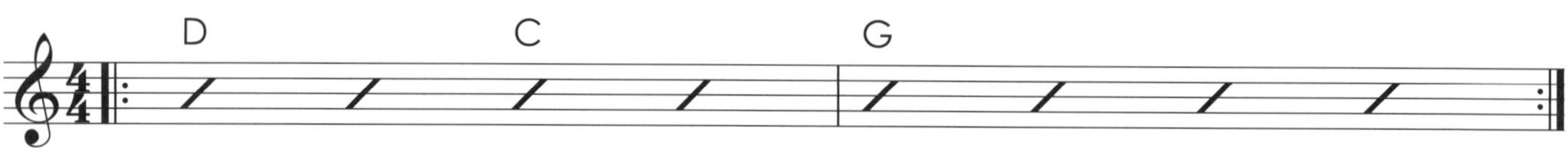

strings:	4	2	3	1	5	2	3	1	6	2	3	1	6	2	3	1
fingers:	p	m	i	a	p	m	i	a	p	m	i	a	p	m	i	a
count:	1	&	2	&	3	&	4	&	1	&	2	&	3	&	4	&

After you get a grasp of these patterns (literally and figuratively), you can start to explore creating combinations of your own. Take any chord progression and see what it's like to use different variations of fingerpicking patterns.

Remember to pay attention to the possibilities you have with different string sets for the chords you are playing.

Here's an example that has a slight variation the second time around with the C chord string set, so that's why it's written over four bars. This demonstrates a common occurrence of variation in music... you don't always have to play a repeated pattern exactly the same way each time.

Ex. 3

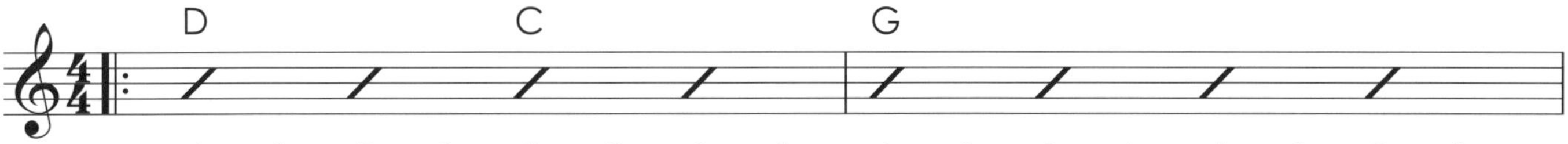

strings:	4	1	2	3	5	2	3	4	6	2	3	4	6	1	2	3
fingers:	p	a	m	i	p	a	m	i	p	a	m	i	p	a	m	i
count:	1	&	2	&	3	&	4	&	1	&	2	&	3	&	4	&

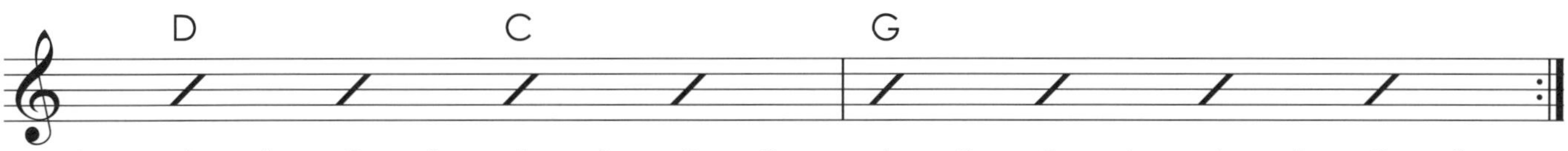

strings:	4	1	2	3	5	1	2	3	6	2	3	4	6	1	2	3
fingers:	p	a	m	i	p	a	m	i	p	a	m	i	p	a	m	i
count:	1	&	2	&	3	&	4	&	1	&	2	&	3	&	4	&

Lesson 47

Learn how to create longer fingerpicking patterns

The fingerpicking patterns you've used so far were short—only four notes long. Let's create some longer patterns to make it more interesting.

Here is the fingerpicking pattern:

p i m i a i m i

Spend some time learning that on just the open strings.

Here is the pattern with the chord progression:

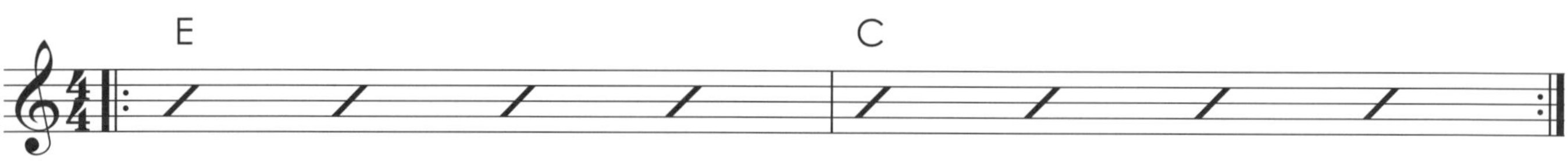

strings:	6	4	3	4	2	4	3	4	5	4	3	4	2	4	3	4
fingers:	p	i	m	i	a	i	m	i	p	i	m	i	a	i	m	i
count:	1	&	2	&	3	&	4	&	1	&	2	&	3	&	4	&

The only difference with the string sets between the E major chord and the C major chord is that the thumb moves between the 6th and 5th strings.

So just like you did with the strum patterns and chords, you want to combine different patterns with different chords. Now that you have the basic idea about fingerpicking, start to come up with your own patterns. Write them down and build a vocabulary of patterns you like.

Explore, experiment and create!

Lesson 48

Confidently know the fret numbers

We have looked at how so much of music and guitar playing involves numbers. It is important to be adept with all this labeling.

Now is a good time to make sure you confidently know the fret numbers because you will soon be utilizing the entire fretboard. If you are still tentative with what each fret's number is, you will have a tough time learning and playing music freely. So here is a simple drill to get this down.

Fret Numbers Drill:

- Choose a string—it doesn't matter which one because you are focusing just on the frets and their numbers
- Randomly place your first finger on the string at any fret
- Call out the fret number
- Repeat with a different fret location

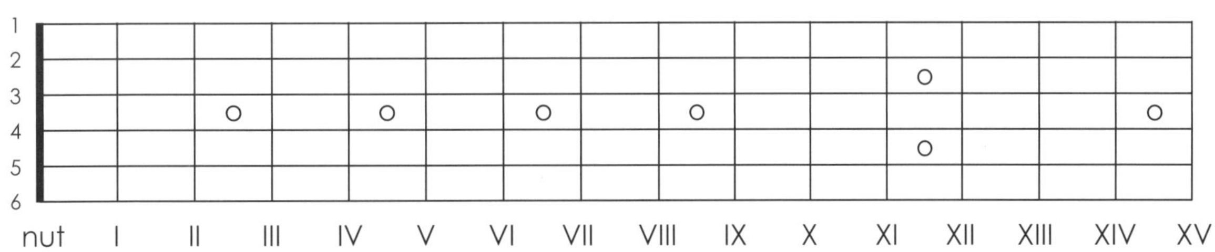

I have noticed that it is easy to get caught up in learning something and forget to remember certain *simple* things along the way. You might find that you get a little unsure of the fret numbers as you go up the neck.

Do this for just a few minutes every time you pick up the guitar and soon you will confidently know what fret number your hand is at. It will seem like you don't even have to think about it.

Lesson 49

Learn some more dominant 7th chords

It's time to increase your chord vocabulary to include some more chords from the dominant 7th family. These chords are used in all styles of music but especially in blues, rock and country music.

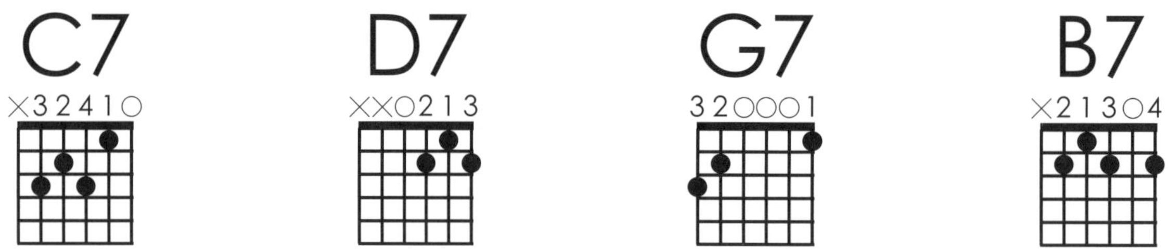

Remember to use the process for learning new chords:

- Grab chord one string at a time... *What string?*
  What finger?
  What fret?

- Double-check technique... *Thumb behind the neck*
  Fingers are arched
  Fingertips are snug behind the frets

- Strum through chord... *One string at a time, to hear that each note is ringing clearly (make sure you strum the correct number of strings)*

- Make adjustments, if necessary... *Make sure there's enough clearance between the backs of your fingers and strings that are supposed to be ringing*

Learn to play two chord progressions that use dominant 7th chords

Lesson

50

When you learn a new chord, it is a good idea to use it in a musical example or song right away so that your brain, ears and fingers get the chord down in a practical manner.

Here are two chord progressions that give you a chance to utilize the new dominant 7th chords from the previous lesson.

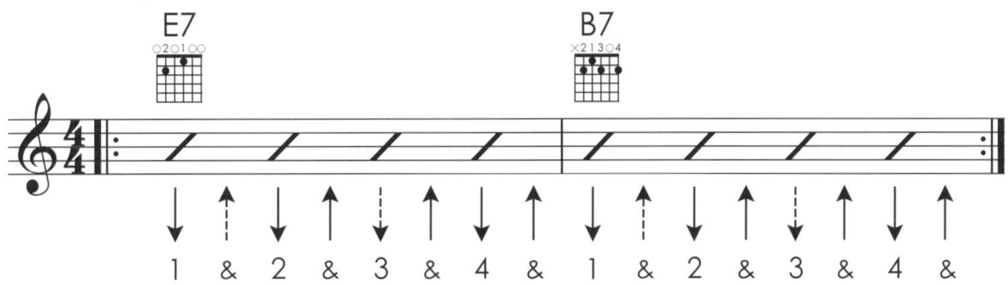

This next progression utilizes all down strums, which is actually a common way to strum and it creates a different "feel" for the steady 8th-note rhythm. There is also an accent on beats 2 and 4 of each bar.

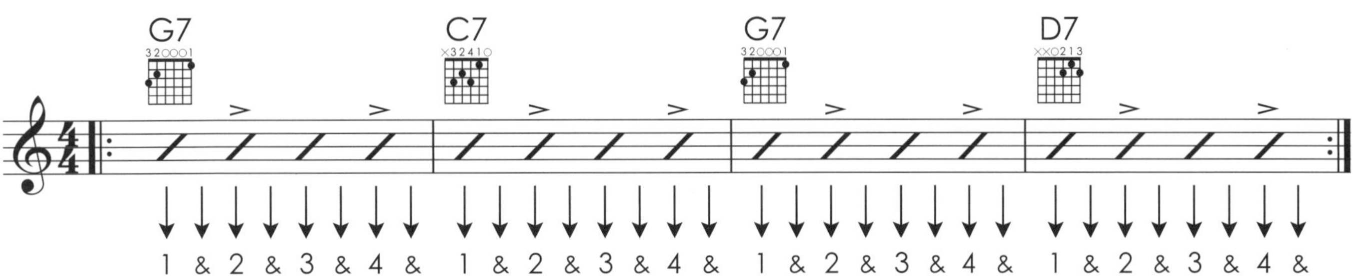

Lesson 51

Learn to play a full barre chord: major

This is an introduction to playing full barre chords, which are extremely common in guitar playing. They require a little extra attention and are well worth the effort.

Lay your first finger across all six strings at the 3rd fret. Roll the finger a little bit to the left. Keep your thumb behind the neck for leverage.

Make the shape in front of your 1st finger with the remaining fingers. (This shape is the same as the E major chord down in open position, meaning down by the nut, but you're using the 2nd, 3rd and 4th fingers).

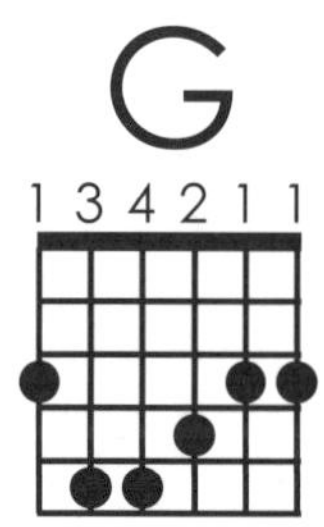

For now, just practice forming this chord at the third fret. Go through the usual process for learning a new chord, making adjustments if necessary, until all the strings ring clearly.

The letter name of this chord is based on the 6th string. The note at the 3rd fret on the 6th string is the note G, so this barre chord is a G major chord.

This chord is a moveable shape. You can play it at any fret (but more about this later).

Again, just for now, practice forming this chord at the 3rd fret.

Learn to play two more barre chords: minor & dominant 7th

Here are two more barre chords, G minor and G dominant 7th:

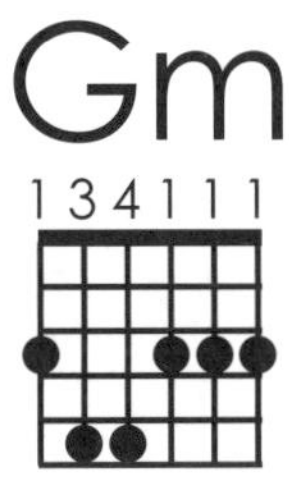

Again, just for now, practice forming these chords at the third fret.

Notice how the shape you are playing in front of your 1st finger is the same shape as the E, Em, and E7 chords you learned in the beginning. With the barre chords, your 1st finger is holding the strings that the nut was holding with the open E chords.

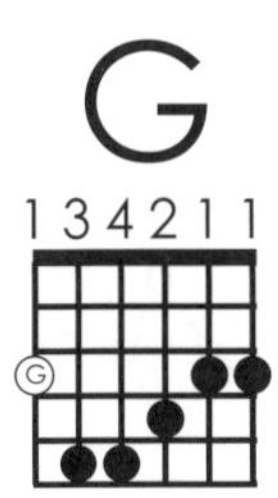

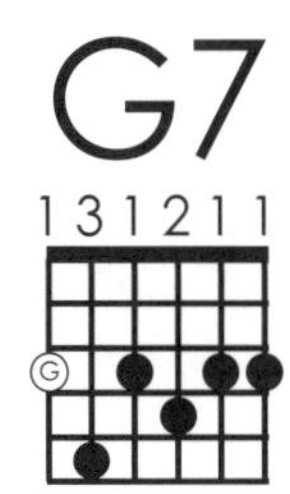

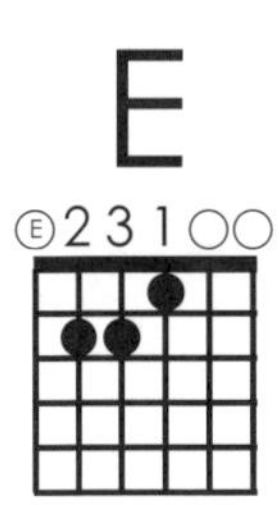

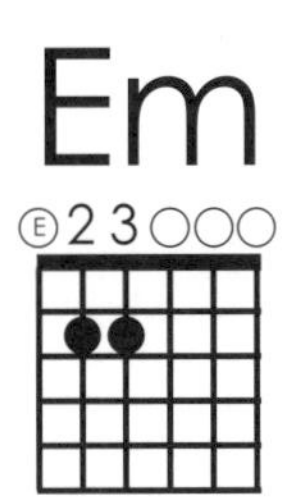

The brain really likes to relate new things (new chord shapes) to things you already know (chord shapes you'e been playing for awhile now). This helps you learn faster and at a deeper level. Always strive to *make connections* with all of the information you are learning in this course. It makes a huge difference in how fast you progress on your path of taking your guitar playing skills to a higher level.

Okay, once you get familiar and comfortable with playing these chards at the 3rd fret, start practicing playing all three barre chords at different frets.

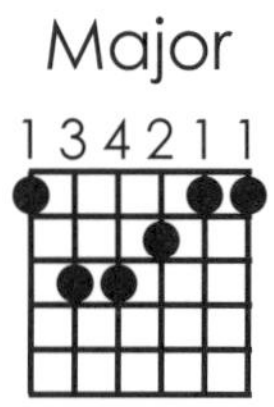

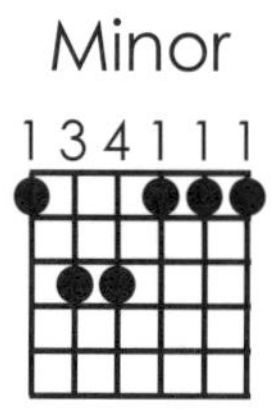

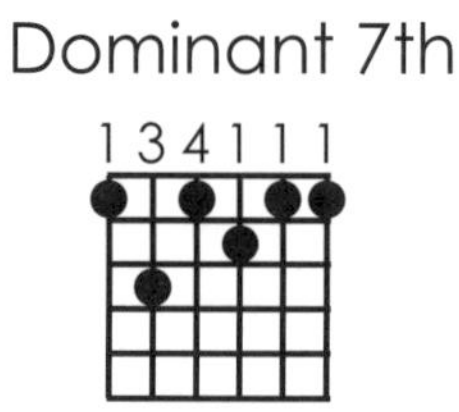

Just choose one of the three barre chords, choose any fret, and then form the chord at that fret. This will give your hand the experience of playing these chords around the fretboard, which is what you'll be doing when you use these chords in songs.

Pay most attention to what fret your 1st finger is on. Use the fret markers to keep track of fret numbers.

We've already mentioned that the note name on the 6th string is the letter name of these chords. We will soon be getting deeper into all of that.

For now, you just want to focus on getting your hand comfortable with playing these three barre chords all around the neck. Understanding the names of the chords will come later.

Start to develop right hand picking technique: picking one note at a time

Lesson **53**

This is an introduction to picking one string at a time, which is the same as saying picking one *note* at a time. You've actually done this already with the fingerpicking technique, but now we will learn to do it with the pick.

This exercise is *extremely* simple and is designed to prepare you for the more organized right hand picking exercises that are in the near future for you.

Simply pick individual strings with your pick *randomly*, *yet intentionally*. This means that you can pick any string you want, in any order, using either a downstroke or an upstroke.

You can pick each string in order from high to low, skip strings, use all downstrokes, use all upstrokes or use alternating strokes—really anything you can think of.

We could call this "mindful randomness". It is a good way to initially introduce a technique to your hand because you're not too focused on "doing it right" and you can pick any string in any order, so there is no "right".

You do want to be paying attention to how you hold the pick and making sure you have control, of course.

Maybe you can think of the string number in your mind as you play it. This will develop your cognitive skills, which are important because when you are working on music, you sometimes want to *know* what you are doing.

I suggest you do this exercise for two to three minutes per practice session (or longer).

Lesson 54 Learn the "Percussive Muted Strum"

Percussionists and drummers make music simply by hitting things. It always contributes a lot to the overall feel and "groove" of the music when you add some percussion to the sound. You can do this yourself with the guitar.

If you watch guitarists playing rhythm guitar (strumming and chords), you may notice that sometimes their strumming is really *rhythmic*. This "rhythmicness" is achieved by adding a simple percussive sound, created by hitting the muted strings with the right hand.

We shall call this "percussive muted strumming", but you want to know that this is not an official music or guitar term.

Take your pick and hit the open strings and make sure the side of your right hand hits the strings before your pick. It should make a "thump" noise and there should be no ringing of any of the strings.

Work on getting that sound for a bit. The secret is to not over-think it—just make the motion and go for the sound.

Now, grab an E major chord. Then do the percussive muted strum and immediately do an up strum. Work on this for a few minutes. Next, take this strum pattern we'e worked with before and review it. Spend a few minutes strumming it and getting comfortable with it.

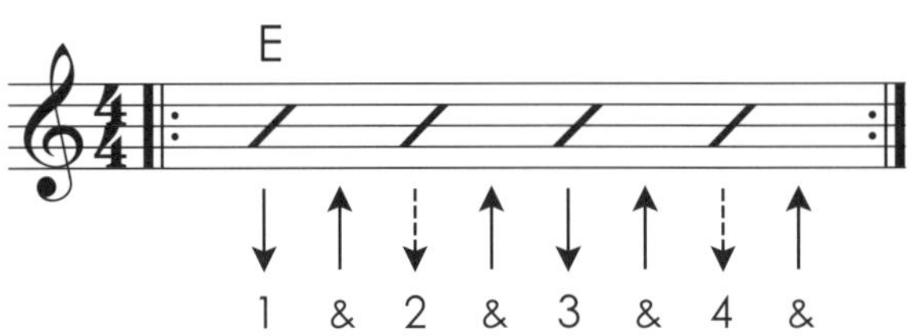

Let's put this percussive muted strum into the strum pattern and see how it all sounds together.

M = percussive muted strum

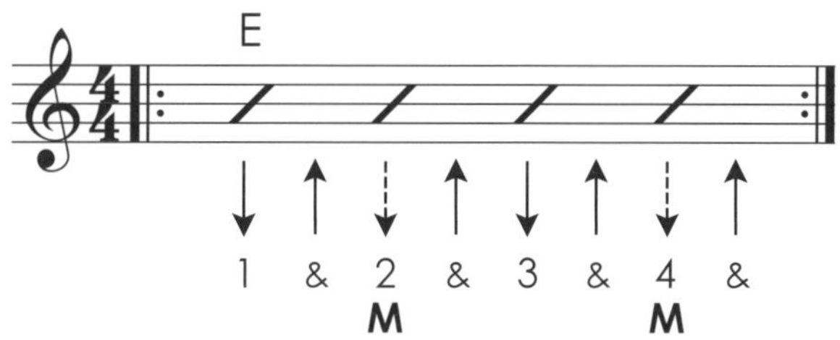

By putting the muted strum on beats 2 and 4, we've given the strum pattern extra groove and rhythmic feel.

By the way, beats 2 and 4 in a bar of 4/4 are referred to in music as the **backbeat**, which is the foundation for most rhythmic music: rock, funk, pop, dance, reggae, etc. The percussive muted strum in this strum pattern emphasizes the back beat and therefore is very effective in creating a heightened rhythmic element to the strumming.

Here's another example. Again, work with the strum pattern as it is for a few minutes to get comfortable with it, then add the muted strum on beat 3.

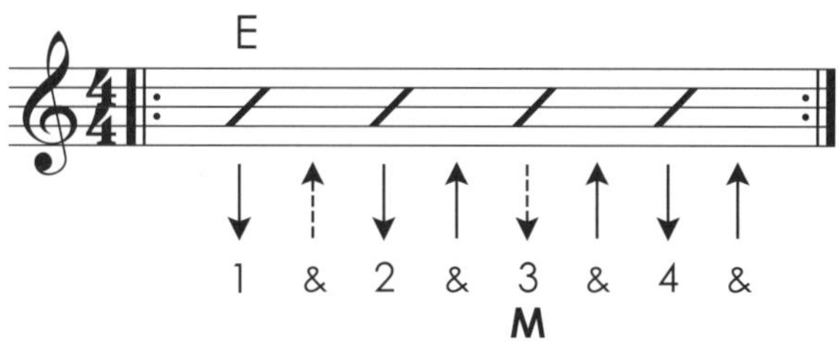

Experiment by putting this percussive muted strum into any of the strum patterns we worked on so far (both 8th-note patterns and 16th-note patterns). You can substitute a muted strum for any *down arrow*.

This approach to strumming can add a lot of energy to your rhythm guitar playing.

Lesson 55

Learn another major barre chord

This barre chord is a bit different for a few reasons—mostly in that you are not actually barring with the 1st finger this time, you are barring with the 3rd finger. Another difference is that the note on the 5th string (not the 6th) is the letter name of this chord. Also, this chord only has four notes in it.

Start by putting your 1st finger across the 3rd fret, and have the tip of your finger touching the 6th string to mute it. Don't press down with your whole finger—you are actually just going to be holding down the 5th string while the back of your 1st finger is merely *laying* on the 4th, 3d, 2nd and 1st strings.

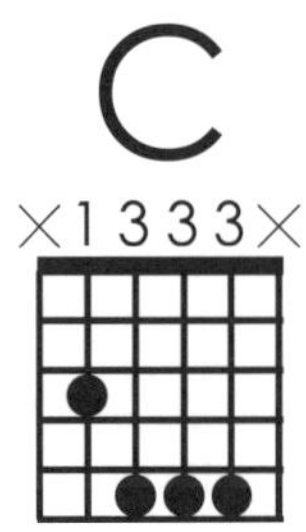

Now take your 3rd finger and put it on the 4th, 3rd and 2nd strings, two frets up from your first finger (in this case, the 5th fret).

Notice in the diagram that the 1st string has an X above it—your 3rd finger is actually going to come up just a bit so that it is muting the 1st string.

Now make sure that your 1st finger is holding down the 5th string on the 3rd fret and your third finger is holding down its three strings and give it a strum.

Make any adjustments necessary so that the all the notes are ringing clearly.

Like you did with the other barre chords so far, once you get familiar and comfortable with playing this chord at the 3rd fret, start playing it in various positions up and down the fretboard.

Lesson 56

Learn another minor & dominant 7th barre chord

These next two barre chords are going to complete your set of six barre chords that you will be working with a lot. There are thousands of barre chords on the guitar, but these six will get you through a lot of songs. They are extremely useful to the modern guitarist.

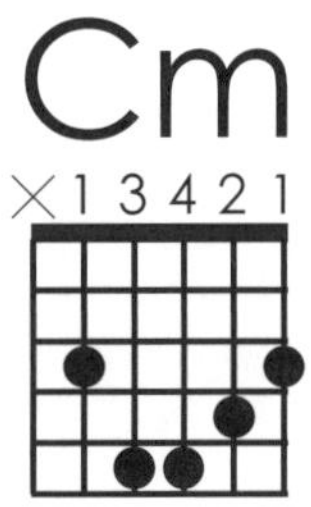

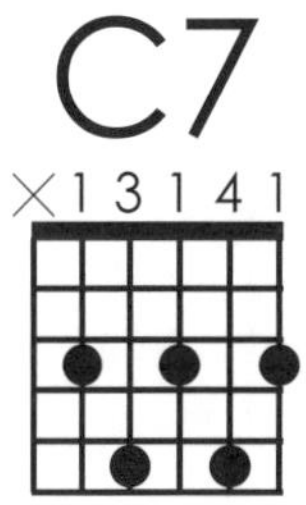

By now you know the procedure for learning new barre chords. As always, give yourself time to learn them with your fingers and your brain by playing them at the 3rd fret, and then start playing them around the fretboard.

So here are all six of the barre chords presented in one place:

Major
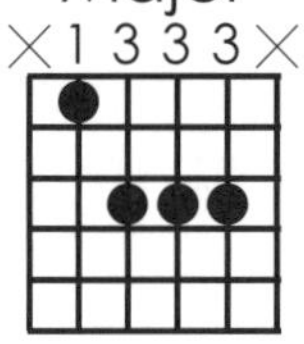

Minor
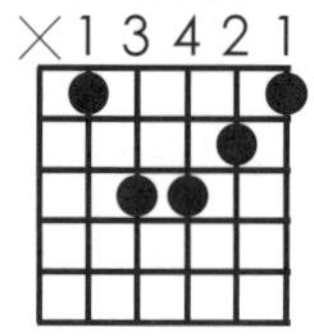

Dominant 7th
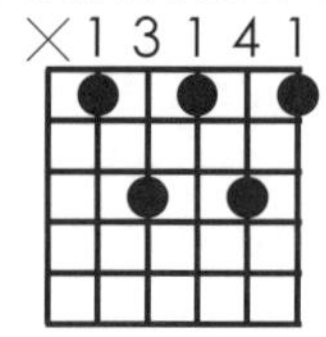

Major
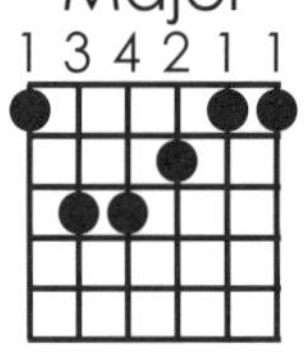

Minor
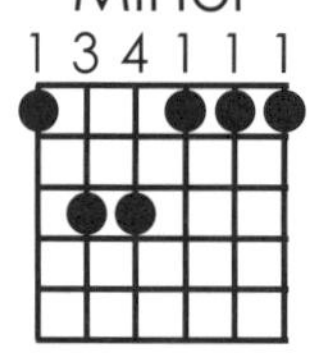

Dominant 7th
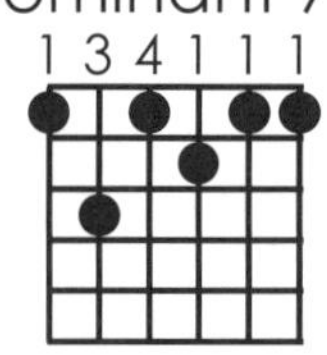

There are two major barre chords, two minor barre chords and two dominant 7th barre chords. Work with all six like you did in Lesson 52.

Just choose one of the six barre chords, choose any fret and then form the chord at that fret. This will give your hand the experience of playing these chords around the fretboard, which is what you'll be doing when you use these chords in songs.

Pay most attention to which fret your 1st finger is on. Use the fret markers to keep track of fret numbers. Remember, on most guitars the markers are on the III, V, VII and IX frets.

For now, you just want to focus on getting your hand comfortable with playing these six barre chords all around the neck. Understanding the names of the chords will come later.

Next, we will learn a little bit of music theory so you can identify these chords with ease. Soon you will be a formidable rhythm guitarist!

Learn some more music theory: sharps & flats

Lesson **57**

It is amazing how well someone can play the guitar without knowing any music theory.

However, with just a *little* bit of fundamental theory, you will really be able to find your way around your instrument. And that makes a huge difference in understanding the music you are playing— you will play at a higher level, you'll learn songs faster and be able to create your own music easily. It is definitely worth the effort. So let's now learn about sharps and flats.

♯ = **sharp**
raises the note a half step, which is one fret

♭ = **flat**
lowers the note a half step, which is one fret

So you can sharp any note and you can flat any note.

A♯	**B♯**	**C♯**	**D♯**	**E♯**	**F♯**	**G♯**
A	**B**	**C**	**D**	**E**	**F**	**G**
A♭	**B♭**	**C♭**	**D♭**	**E♭**	**F**	**G♭**

Fretboard examples:

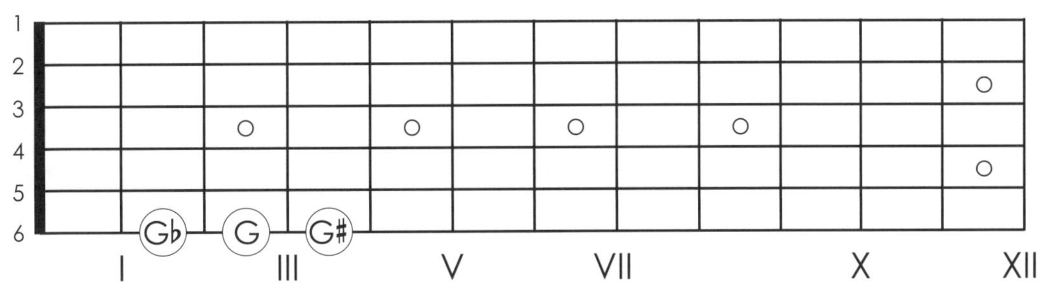

Note: The orientation of this neck diagram is different than my guitar neck in the video. Your fretboard is upside down and opposite to it.

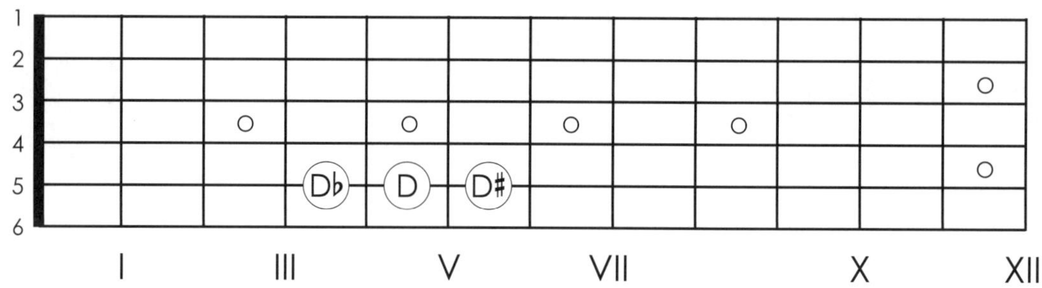

Note names can get a little interesting because a lot of the notes have more than one name. Let's take a look at that...

enharmonic = *same note, different name*

Example of enharmonics:

D♭ = C♯ (or you can also say C♯ = D♭)

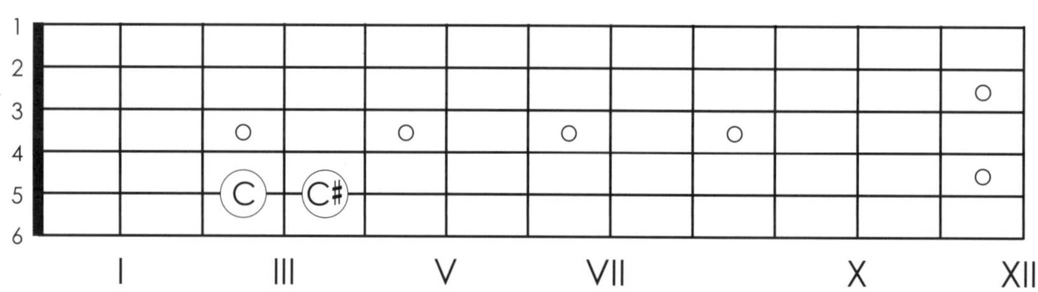

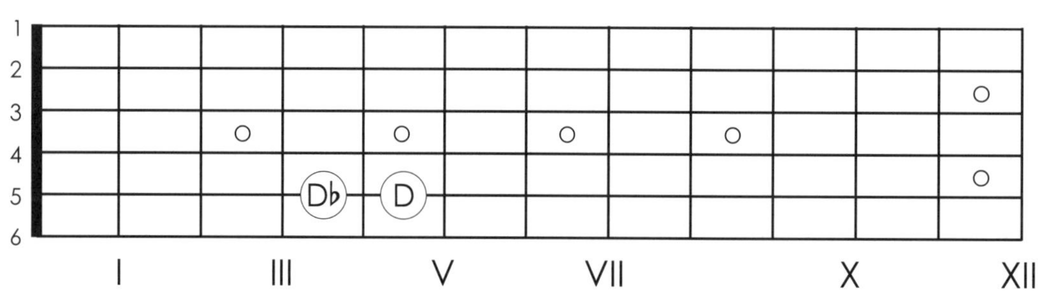

Now remember that E and F and B and C are a half step apart.

So that means...

F♭ = E   **E♯ = F**   **B♯ = C**   **C♭ = B**

That might seem a little strange to use a sharp or flat when you could just call it a plain letter, but there is a system to music theory and this is how it all works out. It will be easiest for you to go along with this note naming system because the whole planet uses it.

Here are all of the possible enharmonics:

A♯ = B♭
B♯ = C
C♭ = B
C♯ = D♭
D♯ = E♭
E♯ = F
F♭ = E
F♯ = G♭
G♯ = A♭

I understand that it might not make sense to have more than one name for a single note, but there is a very good basis for all of this. Every musical instrument uses this system of note naming. In order for you to totally understand this, you would have to possess a much deeper knowledge of how music theory works and it is not necessary for you to get into all of that right now.

I suggest you just continue getting a solid grasp of the plain note names—A B C D E F G—on the 5th and 6th strings (soon you will start working on the rest of the strings) and then spend some time getting acquainted with the sharps and flats for each note. Trust that this will all become clear the more you work with it. Down the road you will see how all this will benefit you as it takes your guitar playing to a much higher level.

Lesson 58 Learn how to identify barre chords

It is now time to complete your understanding of barre chords and how they are named. First, we need to learn another theory term:

root = *the letter name of the chord*

The term root (sometimes called the **tonic**) refers to the letter name of the chord.

Here are the three barre chords whose roots are on the 6th string. When you play them at the 3rd fret, their roots are G because that is the name of the note on the 3rd fret, 6th string.

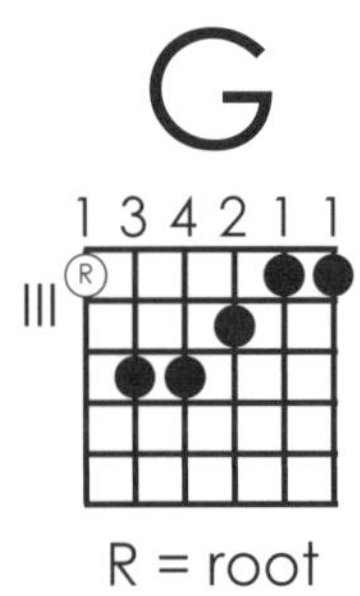

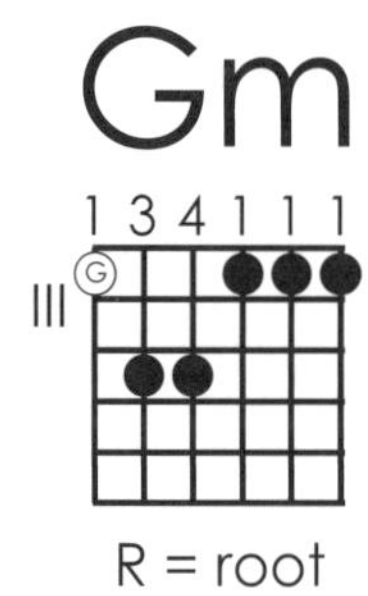

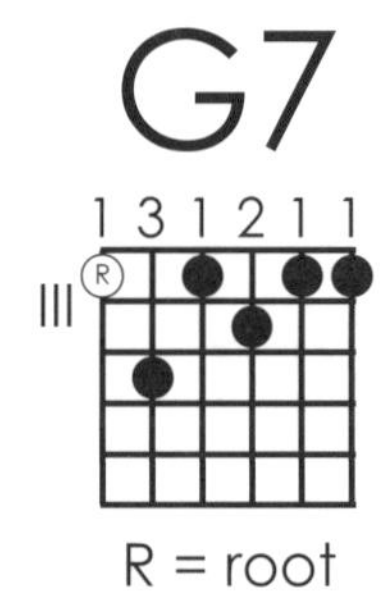

The Roman numeral "III" next to the chord diagram designates that line is now the 3rd fret. Using a number like this with the chord diagram enables us to write out chords that are located at any fret.

As it turns out, all the chords you've learned so far have their root as the lowest note in the chord (no Roman numeral this time—the dark line at the top of the diagram designates it as the nut):

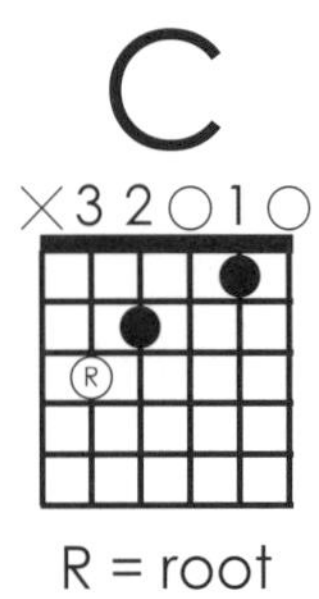

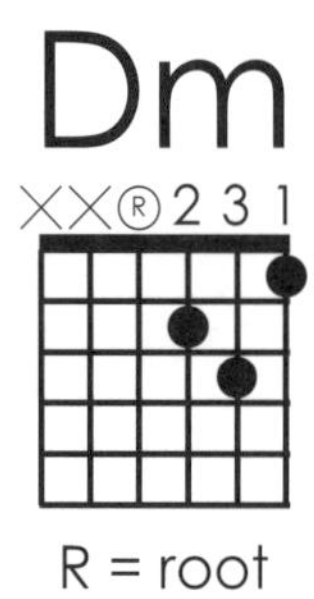

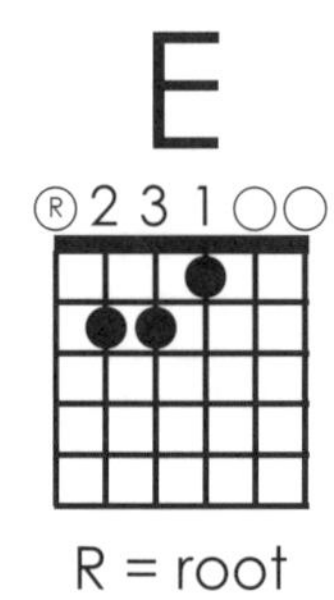

Important!

You need to know that not *all* chords in music have the root as their lowest note. But all the chords we've dealt with so far have the lowest note as their root.

Here are all six barre chords. Their roots are on the lowest string of the chord.

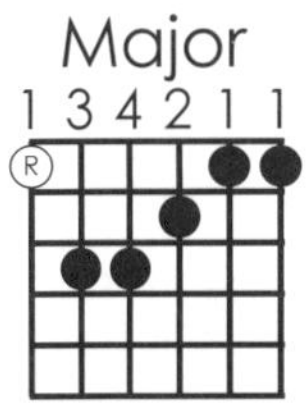

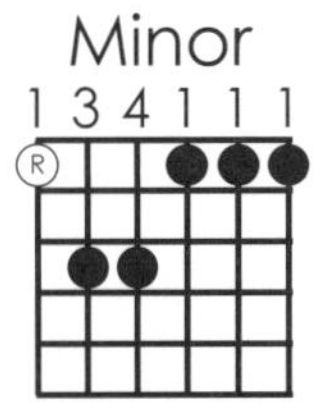

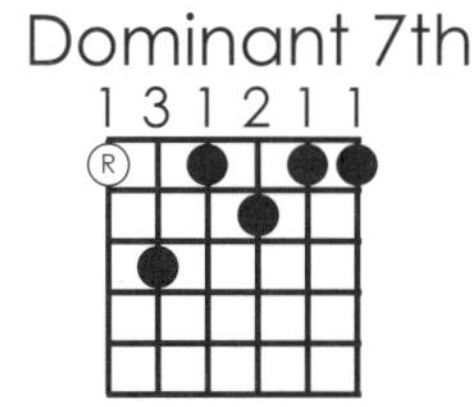

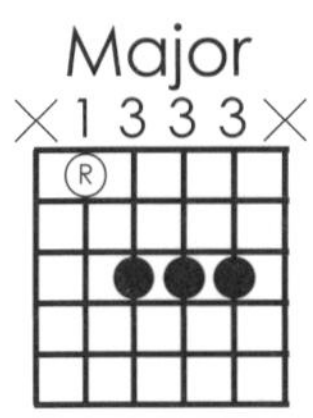

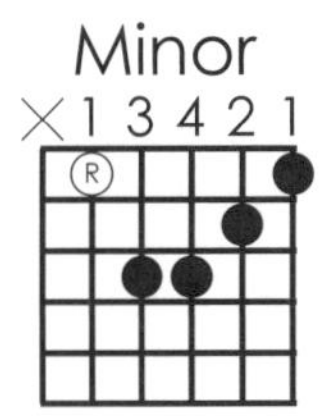

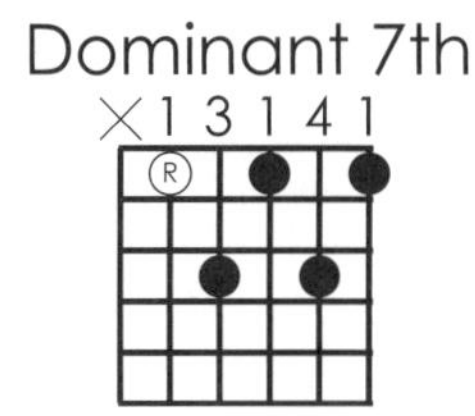

So...

You have three barre chords—major, minor and dominant 7—with the root on the 6th string. And, you have three barre chords—major, minor and dominant 7—with the root on the 5th string.

Another way to look at it...

You have two major barre chords, one with the root on the 6th string and one with the root on the 5th string. You have two minor barre chords, one with the root on the 6th string and one with the root on the 5th string. You have two dominant 7 barre chords, one with the root on the 6th string and one with the root on the 5th string.

The procedure for becoming fluent with these barre chords is simple. Spend time playing each of the six barre chords at various frets and identify the root.

Procedure:

- Choose any of the six chords
- Choose any fret (keep in below the XII fret)
- Play that chord at that fret and identify its root
- Repeat this process with each of the six barre chords at three or four different frets

Here are some examples:

B

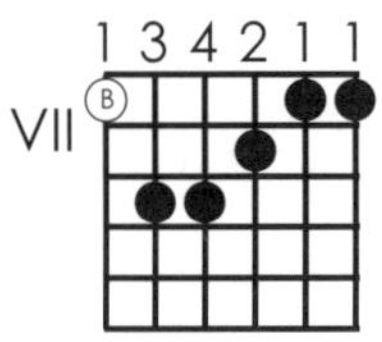

F

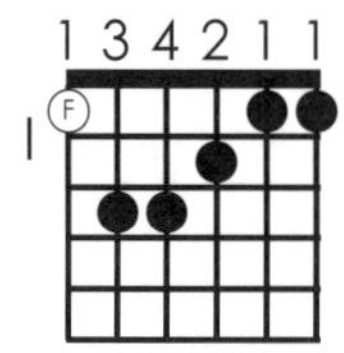

D

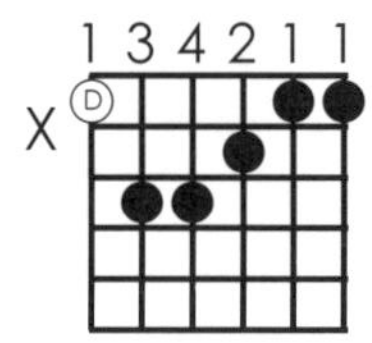

Major barre chords— root on the 6th string

E

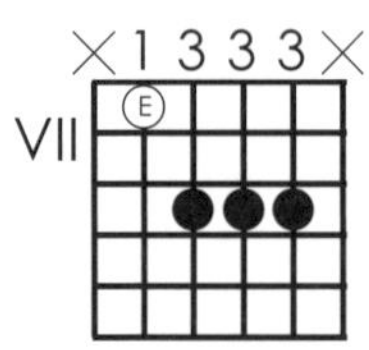

Major barre chord—
root on the 5th string

Bm

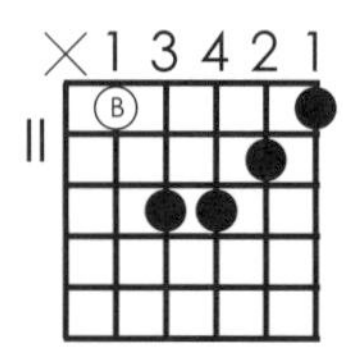

Minor barre chord—
root on the 5th string

F7

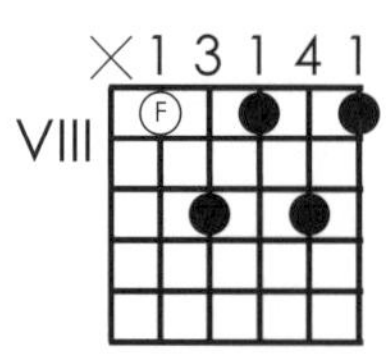

Dominant 7 barre chord—root on the 5th string

Sometimes you will choose a fret whose name is an **enharmonic**, so in that case the barre chord will have two letter names.

Here are some examples:

F♯m

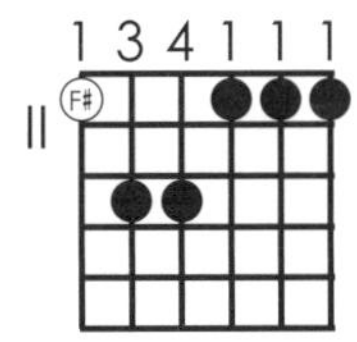

G♭m

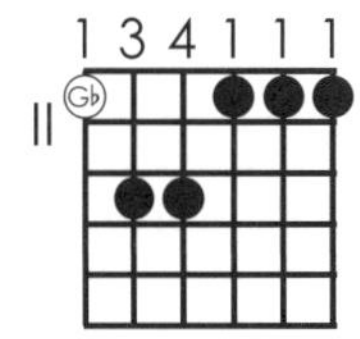

B♭7

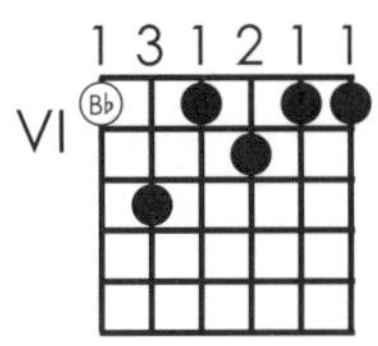

A♯7

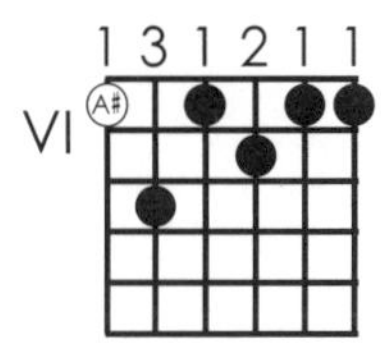

E♭7

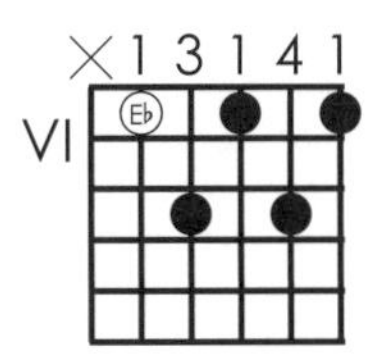

D♯7

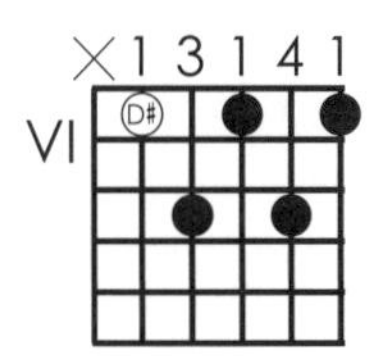

For now, when you play a barre chord at a fret that has an enharmonic (two names), just know *both* names. Later on, when you are working on songs, you will see that usually only one of the names is what you will actually call any particular chord like this.

I assure you, the barre chords are worth the time you put into learning them. With these six chords, you can rule the world!

Lesson

59 Learn how to use barre chords in chord progressions

Let's get right to using the barre chords in actual chord progressions. Here is a chord progression we have worked on a few times so far. This time we will use barre chords to play it.

These are the barre chords we'll use first:

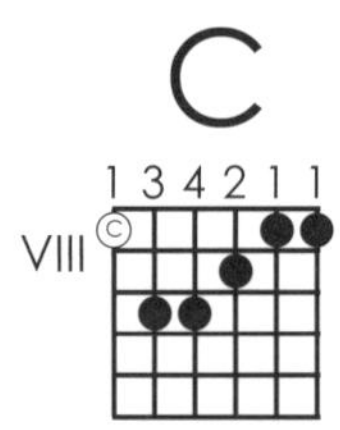

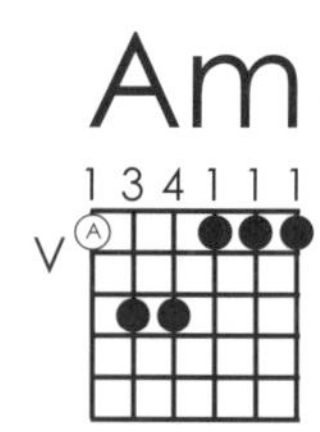

Let's just strum it with a basic steady eighth note strum.

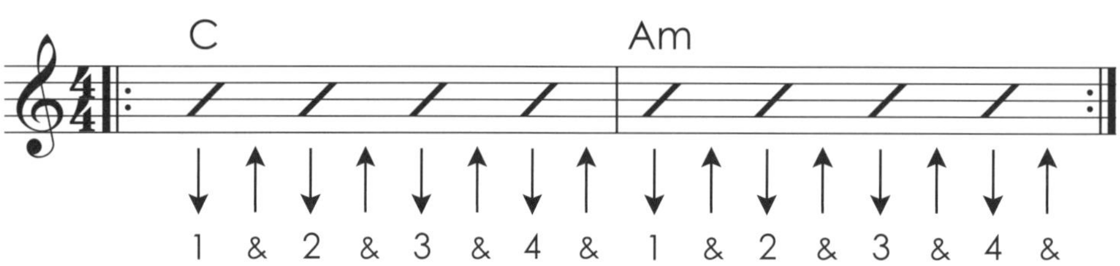

You could also use this C major barre chord:

It's a little closer to the Am and thus easier to get back and forth from.

Let's try a fingerpicking pattern with it:

strings:	6	4	3	2	3	4	3	2	6	4	3	2	3	4	3	2
fingers:	p	i	m	a	m	i	m	a	p	i	m	a	m	i	m	a
count:	1	&	2	&	3	&	4	&	1	&	2	&	3	&	4	&

This next one is a typical progression found in rock music. Using all downstrokes gives it a more driving rhythmic feel.

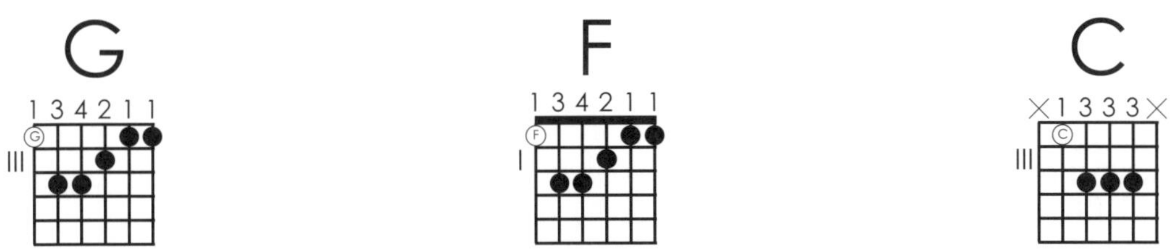

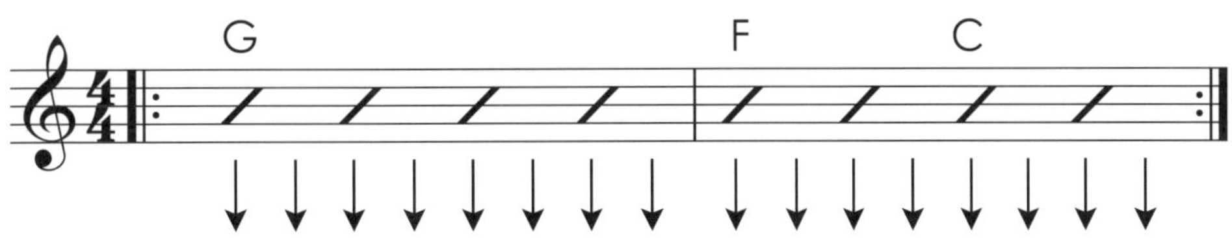

1 & 2 & 3 & 4 & 1 & 2 & 3 & 4 &

One more example:

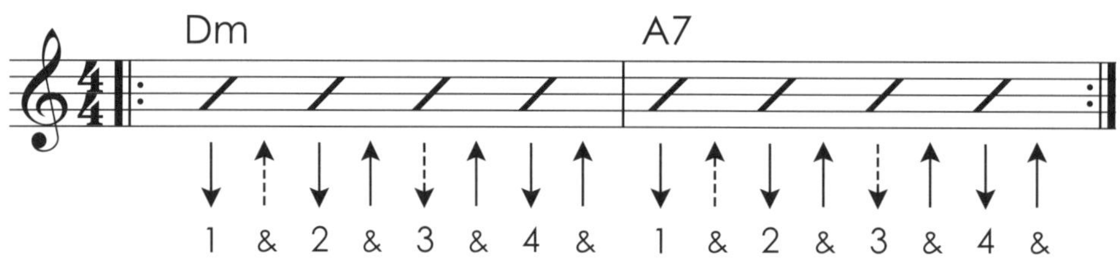

Notice that you now have more than one way to play a lot of these chords. This will be of great use to you as you learn (and write) songs. You have prepared yourself for playing so much music with the chord vocabulary you have developed in these lessons.

Spend some significant time exploring possibilities with barre chords. Mix and match any of these six barre chords with any of the chord progressions, strum patterns and fingerpicking patterns. This is a great way to build your technique as a guitarist.

Lesson 60

Learn Right Hand Picking Exercise #1

Soon we will be working on scale vocabulary, so it is a good idea to prepare for the specific techniques necessary to play scales. Right hand picking technique is very important to playing scales with accuracy and speed. So we are now going to address the particulars of how to develop an effective approach to right hand picking technique.

This simple exercise will enable you to focus on your right hand and on accurate picking. Here are the right hand picking symbols:

⊓ = downstroke   V = upstroke

Four notes per string:

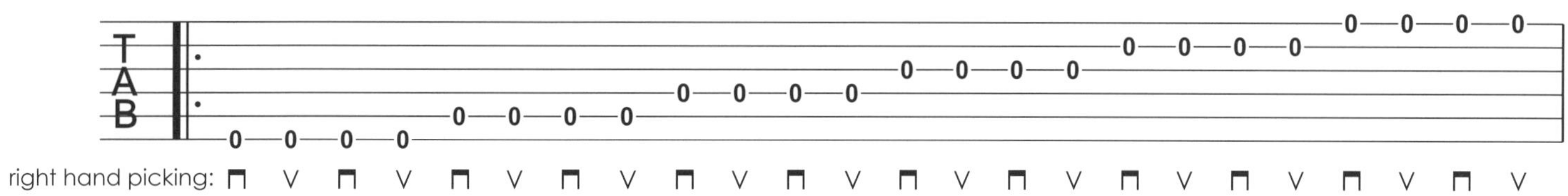

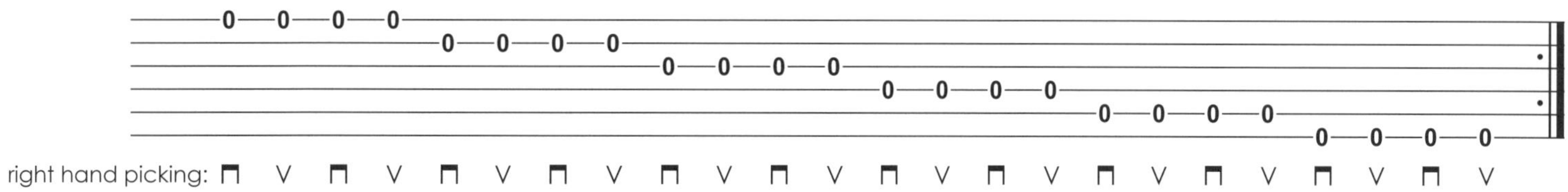

To help stabilize your hand while it is picking, you can anchor the hand on the strings. But you must do it in a specific way:

When picking strings 6, 5, and 4,
rest the back of the curled-in fingers
on strings 3, 2, and 1

When picking strings 3, 2, and 1,
rest heel of hand
on strings 6, 5, and 4

Set a timer and do this exercise for five minutes at a time.

Learn Right Hand Picking Exercises #2 & #3

Lesson **61**

Here are two more exercises to get your right hand picking up to speed. Remember, it's all about consistent alternate picking.

Two notes per string:

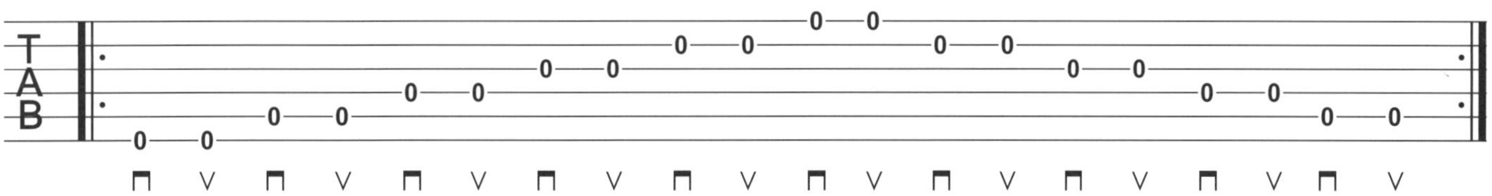

Three notes per string:

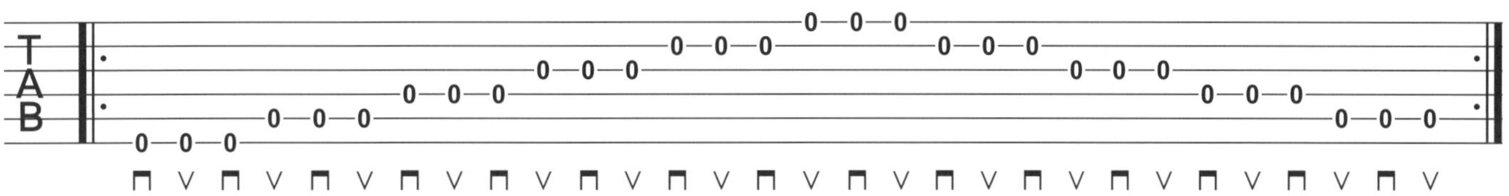

After you get comfortable with the three picking exercises, add foot tapping. You will tap your foot on the first note of each grouping, like this:

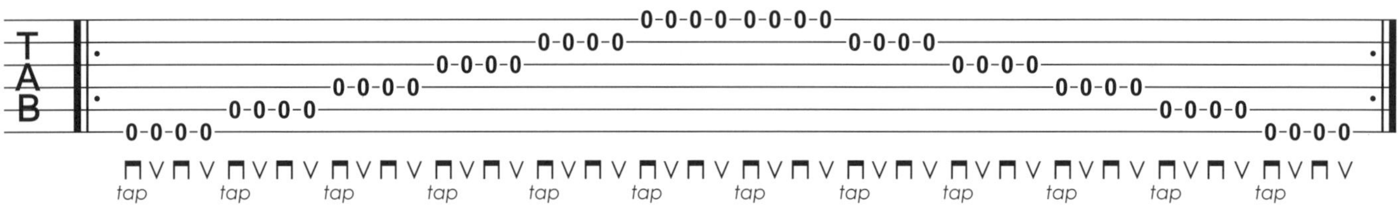

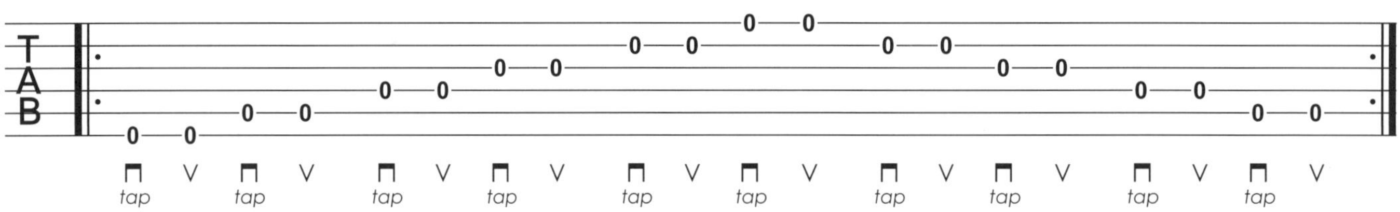

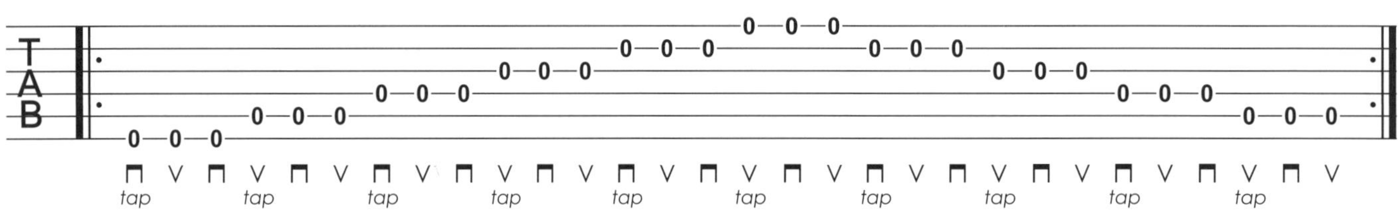

Learn the Pseudo-Chromatic Exercise

Lesson 62

This is a very basic exercise that will introduce you to the techniques necessary to play scales on the guitar. It utilizes all four fingers and is an excellent way to build left hand finger agility.

Here's what the notes look like on a neck diagram:

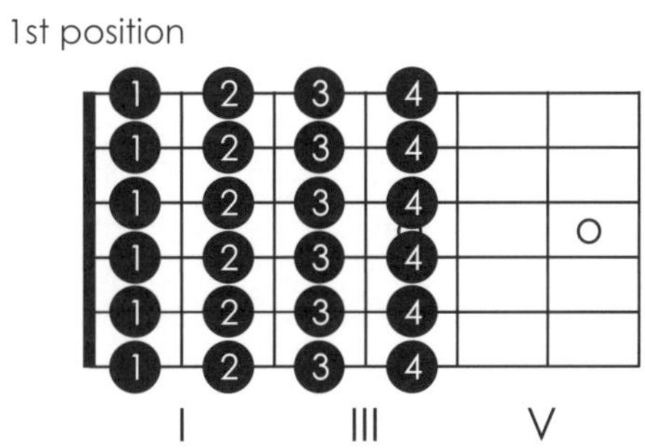

Here's what the notes look like on tablature:

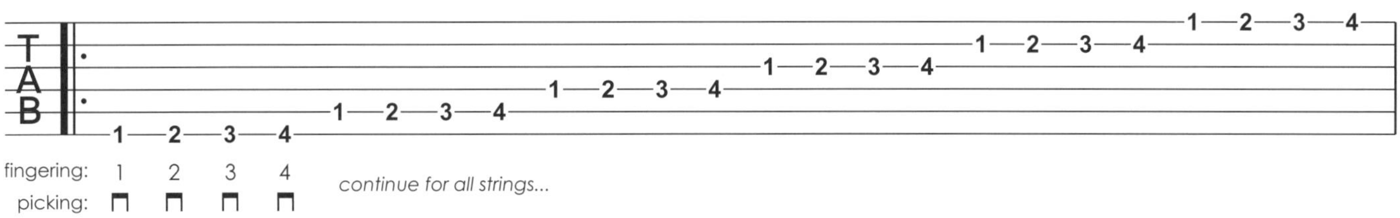

Here are some particulars you want to pay attention to:

- *For the right hand picking, use all down strokes (at first)*
- *When ascending, keep fingers down on the strings*
- *When descending, keep fingers low over the strings*

Start off playing this very slowly. Actually, don't even play it in tempo. Then, after awhile when you get comfortable with the exercise, you can play each note evenly.

Play this exercise ascending and descending at every fret up the neck in every **position**.

position = *determined by what fret your first finger is on, on any string*

Variation: play this exercise up one position then down the next, continuing up the fretboard.

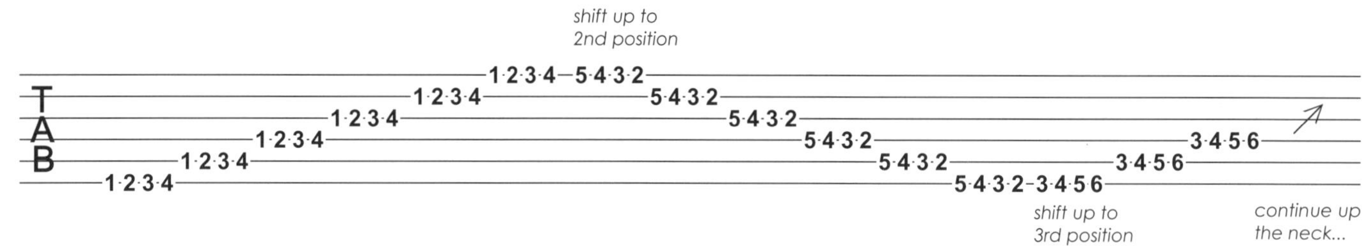

Here's another variation: use alternate picking with the right hand. This means you'll be picking *down up down up* on each string.

Important!

Wait until you are comfortable with all aspects of the left hand before you add alternate picking to the exercise.

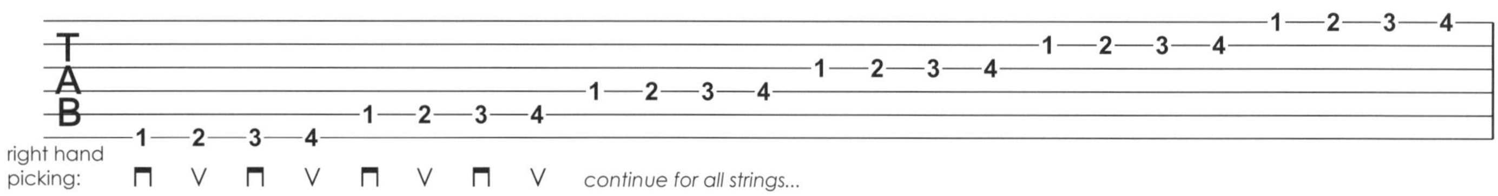

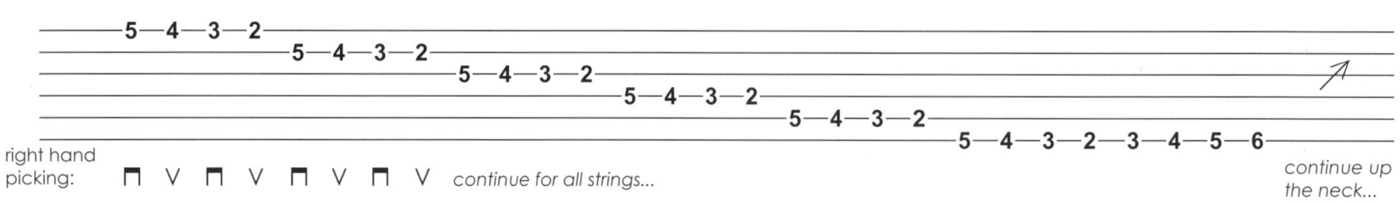

Learn the note names on the 4th, 3rd, 2nd & 1st strings

Lesson 63

Now it is time to learn the note names on the rest of the strings. Knowing the note names on your instrument is probably one of the most important skills to develop as a musician.

You will undoubtedly notice that the note names on the 6th and 1st strings are the same. But they don't sound exactly the same—they are two octaves apart.

octave = *same note name,*
but higher or lower pitch

You are going to utilize the same drill you used for the 5th and 6th strings to learn the remaining strings.

Drill:

- Choose a note name randomly (**C**, **D**, **E**, **F**, **G**, **A**, **B**)
- Find that note on the string and play it with your 1st finger
- Choose another note name, find it and play it (*go slowly*)
- Continue in this manner for at least five minutes

Important!

Work on the strings one at a time and do not move on to the next string until you've mastered the previous strings. Otherwise, your brain will just get all confused when it tries to keep track of the same seven letters at different frets on six different strings.

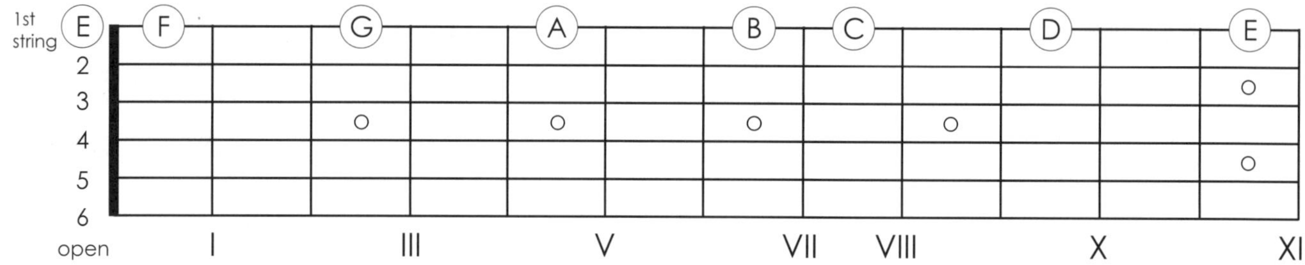
1st string
E F G A B C D E
2
3
4
5
6
open
I III V VII VIII X XII

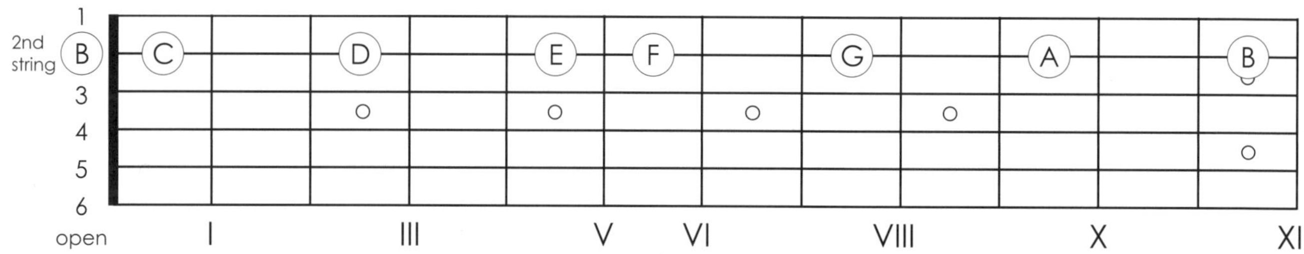
1
2nd string
B C D E F G A B
3
4
5
6
open
I III V VI VIII X XII

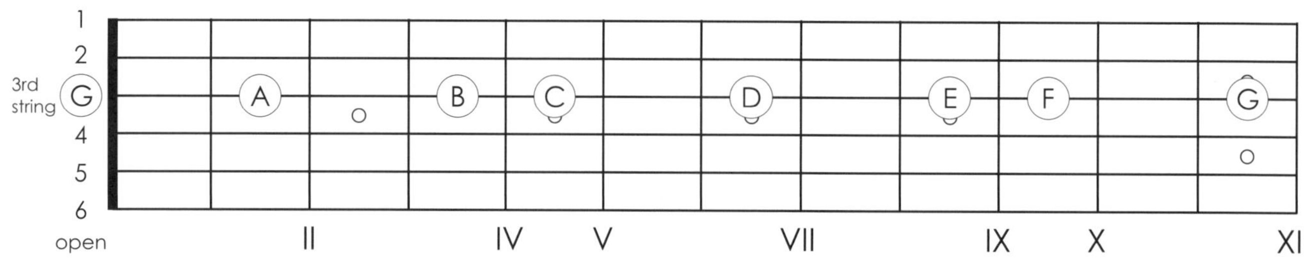
1
2
3rd string
G A B C D E F G
4
5
6
open
II IV V VII IX X XII

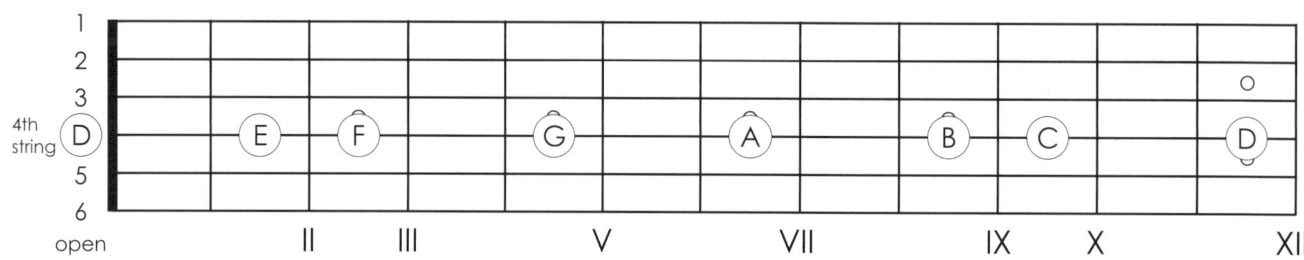
1
2
3
4th string
D E F G A B C D
5
6
open
II III V VII IX X XII

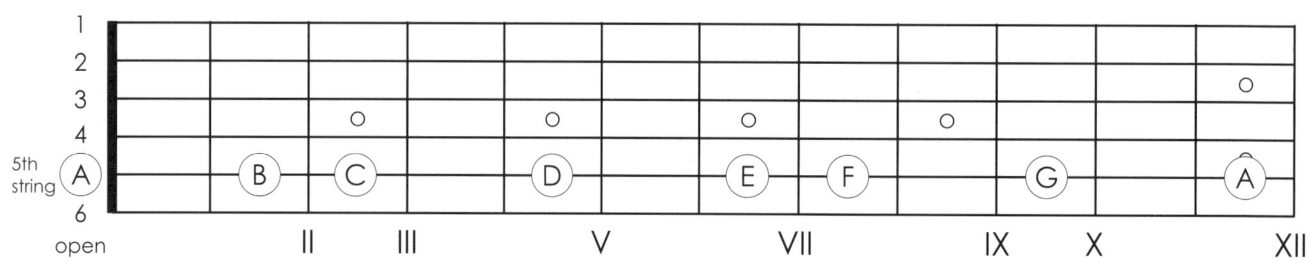
1
2
3
4
5th string
A B C D E F G A
6
open
II III V VII IX X XII

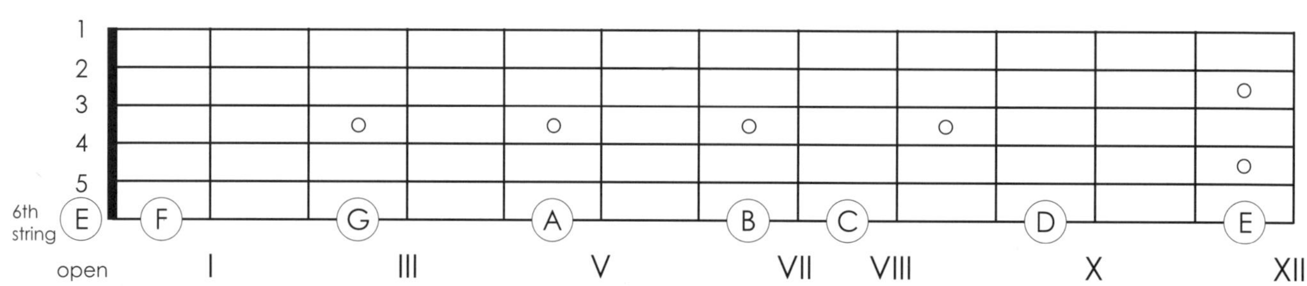
1
2
3
4
5
6th string
E F G A B C D E
open
I III V VII VIII X XII

Learn to play hammer-ons

Lesson

64

Hammer-ons are another way to get from one note to another note on the same string. The name is somewhat literal because you pick the lower note with your right hand and then "hammer" your fingertip onto the higher note. These exercises will benefit you greatly in building strength in your left hand fingers.

Here are some particulars that you want to pay attention to:

- Pick the lower note and hammer on the finger to the higher note
- Keep the lower finger down on the string
- Do each pair of fingers four times on all six strings
- Practice these exercises in various positions: I, V, IX, XII, XV

Here are all the possible pairs of fingers:

1–4
1–3
2–4
1–2
2–3
3–4

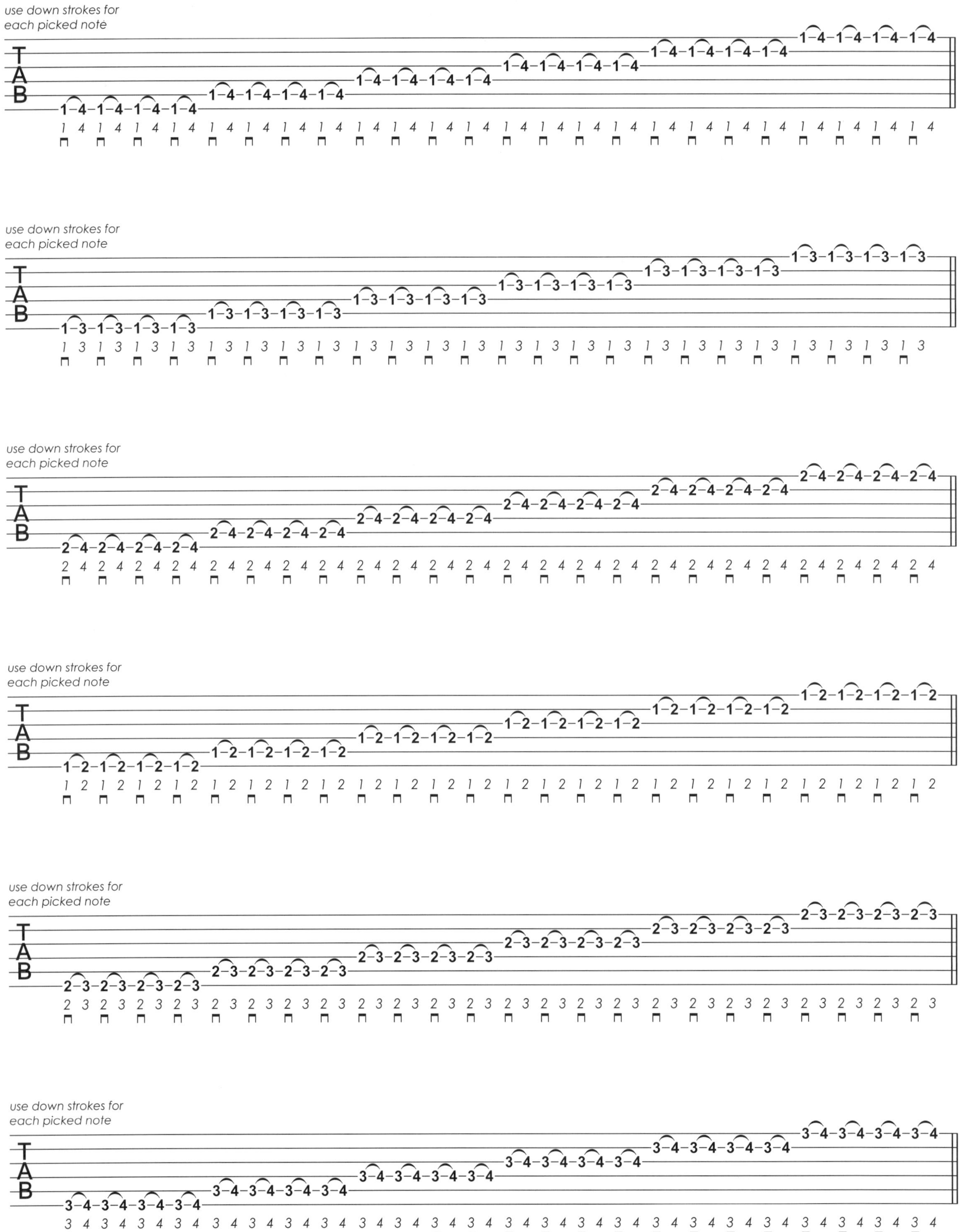
use down strokes for each picked note
use down strokes for each picked note
use down strokes for each picked note
use down strokes for each picked note
use down strokes for each picked note
use down strokes for each picked note

Lesson 65

Learn to play pull-offs

Pull-offs are similar to hammer-ons. They are also another way to get from one note to another note on the same string. However, whereas hammer-ons go from a *lower* to a *higher* note, pull-offs go from a *higher* to a *lower* note. So the action involved is different. With pull-offs, you do a slight downward flicking motion with your finger. This makes the resulting note clearer.

Here are some particulars you want to pay attention to:

- Pick the higher note and pull-off the finger to the lower note
- Keep the lower finger down on the string
- Do each pair of fingers four times on all six strings
- Practice these exercises in various positions: I, V, IX, XII, XV

Here are all the possible pairs of fingers:

4–1
3–1
4–2
2–1
3–2
4–3

use down strokes for each picked note

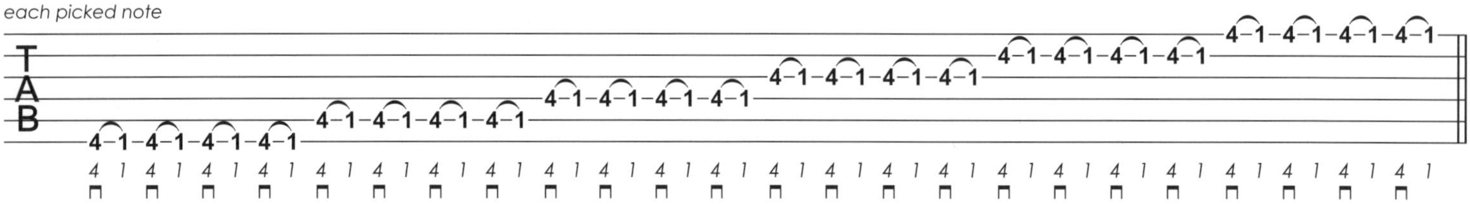

use down strokes for each picked note

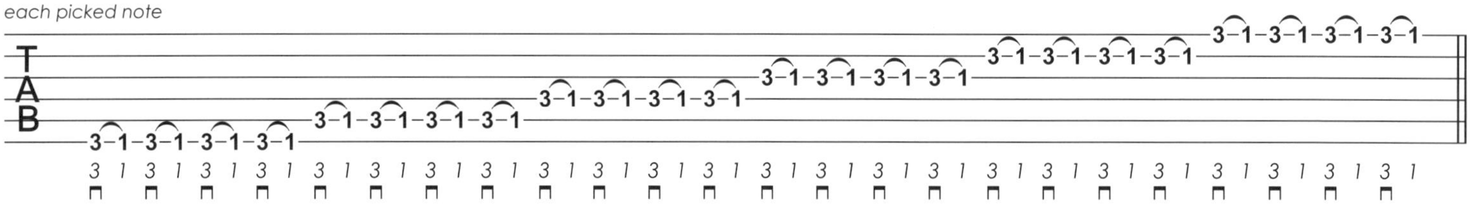

use down strokes for each picked note

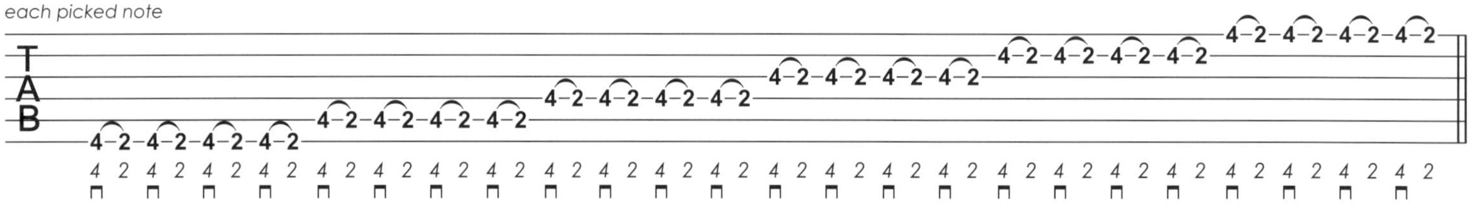

use down strokes for each picked note

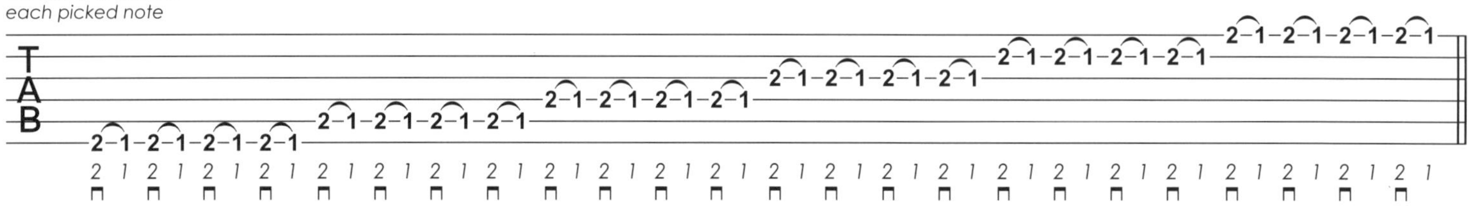

use down strokes for each picked note

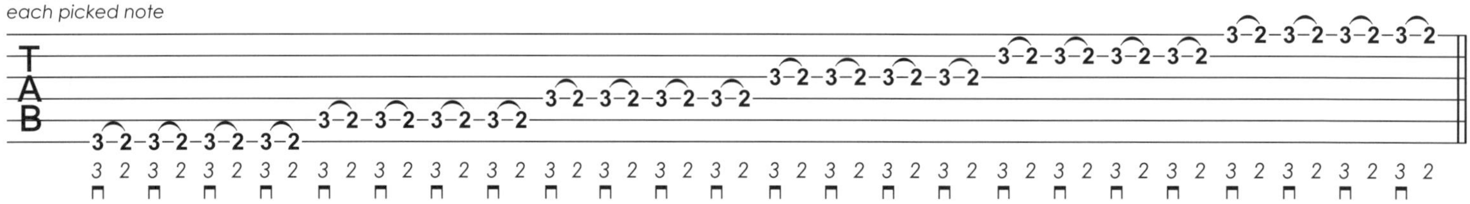

use down strokes for each picked note

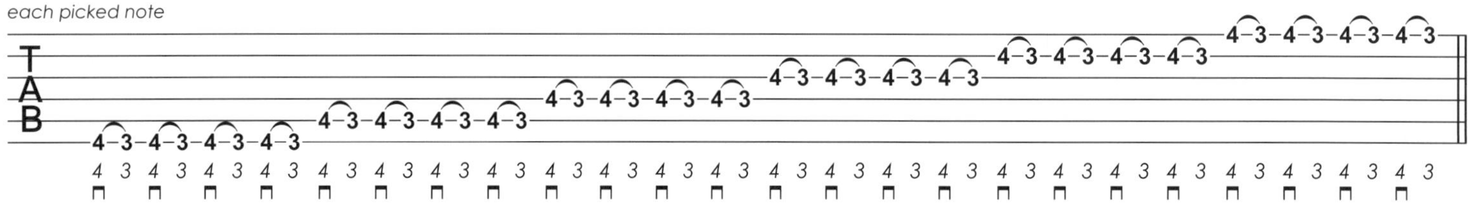

Lesson 66

Learn about slash chords

The chord symbols for slash chords can be a little intimidating. But as it turns out, these chords are common in music and quite often are just as easy to finger as any of the chords you already know.

slash chord = *chord / lowest note in the chord*

Here are some examples of common slash chords.

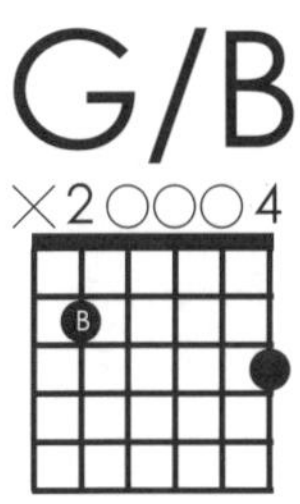

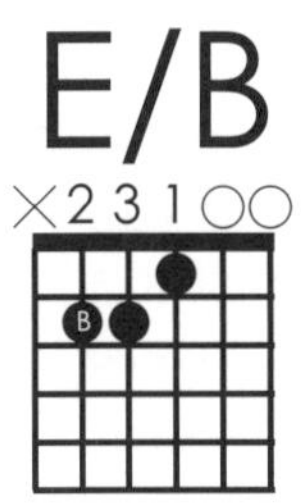

Here are two examples of slash chords being used in a chord progression. Notice how an interesting bass line is created by changing the lowest note of the G major chord in Example 1 and the D major chord in Example 2.

Example 1:

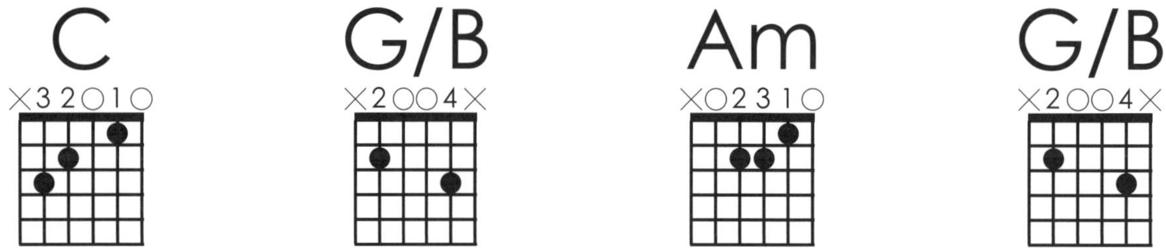

Example 2:

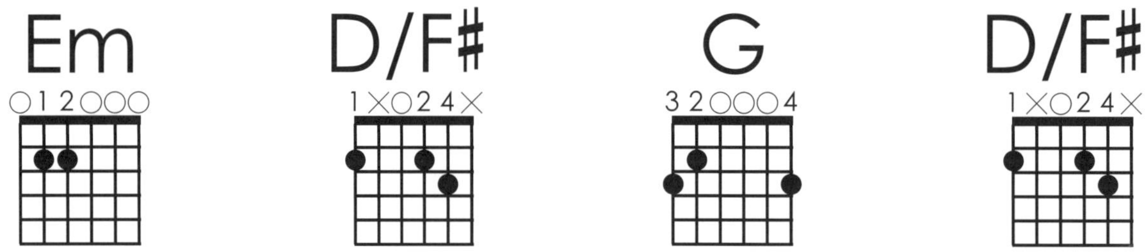

Just so you know, it is common to hear people refer to slash chords as
"G with B in the bass" and also "G over B".

Learn the Minor Pentatonic Scale Pattern #1

There are many different types of scales used in many different types of music. Out of all the scales, the minor pentatonic scale is one of the most common.

You are going to learn this scale in a way that you will eventually be able to play it in any key, anywhere on the fretboard. This skill will enable you to create music freely and easily.

This is the first of the five patterns for minor pentatonic:

G Minor Pentatonic Scale Pattern #1

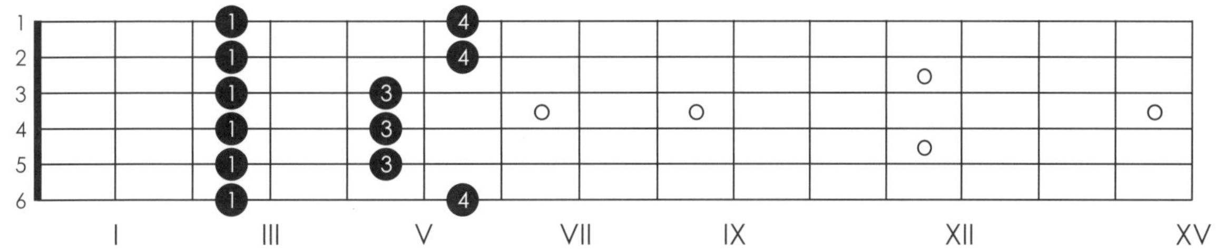

Important!

Make sure you start off very slowly to give your brain and your fingers time to learn the pattern. Begin by playing the pattern one note at a time, so slowly that you can think about each note you are playing.

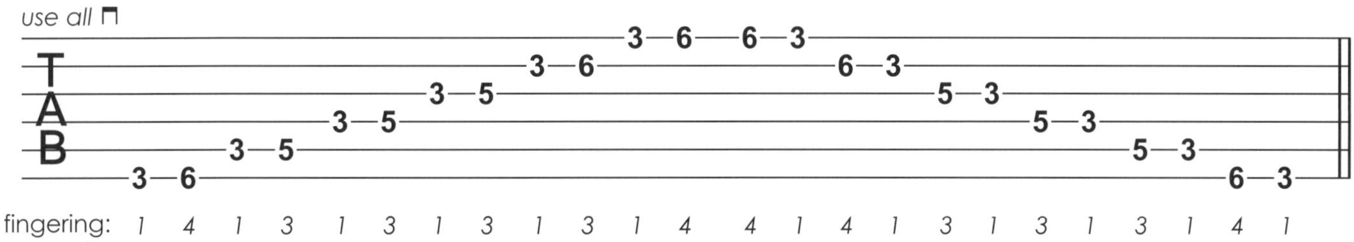

Here are the actual note names in the pattern.

G Minor Pentatonic Scale = G B♭ C D F

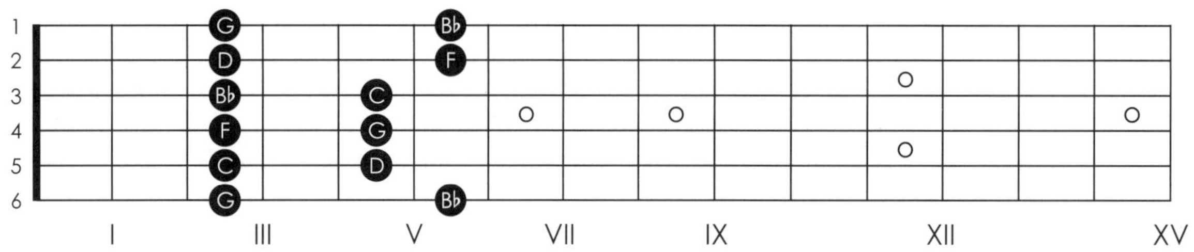

A scale pattern on the guitar represents all the notes of that scale that occur in, and around, that fretboard position.

More about this later—I just wanted to show you what this will all eventually look like to you after you've been working with these scale patterns for a while.

When learning a new scale pattern:

- Go slowly! No tempo, just one note at a time
- Multiple passes, ascending and descending
- Strive for ten or more accurate repetitions
- Focus on fingering for now—note names will come later

Learn the Minor Pentatonic Scale Pattern #2

This is the second of the five patterns for minor pentatonic:

G Minor Pentatonic Scale Pattern #2

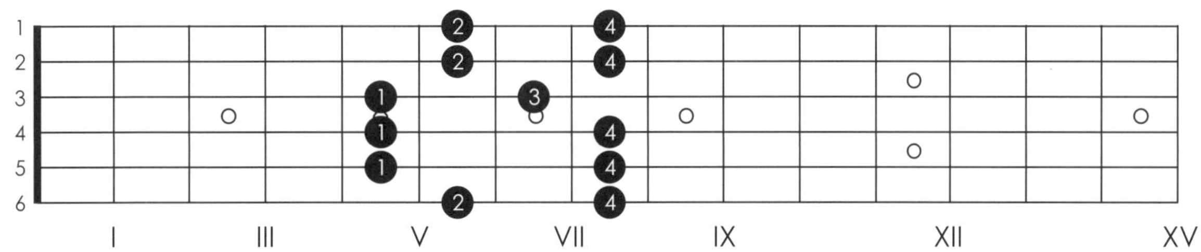

Notice how pattern #1 and pattern #2 overlap—the notes on the 5th and 6th frets are the same.

Also, remember that term, **position**. It refers to the fret number your *1st finger* is at. In this case, with pattern #2, you are in V position (5th) and you start the pattern with your 2nd finger on the 6th fret of the 6th string.

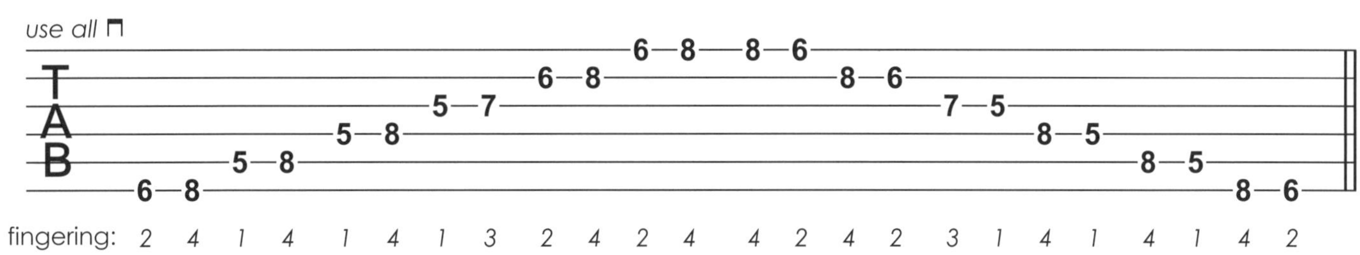

So remember, when learning a new scale pattern:

- Go slowly! No tempo, just one note at a time
- Multiple passes, ascending and descending
- Strive for ten or more accurate repetitions
- Focus on fingering for now—note names will come later

Lesson 69

Learn the Minor Pentatonic Scale Pattern #3

This is the third of the five patterns for minor pentatonic:

G Minor Pentatonic Scale Pattern #3

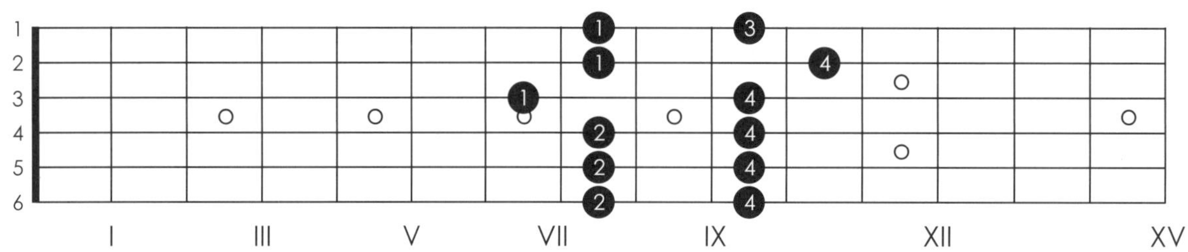

Pattern #3 is a little different than the other four because it has a position shift. This occurs between the 2nd and 3rd strings. Your hand will shift from IX position to X position ascending and then your hand will shift from X position to IX position descending.

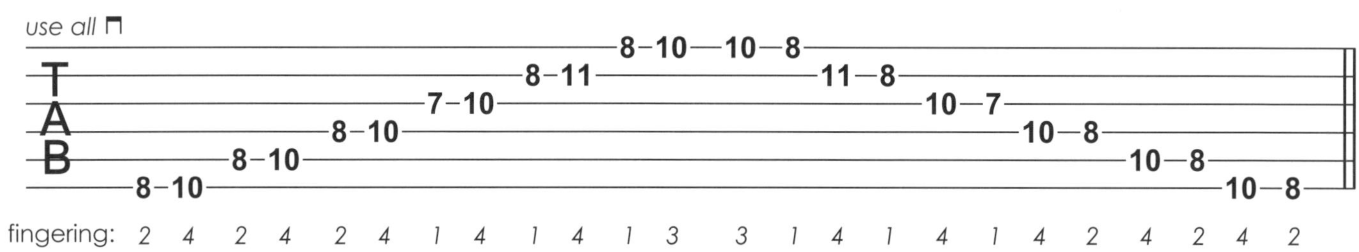

As always, when learning a new scale pattern:

- Go slowly! No tempo, just one note at a time
- Multiple passes, ascending and descending
- Strive for ten or more accurate repetitions
- Focus on fingering for now—note names will come later

Learn the Minor Pentatonic Scale Pattern #4

This is the fourth of the five patterns for minor pentatonic:

G Minor Pentatonic Scale Pattern #4

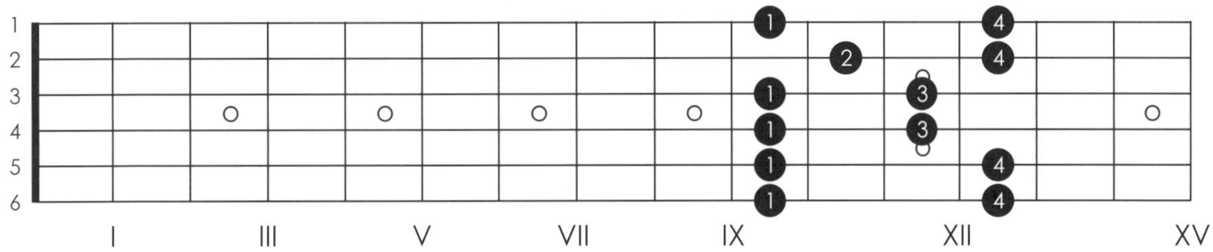

This entire pattern is in X (tenth) position.

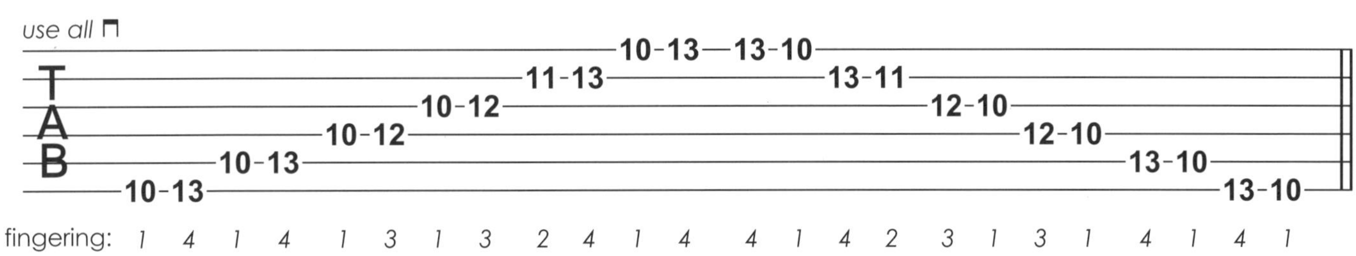

Don't forget, when learning a new scale pattern:

- Go slowly! No tempo, just one note at a time
- Multiple passes, ascending and descending
- Strive for ten or more accurate repetitions
- Focus on fingering for now—note names will come later

Lesson 71 Learn the Minor Pentatonic Scale Pattern #5

This is the fifth of the five patterns for minor pentatonic:

G Minor Pentatonic Scale Pattern #5

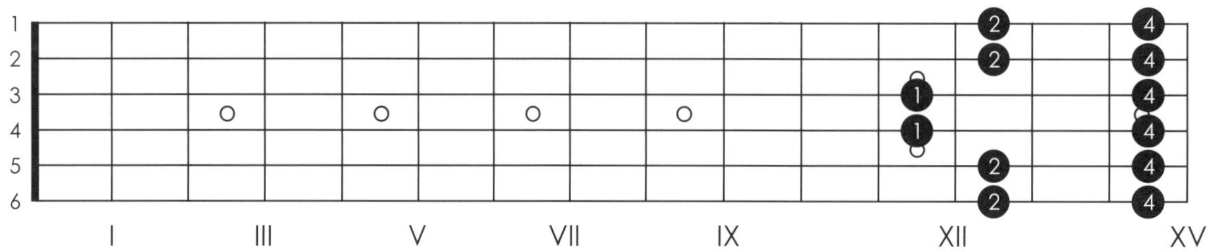

It is important to maintain good posture when playing high up the fretboard. Make sure not to hunch over the guitar. You can actually reach all the notes with your body, arm and hand in their usual position.

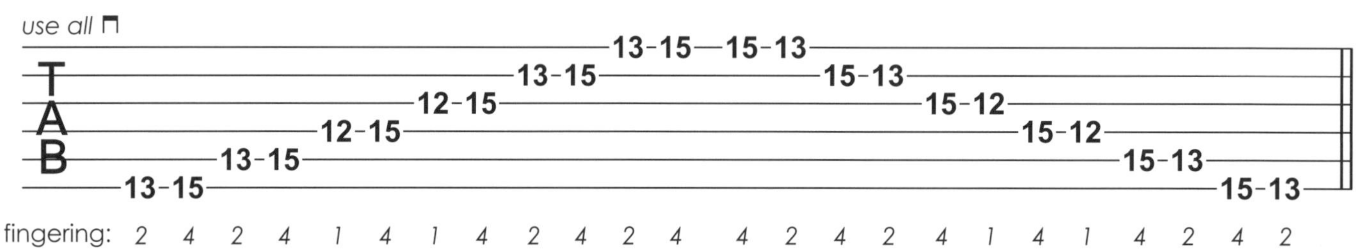

By now you know that when learning a new scale pattern:

- Go slowly! No tempo, just one note at a time
- Multiple passes, ascending and descending
- Strive for ten or more accurate repetitions
- Focus on fingering for now—note names will come later

Learn about tonic shapes

Lesson **72**

Tonic shapes are an excellent way to organize the fretboard so that you always know what key you are in. This enables you to use your musical vocabulary to create music freely.

Let's start with clarifying a few music theory terms:

root and **tonic** mean the same thing: it's the key you're in

Now, what does key mean? Well, there is an in-depth definition based on a lot of music theory, and then there is a simplistic definition, which is a little vague. Let's go with the latter:

key = *a group of notes that belong together, which songs use to create melodies and chords.*

So when someone says that a song is in a particular key, for example "the key of E", they are usually referring to E major and there are certain notes that are used for that key. Songs can also be in minor keys as well, like "the key of A minor."

Essentially, these tonic shapes are fundamentally just octave shapes (**octave** = same note name, but higher or lower). You want to know them by both names: **tonic shapes** and **octave shapes**.

Once again, I am suggesting that you focus on keeping it simple for now and trust that you will learn the details of music theory later, after you've been playing music for a while. This is an effective approach. I've stated before that one of the cooler aspects of learning to play the guitar is that you do not have to really know a lot about music theory in the beginning—it's all about shapes and fingerings and patterns.

Here are the tonic shapes in each pattern:
(all the other note names are here for reference—mainly focus on the tonics)

G Minor Pentatonic Scale Pattern #1

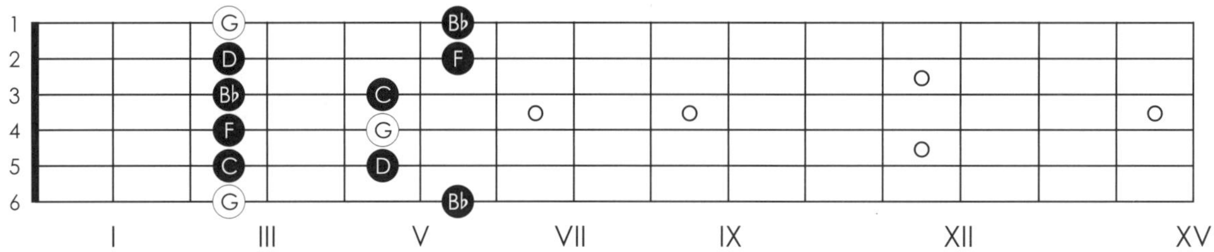

Tonic Shape #1

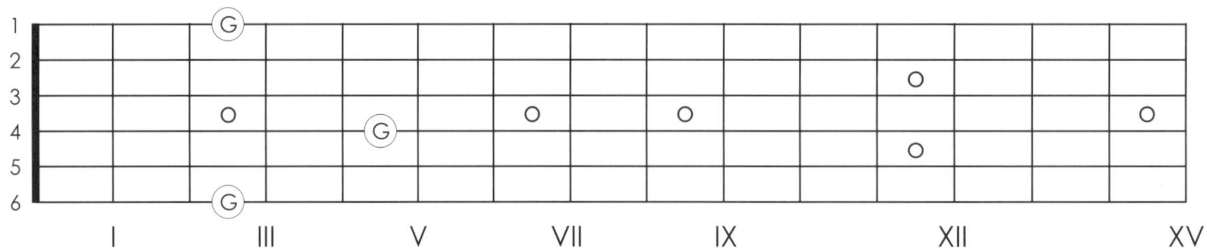

G Minor Pentatonic Scale Pattern #2

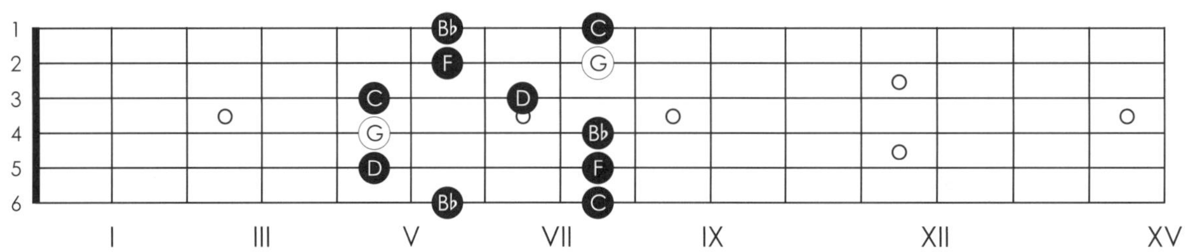

Tonic Shape #2

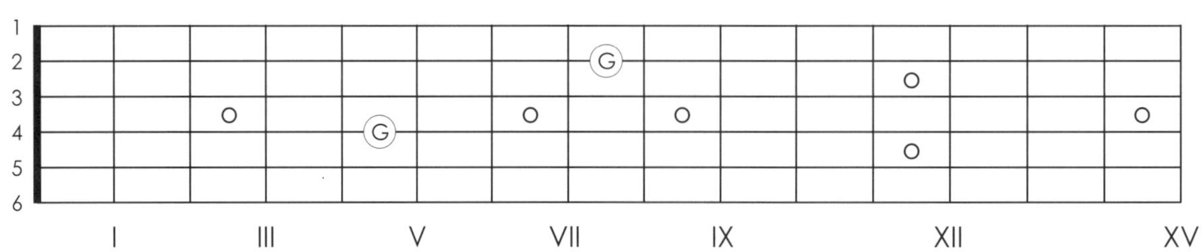

G Minor Pentatonic Scale Pattern #3

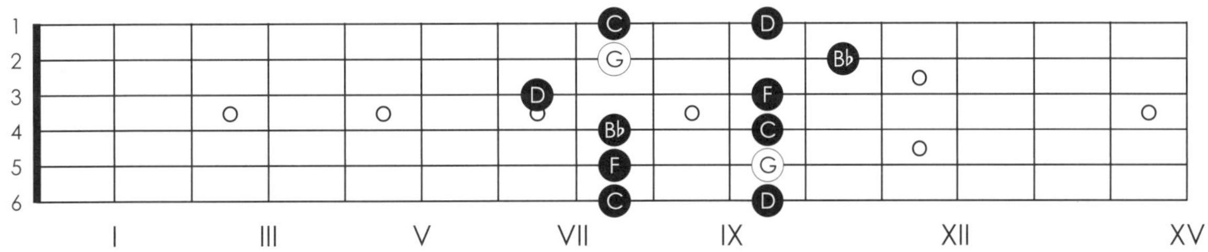

Tonic Shape #3

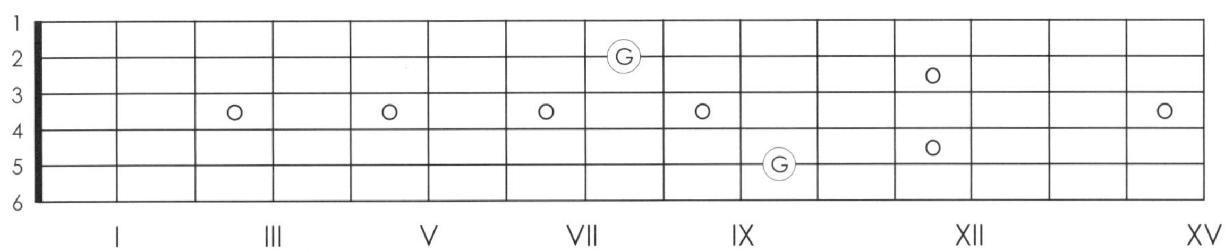

G Minor Pentatonic Scale Pattern #4

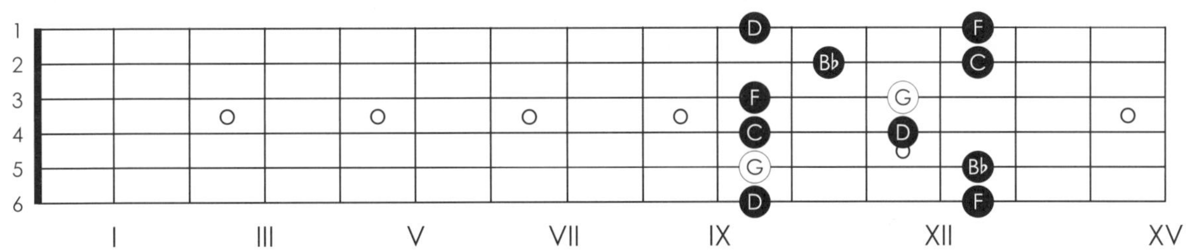

Tonic Shape #4

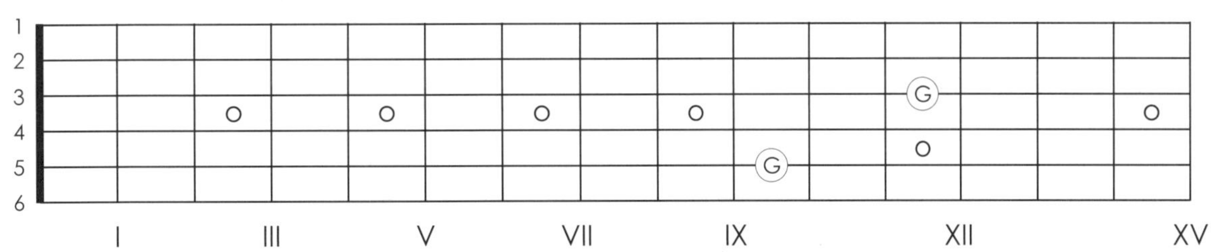

G Minor Pentatonic Scale Pattern #5

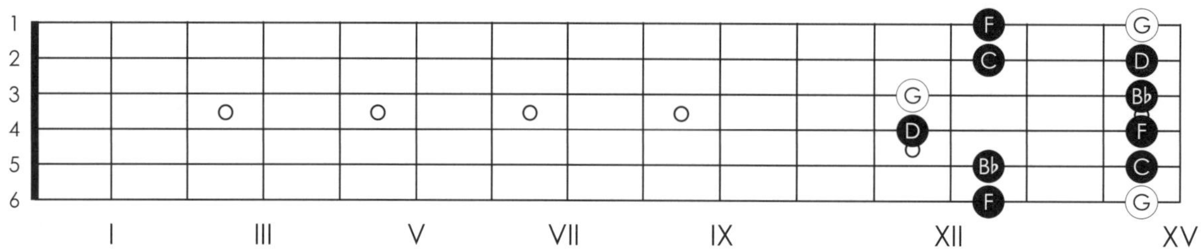

Tonic Shape #5

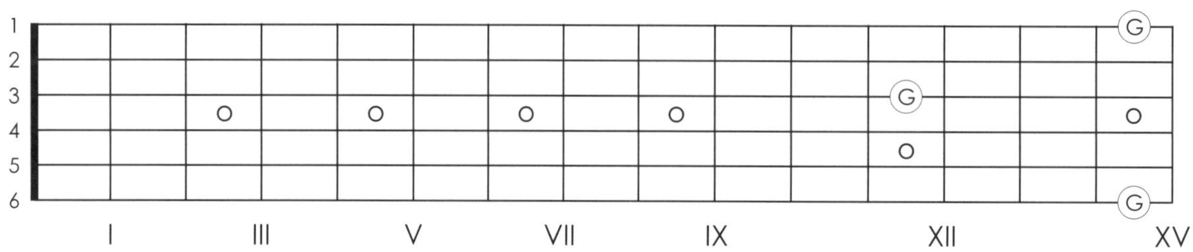

Notice that these tonic shapes overlap: the "left note(s)" of the *higher* tonic shape is/are the same as the"right note(s)" of the *lower* tonic shape.

Also, there isn't any specific fingering for the tonic shapes themselves. It is best if you relate to these shapes by what string the notes are on, along with how many frets apart they are. But when you go to play them by themselves, just use a fingering that makes the most sense. It doesn't always have to correspond to the fingering of the scale pattern they're from, but often that will indeed work.

All of the music vocabulary that you will ever learn (chords, scales and arpeggios) will be based on these shapes. Soon you will be using them to navigate the fretboard and create music in a way where you know exactly what you are doing!

So, get these tonic shapes down solid and be able to play them in any order.

Lesson 73

Learn to play hammer-ons & pull-offs with groups of three fingers

Here are some exercises that will further develop your technique using hammer-ons and pull-offs. They involve doing two successive hammer-ons, or pull-offs, with every combination of three fingers. Let's use the same procedure we did for the previous exercises:

- Pick the lower note and hammer-on the fingers to the higher notes
- Keep the lowest finger down on the string
- Do each grouping of fingers four times on all six strings
- Practice these exercises in various positions: I, V, IX, XII, XV, etc.

Here are all the possible finger groupings of three fingers for hammer-ons:

1–2–4
1–3–4
1–2–3
2–3–4

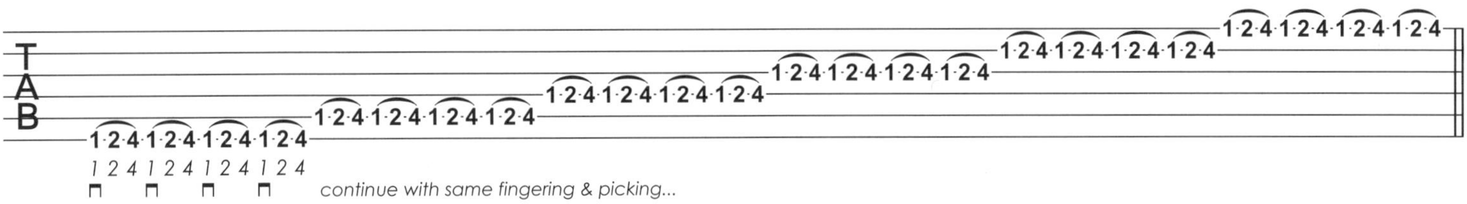

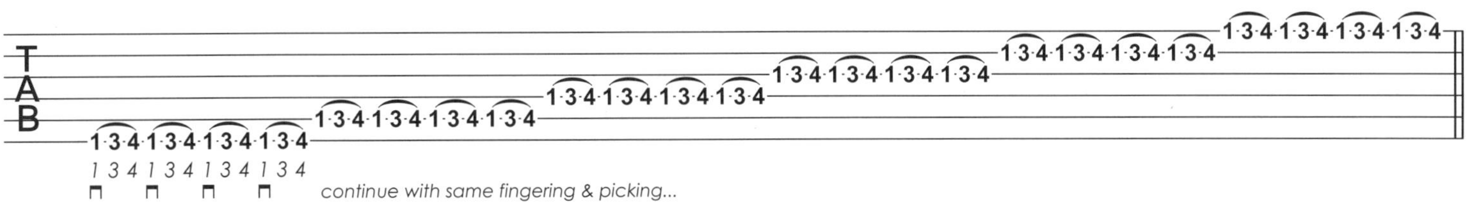

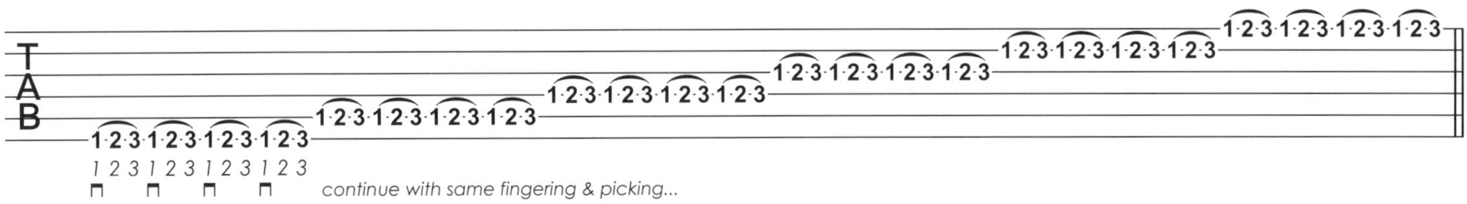

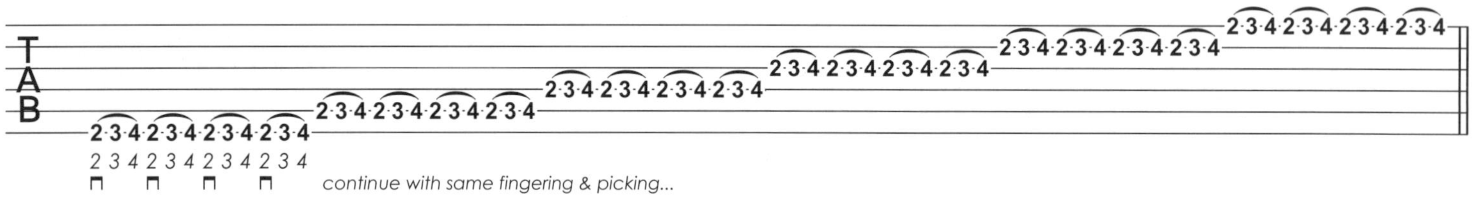

Now let's do the same procedure using pull-offs, except here you will pick the higher note and pull off the fingers to the lower notes.

Important!

Make sure you replace the fingers *simultaneously* before each execution of the pull-off groupings.

Here are all of the possible finger groupings of three fingers for pull-offs:

4–2–1

4–3–1

3–2–1

4–3–2

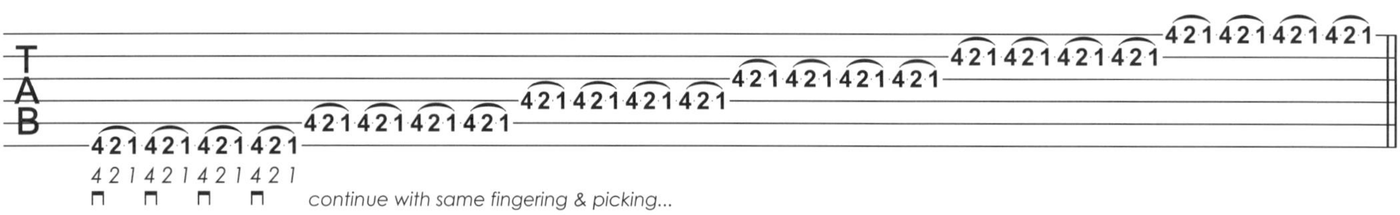

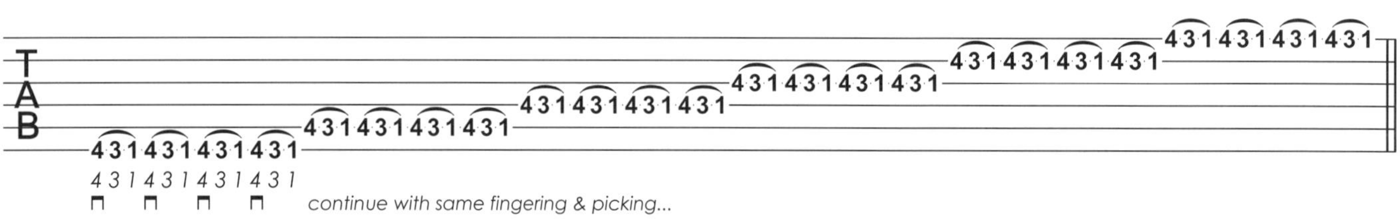

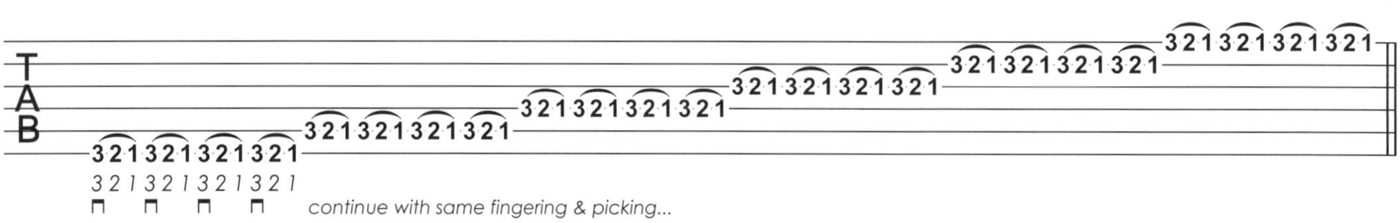

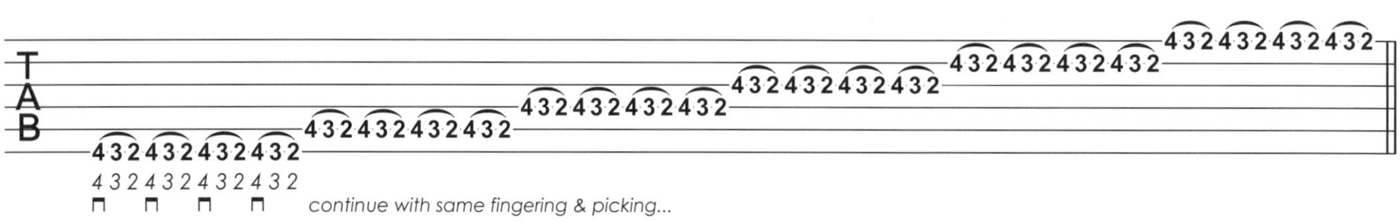

Learn how to play power chords

Lesson 74

Power chords are extremely popular in rock music and are a lot of fun to play. Essentially, they are the "bottoms" of your barre chords—the lower three strings. They function the same way as barre chords in that they are movable and the lowest note represents the chord name.

One thing that is interesting with power chords is that they are neither major, minor or dominant 7th in their quality. So you can actually substitute a power chord for any chord in a chord progression and give it a more "rock" sound.

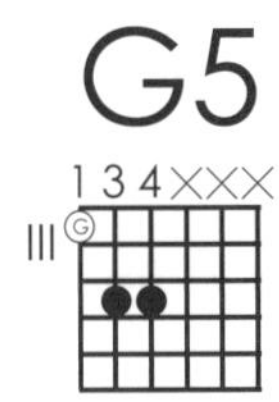

5 = *chord symbol for a power chord*

Here are all of the power chords that you will use in the next chord progression example. They are substitutions for G major, F major and C major:

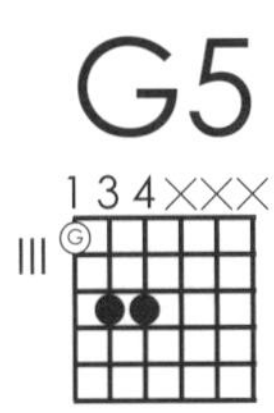

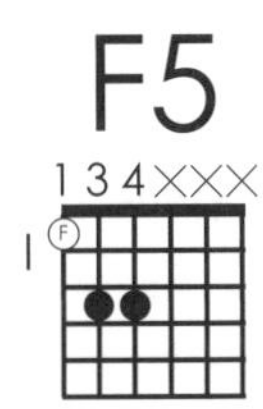

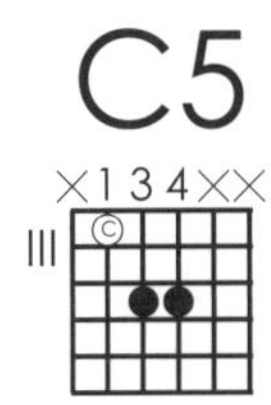

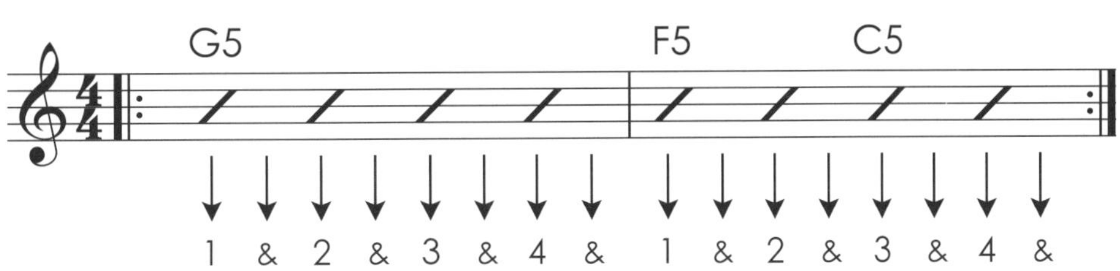

The power chords you will use in the next chord progression example (in this example, the B5 is substituted for a *B minor*):

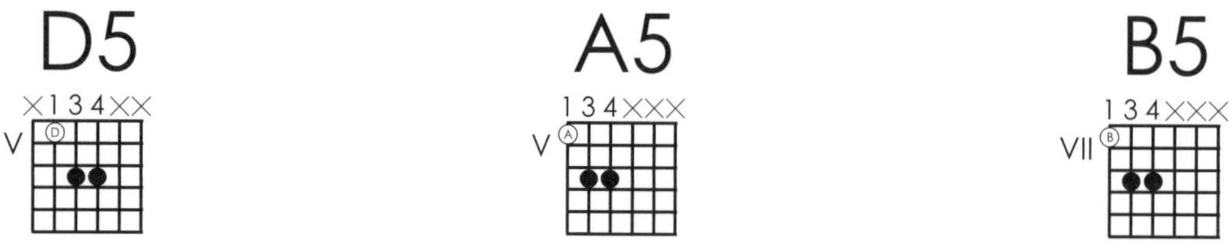

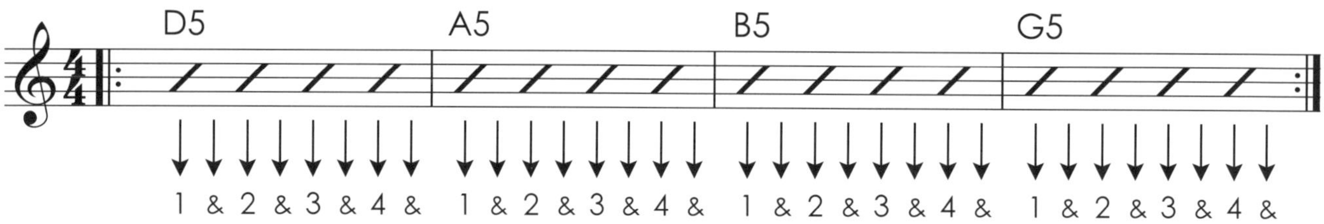

Or you could do the same progression with two beats for each chord:

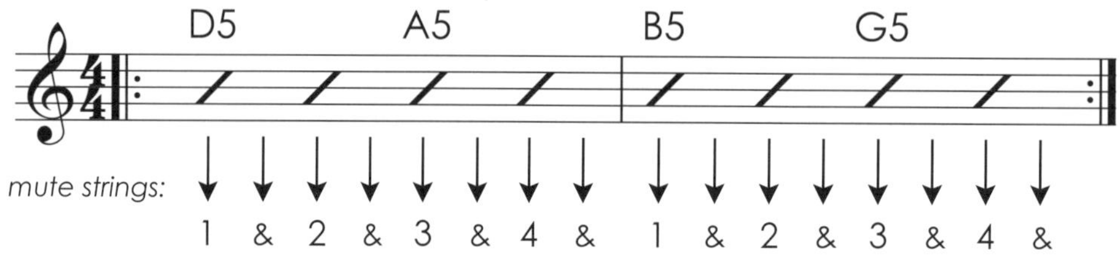

Lay your right hand slightly on the strings close to the bridge to give the chords a muted sound (the heel of your hand should come just a little bit over the saddles). This is a common approach to playing power chords. It gives them a "tighter" sound.

So now you can go back to any of the chord progressions you've worked on so far and experiment with using power chords in place of the full chords. I think you will immediately hear the connection to the sounds you hear used by rock guitarists.

Lesson 75

Learn how to play slides

So far, we've looked at picking notes and also hammer-ons and pull-offs as ways to get from one note to another. You can also get from one note to another by sliding. This technique is very simple and quite often guitar players discover it in their own "organic" way.

You simply pick the first note and slide to the next.

You can go in either direction:

Or you can combine slides:

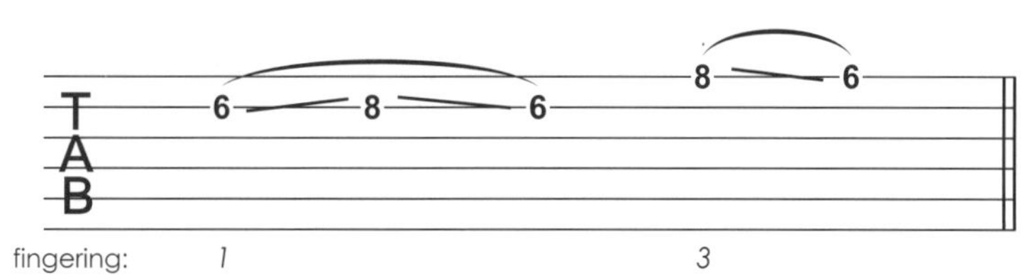

You can slide at any rate of speed from very slow to very fast. And you can slide any distance, as many frets as you want.

Here are two examples using the minor pentatonic scales. This will take you from the bottom note of pattern #1 up to the top note of pattern #5.

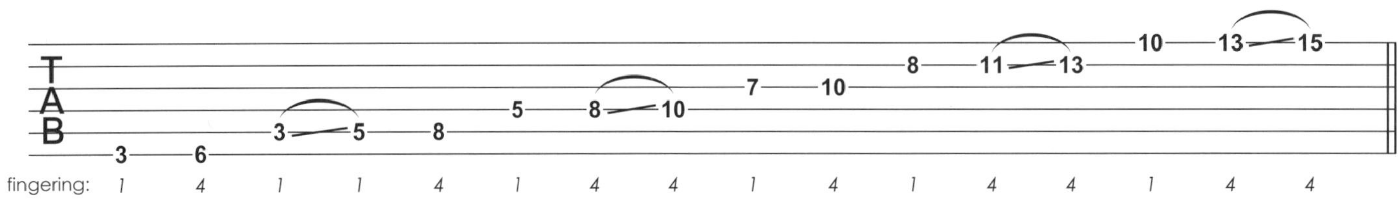

And back down again.

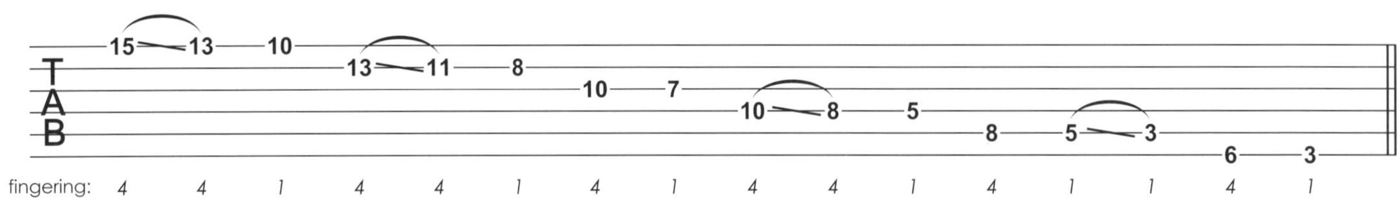

Then you can combine the two into one long phrase that covers quite a bit of the fretboard.

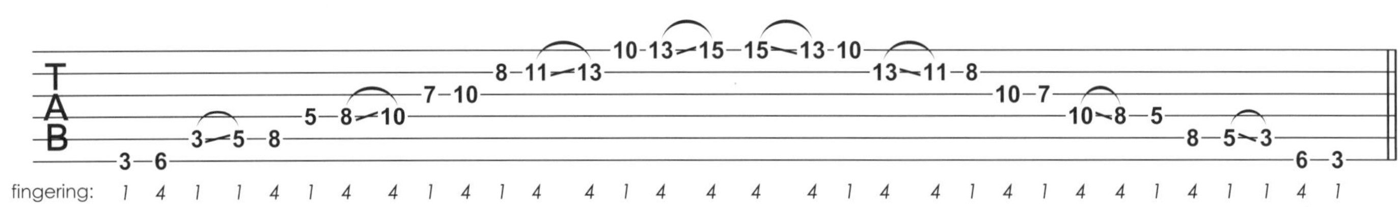

There are many possibilities for you to explore with finding pathways through the scale patterns. After learning these examples, spend some time discovering your own, using sliding technique to get from one note to the next.

Lesson 76

Learn how to combine hammer-ons & pull-offs

Now we are going to combine hammer-ons and pull-offs into one action. This is a very common technique and you will use it frequently when you play guitar solos. These exercises are great for developing finger strength and independence.

All of the same considerations apply here as they did in previous exercises involving hammer-ons and pull-offs:

- Pick the lower note and play the rest of the notes with HO's or PO's
- Keep the lower finger down on the string
- Do each pair of fingers four times on all six strings
- Practice these exercises in various positions: I, V, IX, XII, XV, etc. (here they are written out in V position, just to mix it up a little)

These are all the possible pairs of fingers:

1-4
1-3
2-4
1-2
2-3
3-4

use down strokes for each picked note

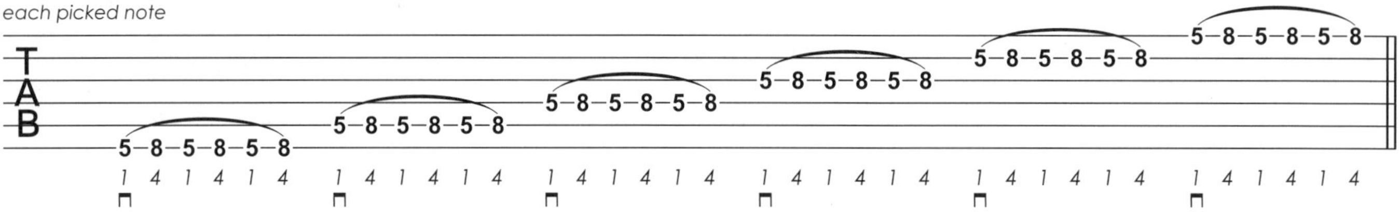

use down strokes for each picked note

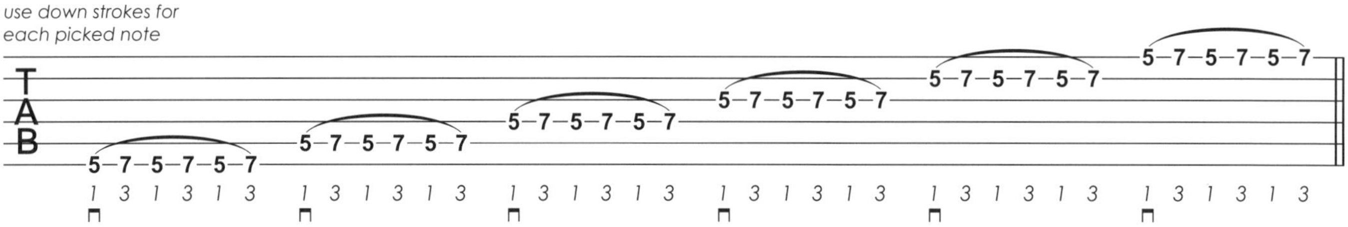

use down strokes for each picked note

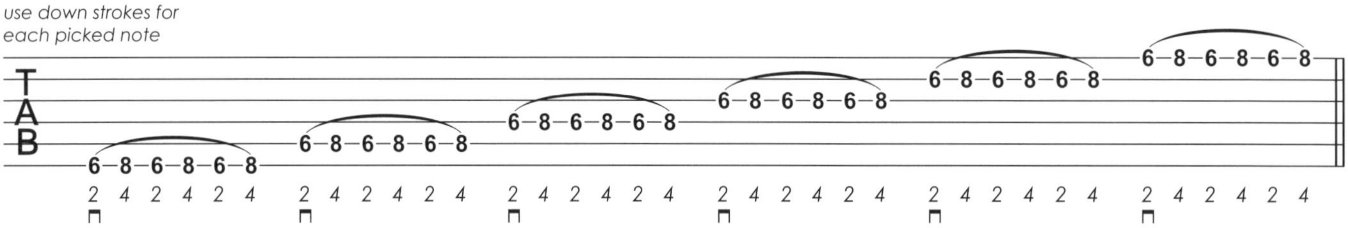

use down strokes for each picked note

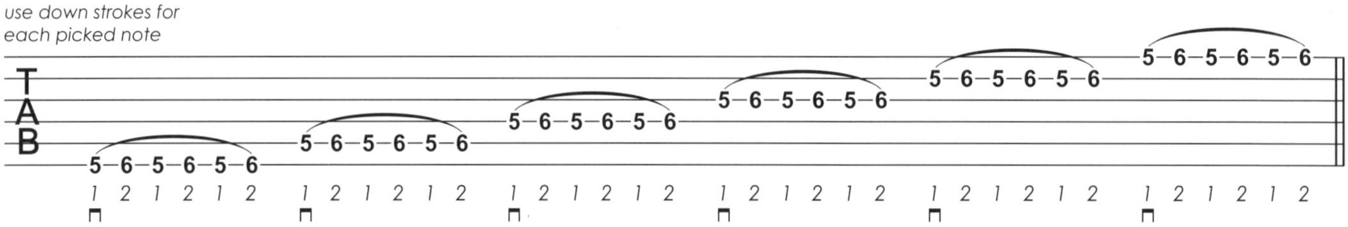

use down strokes for each picked note

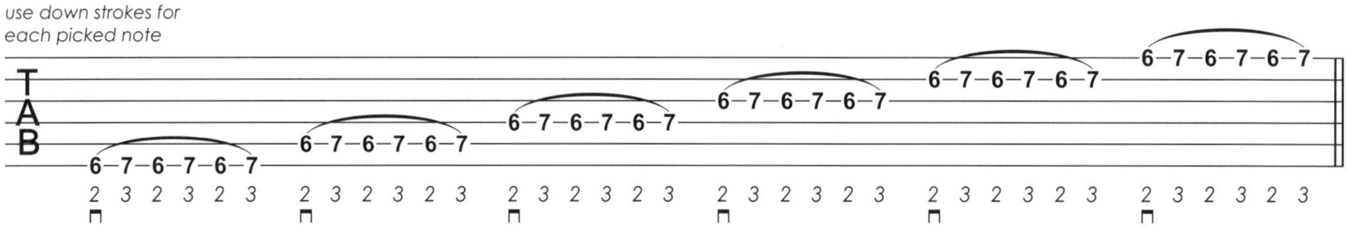

use down strokes for each picked note

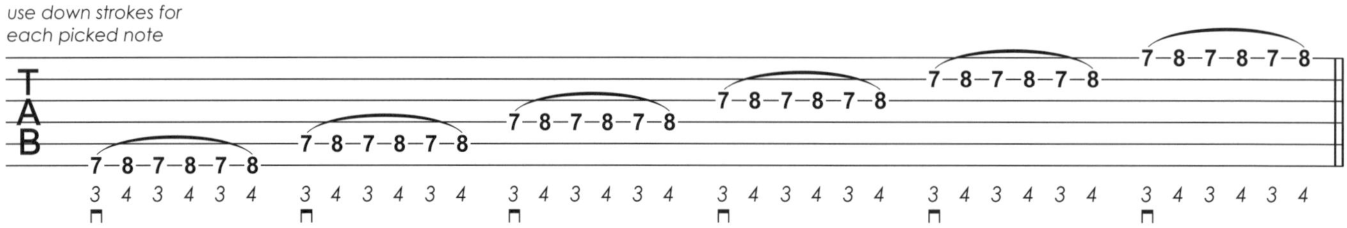

Learn how to bend strings

Lesson 77

Part One

Bending strings is our final way to get from one note to another. This technique adds a lot of character to your guitar playing. It is associated with rock, blues and country music, but you can use bends any time you want. You just need to know the "when and where and how."

Here's the TAB symbol we'll use for a **whole step** bend:

(Be aware, there are different notations out there for this technique in TAB).

In the beginning, you want to just casually explore this new technique. Spend some time bending notes around the fretboard.

Here is a whole step bend on the 2nd string, 6th fret. Using the 3rd finger, bend the string up until the note matches the note two frets higher on the same string.

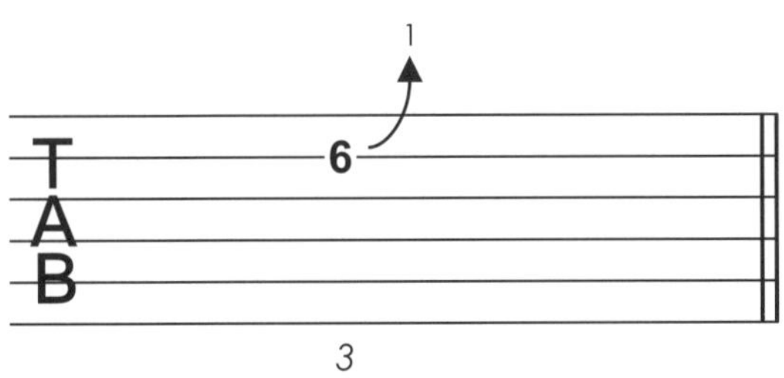

We'll call the note that's two frets higher the "target pitch".

Remember, two frets = whole step.

Important!

Support your 3rd finger with the 1st and 2nd fingers. They're going to help your 3rd finger bend the string.

You can use the fingers to bend, but also explore using the wrist. Hook your thumb over the top of the neck and use the side of your hand against the bottom of the neck as leverage to push the string up. Pivot the hand to bend the string while you support the 3rd finger with your 1st and 2nd fingers.

This technique involves using your ear to determine if your bend is on target or not. Only three things can happen in that regard:

- The bend is too far = sharp
- The bend is too low = flat
- The bend is right on pitch

(Here, the terms "sharp" and "flat"are slang musical terms for whenever a note is out of tune because it is too high or too low).

Here are some more bends on the 1st, 2nd, and 3rd strings.

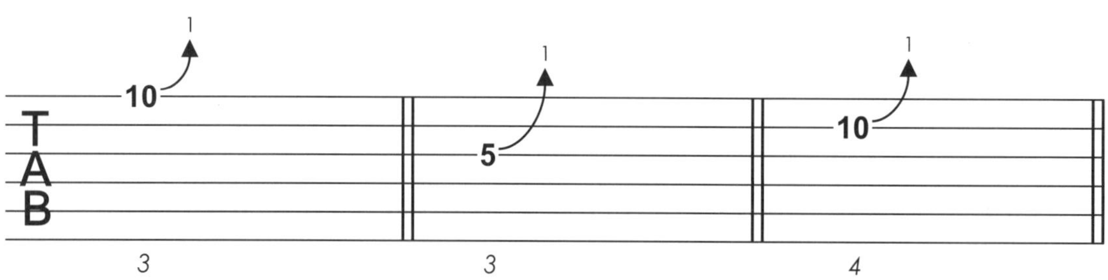

The reality is that you can bend *any* string with *any* finger to *any* pitch. But, as always, it is best to start simply, so do the following:

- Only use either the 3rd or 4th finger
- Only bend the 1st, 2nd or 3rd strings
- Only bend up a whole step (target pitch: two frets higher)

This will give your brain and fingers a chance to get used to this new technique.

Important!

Always be sure to support the finger that's bending with the other fingers. And, always be aware of the target pitch—in this lesson, it will be two frets higher. Play the target pitch frequently to let your ears hear the pitch you are striving to bend up to.

Part Two

Now let's look at the whole step bends that occur within the minor pentatonic scale patterns.

The G minor pentatonic scale has these five notes in it:

G–B♭–C–D–F

So here are the notes we can bend a whole step:

B♭ to C F to G C to D

Again, to keep it simple, we'll just use our 3rd or 4th finger while staying on the 1st, 2nd, or 3rd string. This will keep us on the "upper right hand corner" of each pattern.

These are the bends that are possible in pattern #1.

Here is a bend on the 1st string:

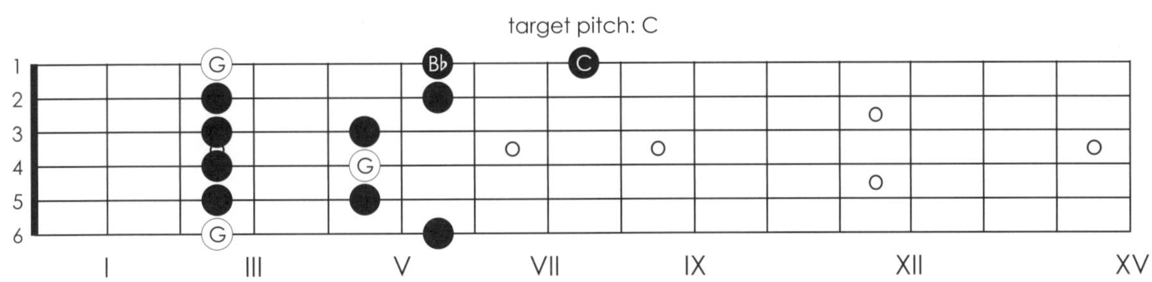

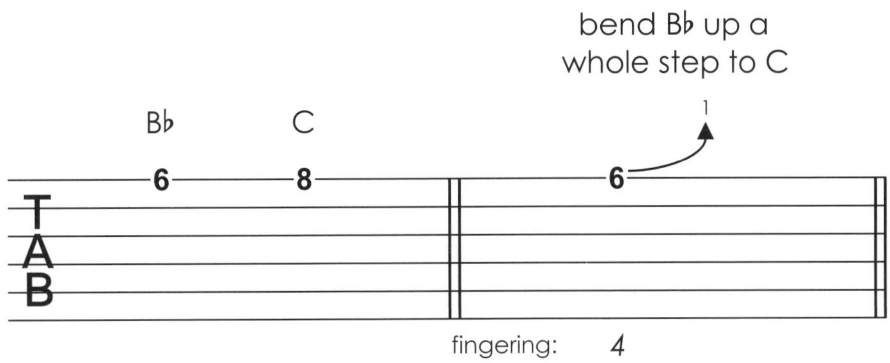

You can see that the target pitch is in pattern #2 (because the patterns overlap).

G Minor Pentatonic Scale Pattern #2

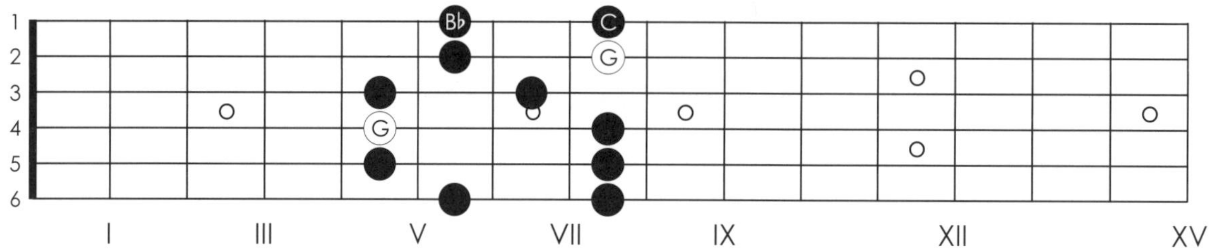

Here is a bend you can do on the 2nd string of pattern #1:

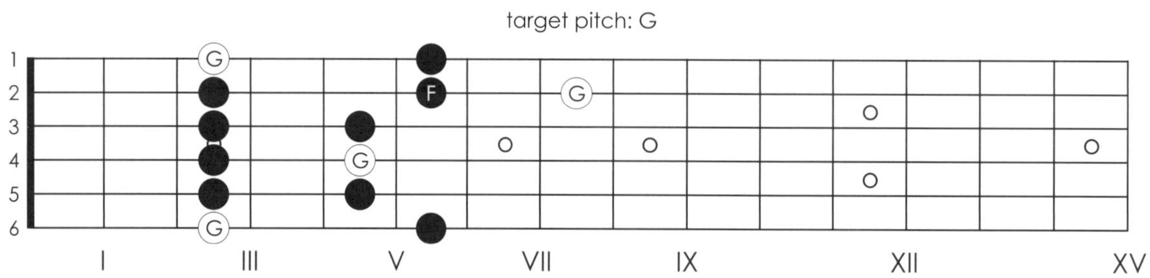

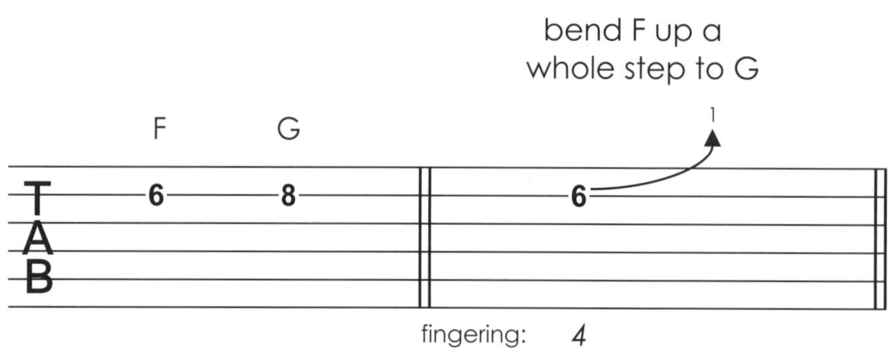

Remember to support your 4th finger with the 1st, 2nd, and 3rd fingers!

Here is a bend you can do on the 3rd string of pattern #1:

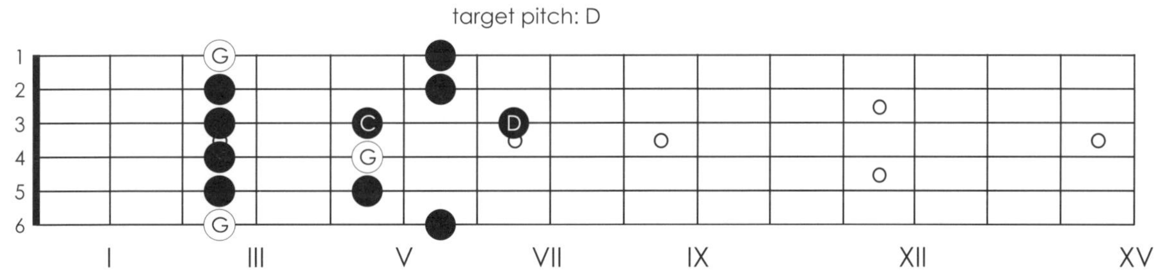

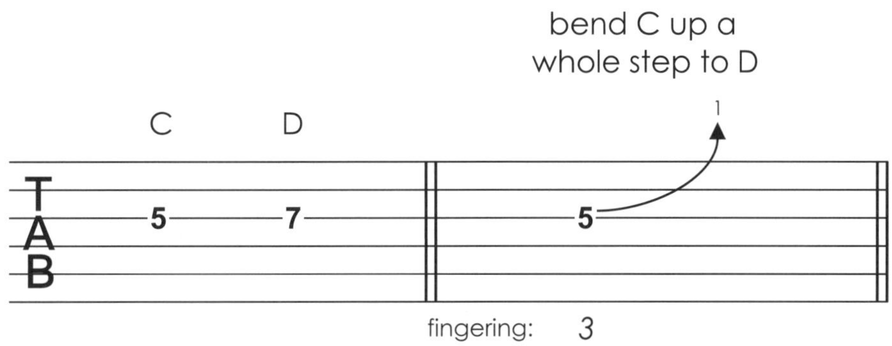

Here are all three of the bends we just looked at:

G Minor Pentatonic Scale Pattern #1:
whole step bends on the top three strings

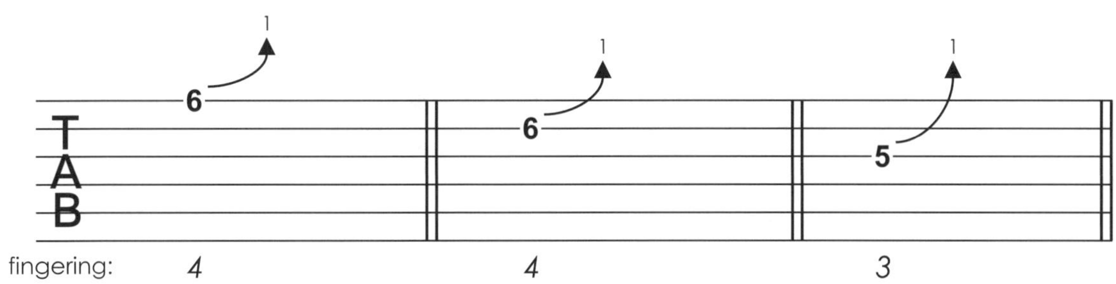

Now let's look at the rest of the patterns and see what notes we can bend.

Here is a bend on the 1st string of pattern #2:

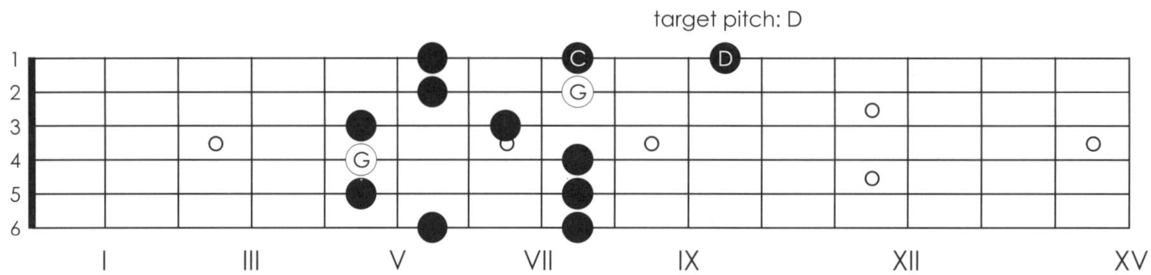

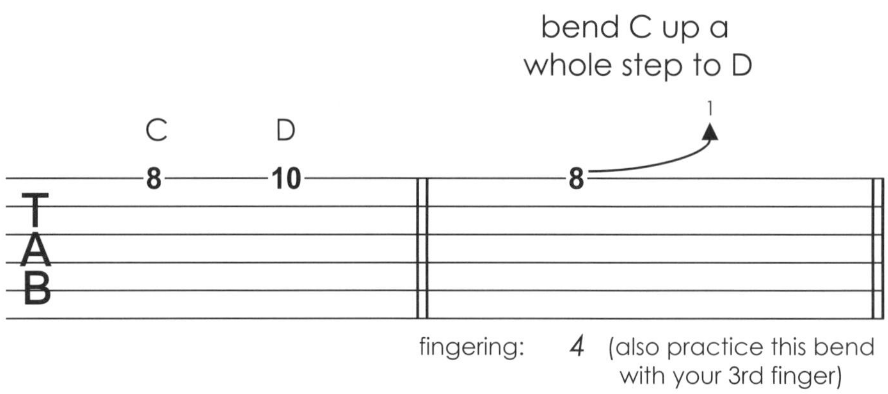

Here is a bend on the 2nd string of pattern #3:

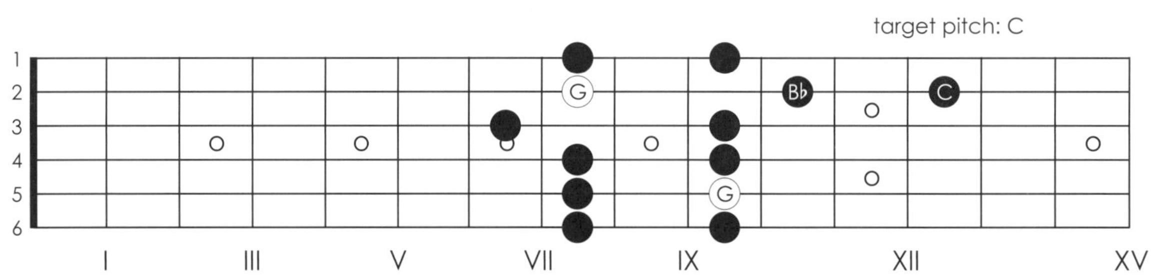

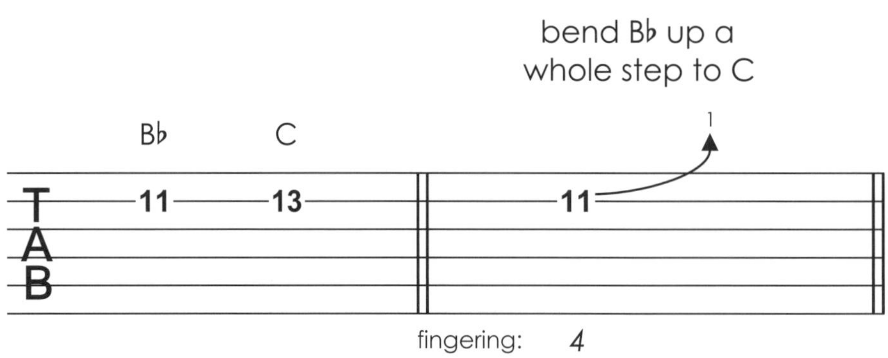

Here is a bend on the 3rd string of pattern #3:

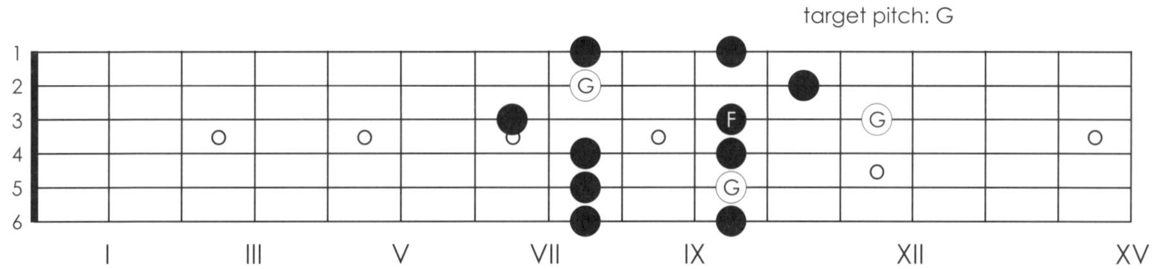

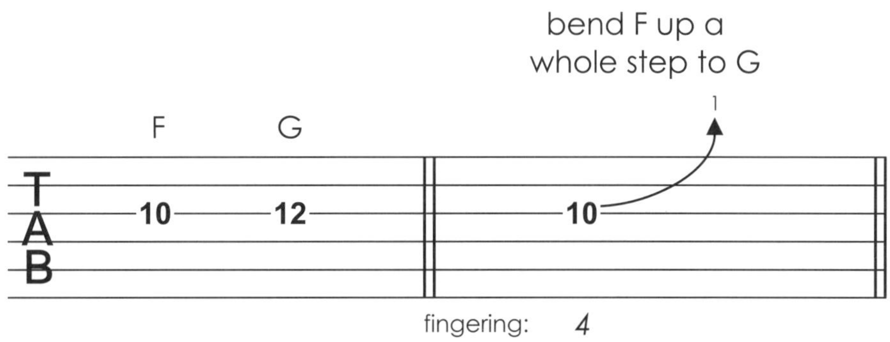

Here is a bend on the 1st string of pattern #4:

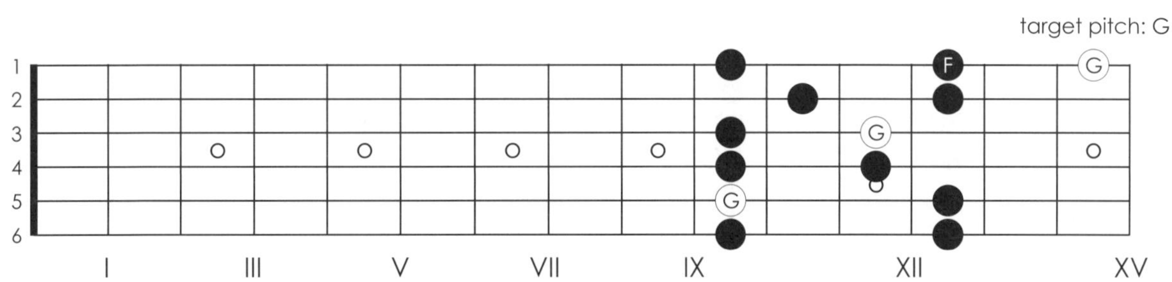

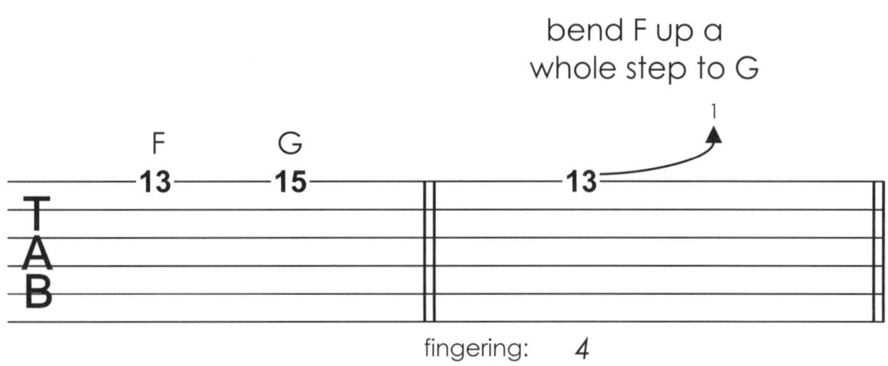

Here is a bend on the 2nd string of pattern #4:

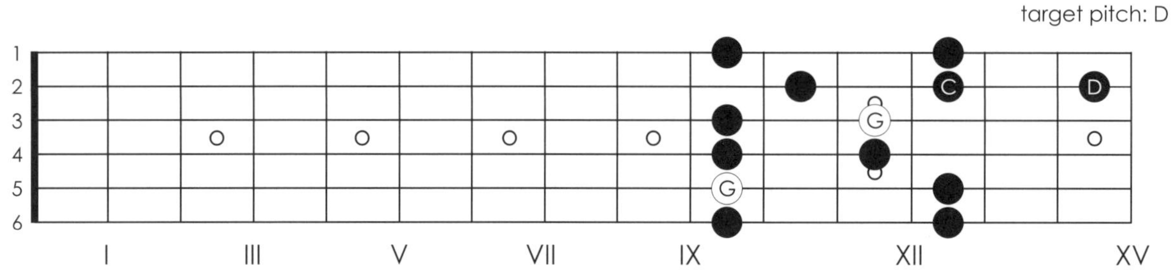

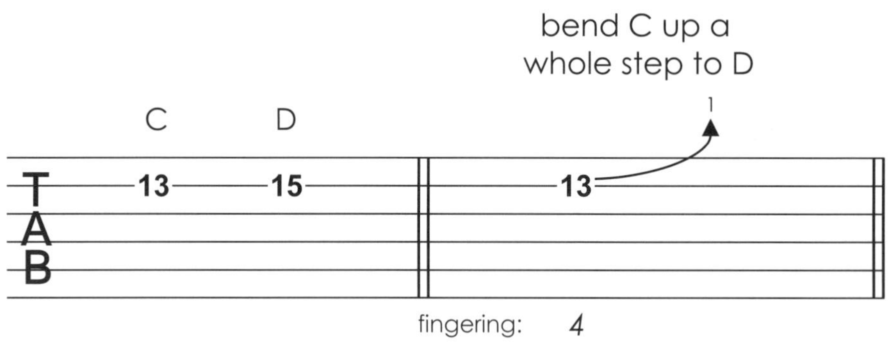

Here is a bend on the 3rd string of pattern #5:

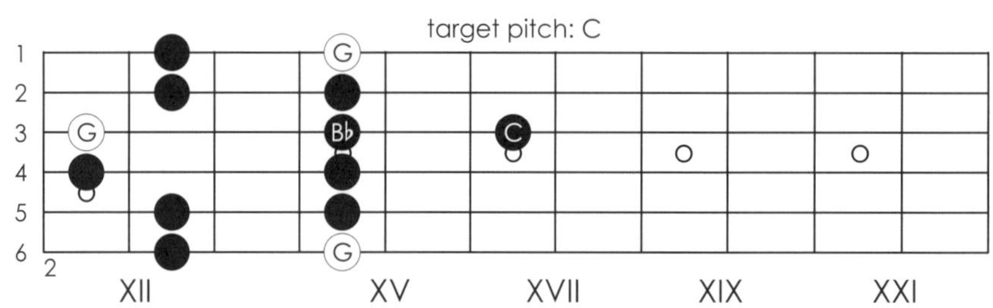

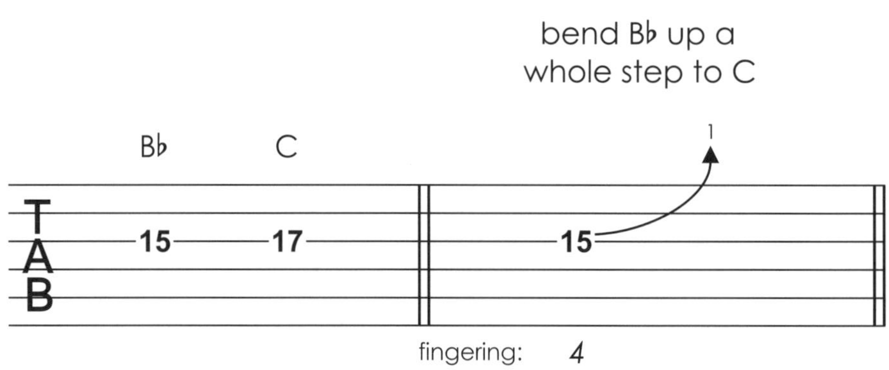

Important!

Practice each bend in this lesson using both your 3rd and 4th fingers.

Each of the five patterns have at least one note that you can bend. Knowing where these bends are gives you a creative edge. It is very common for guitarists to just haphazardly bend any string that they happen to be on and this sometimes results in wrong notes. Give yourself some time to get dialed in to these bends for each pattern. Then when you start using these patterns to play guitar solos, you will be able to create interesting and stylistic music!

Lesson 78 Learn how to use hammer-ons & pull-offs with the Minor Pentatonic Scale Patterns (as well as explore some new fingerings)

Now that you've developed some techniques using hammer-ons and pull-offs, let's apply them to some scale patterns. Since the minor pentatonic scales only have two notes per string, they work well with this approach.

Pattern #1

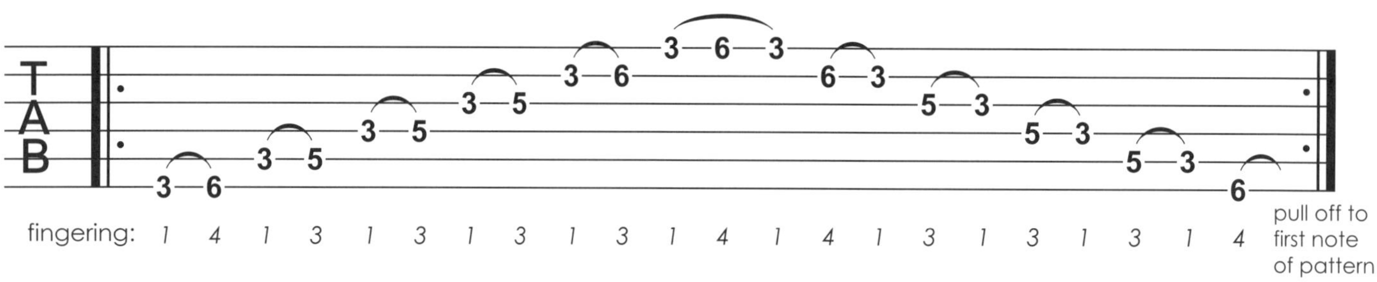

Pattern #2

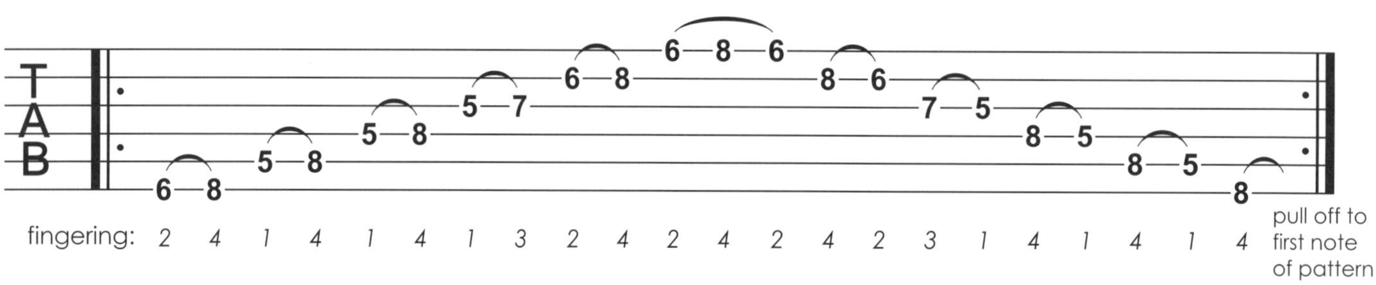

Pattern #3

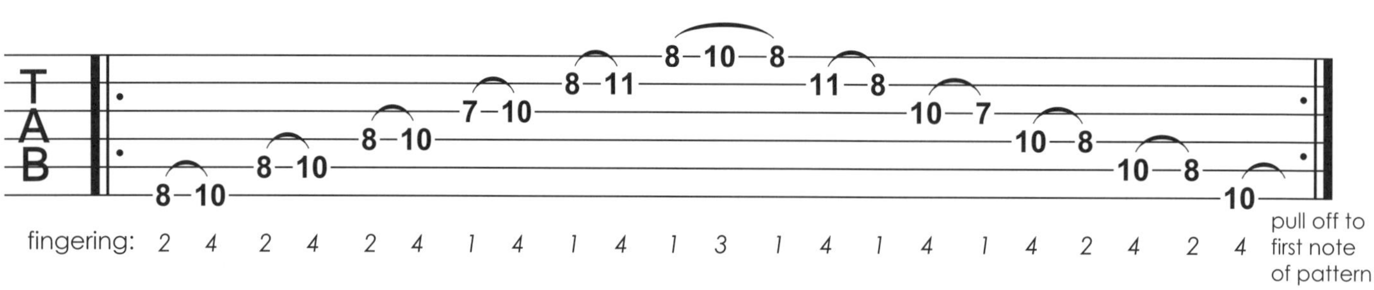

Pattern #4

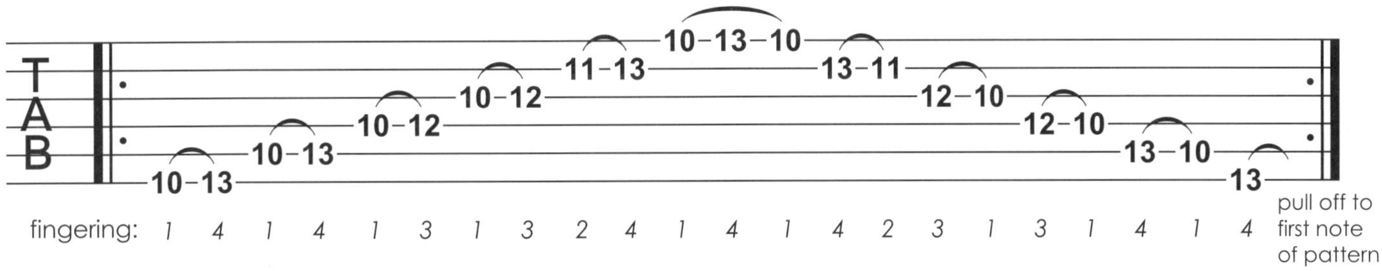

Pattern #5

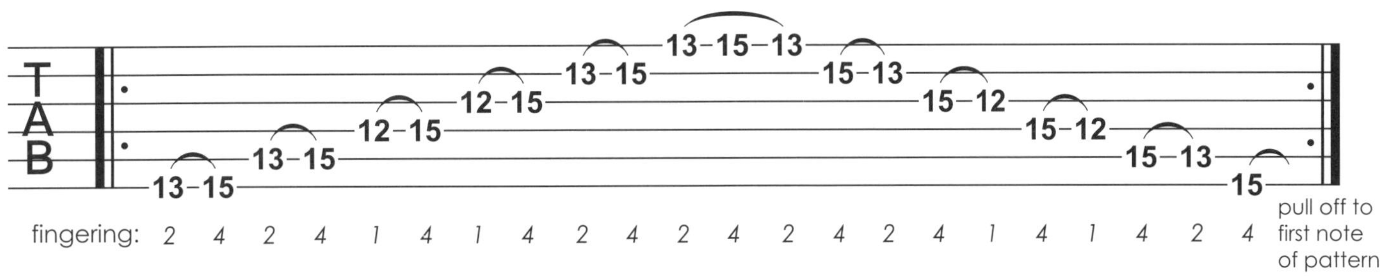

As you progress with your guitar scale technique, you will find that sometimes you will learn more than one fingering for any given scale pattern. Let's now take some time to explore some alternate fingerings for these minor pentatonic patterns.

Essentially, what we'll be doing is swapping out the **2–4** fingerings for **1–3** fingerings. This change of fingering will create more position shifts, but it can ultimately be more comfortable for the left hand.

Pattern #1 does not have any 2-4 fingering so here is pattern #2:

G Minor
Pentatonic Scale
Pattern #2

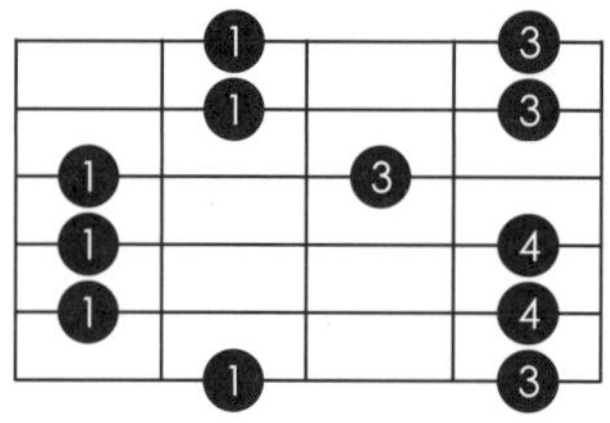

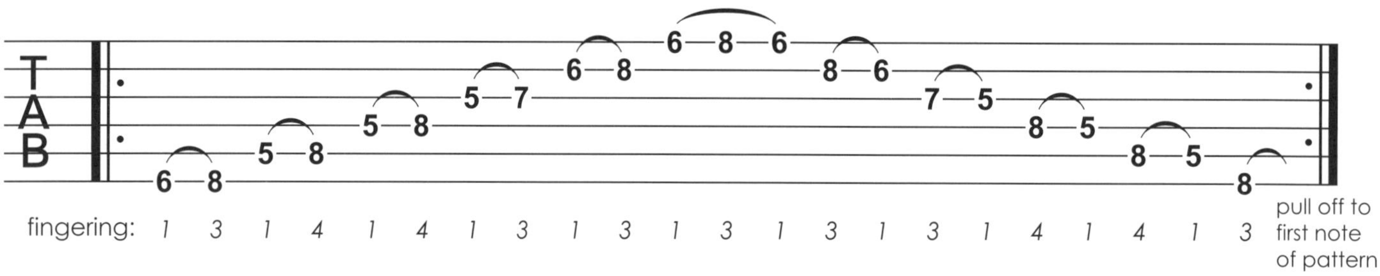

G Minor
Pentatonic Scale
Pattern #3

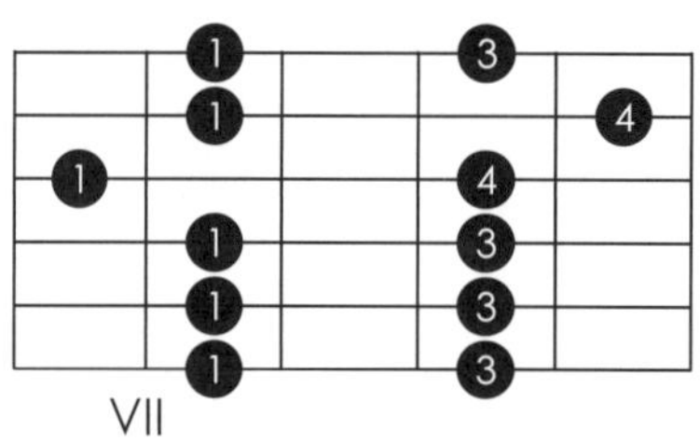

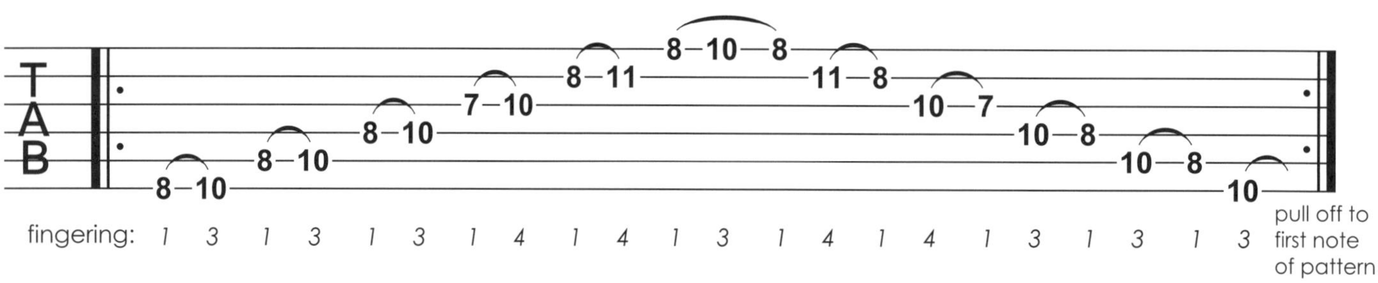

G Minor
Pentatonic Scale
Pattern #4

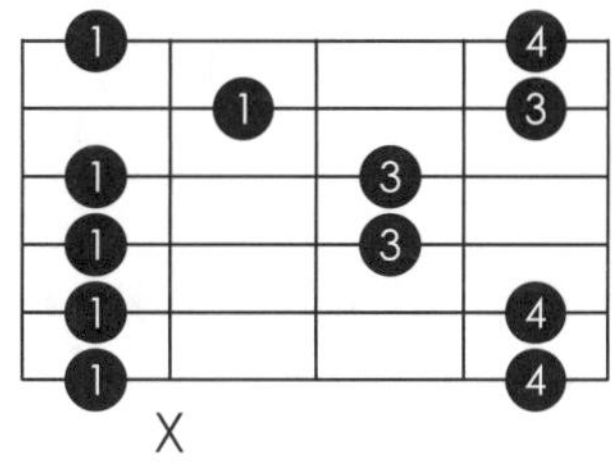

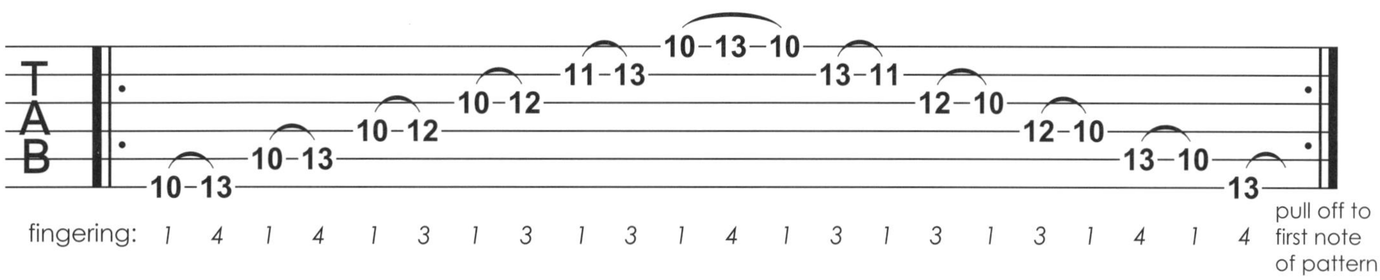

G Minor
Pentatonic Scale
Pattern #5

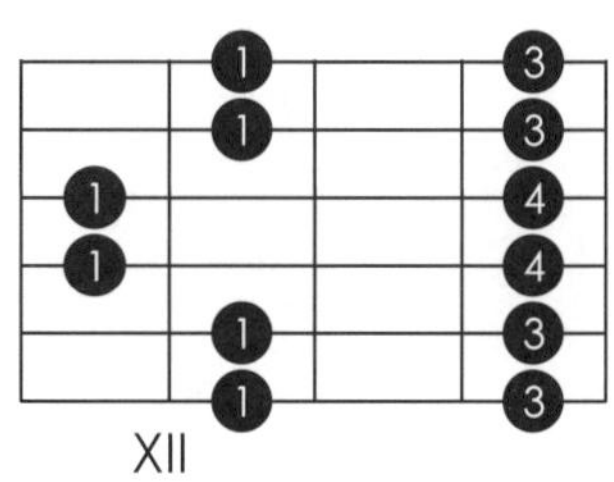

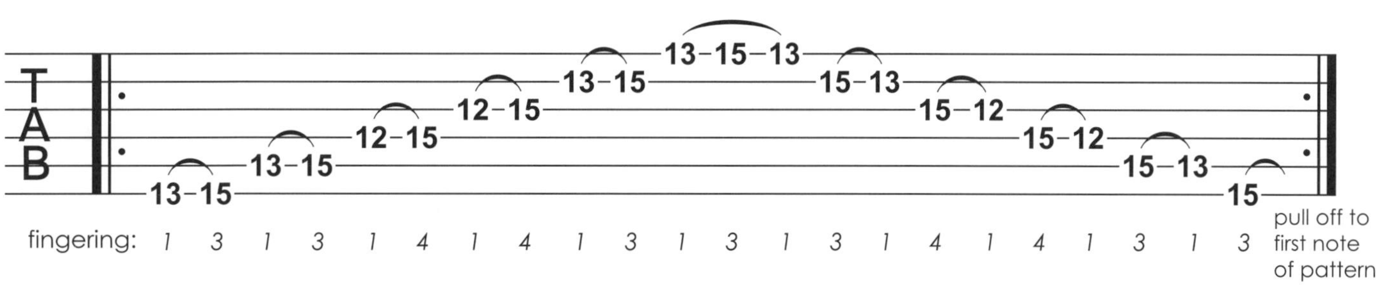

A word about right hand picking...

You may notice that when you can see my right hand in the video, it isn't totally consistent in regards to alternate picking. The reality is, there are many different possible approaches to right hand picking technique depending on what the left hand is doing. I would suggest that as you work with these exercises, you strive to do all downstrokes when ascending the scale, and all upstrokes when descending the scale. This will help your hands coordinate as you focus on the left hand hammer-ons and pull-offs. After your left hand is comfortable with the new fingerings, you can explore other picking strategies.

Lesson 79

Learn how to transpose scales with Transposition Drill #1

Part One

This lesson will show you how to develop a very important skill in playing music on the guitar—moving your scale patterns around the fretboard to different keys. When you change keys, it is called transposing.

transpose = *to change keys*

To do this, you want to use the tonic shapes to navigate the fretboard. That's what they are there for—so you know what key you are in! Whatever the note name of the tonic shape is, that is the key the scale pattern is in.

You've been playing the Minor Pentatonic Scale patterns in the Key of G.

Minor Pentatonic Scale Pattern #1 in the Key of G

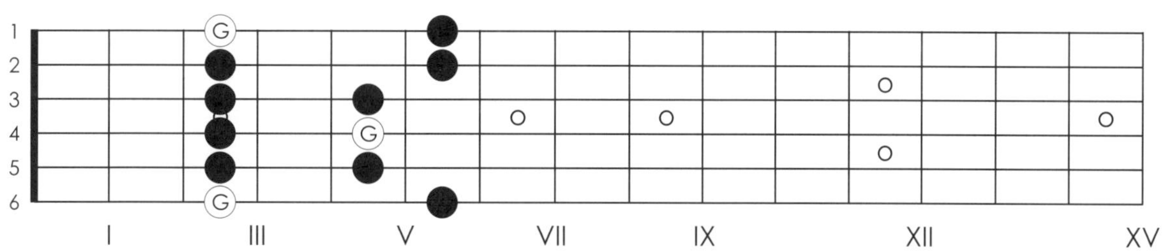

Each pattern has two or three notes in the tonic shape and those notes are G's.

Tonic Shape #1 in the Key of G

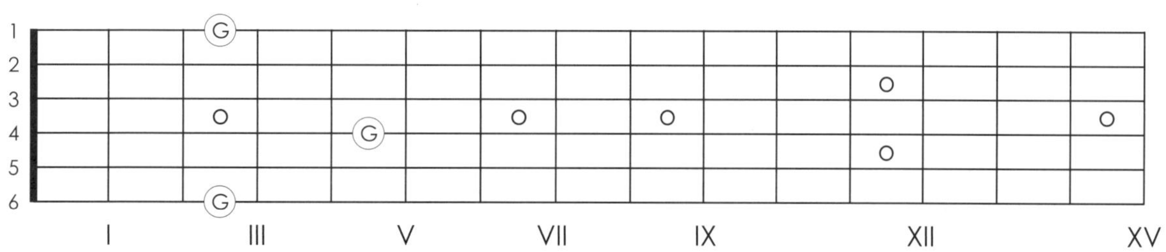

So if you move the pattern to a different part of the fretboard, all the notes in that pattern are going to change, including the tonic shapes. Again, whatever the note of the tonic shape is, that is the key the scale pattern is in.

Here are some examples of transposing pattern #1:

Tonic Shape #1 in the Key of C

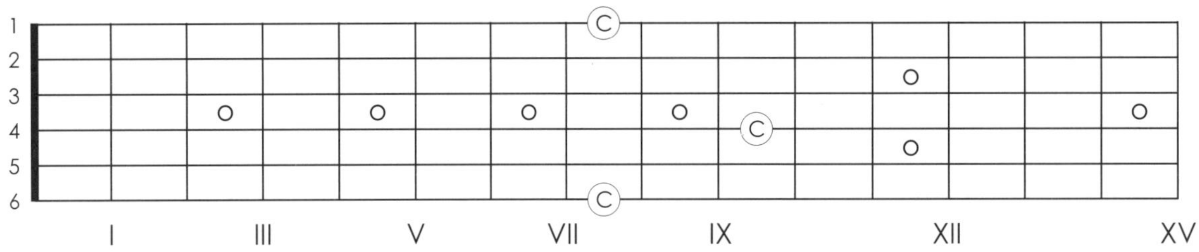

Minor Pentatonic Scale Pattern #1 in the Key of C

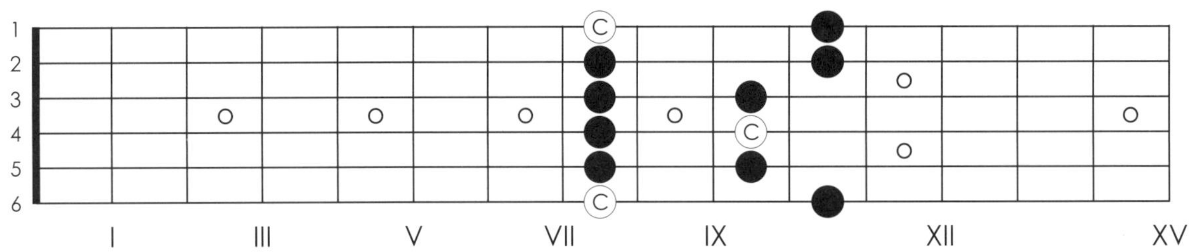

Tonic Shape #1 in the Key of A

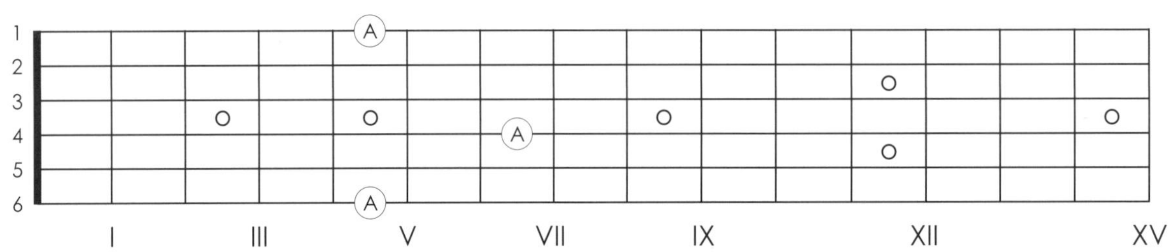

Minor Pentatonic Scale Pattern #1 in the Key of A

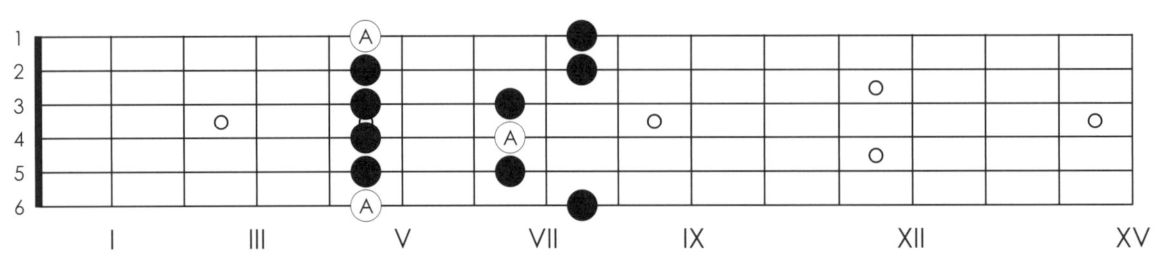

Tonic Shape #1 in the Key of D

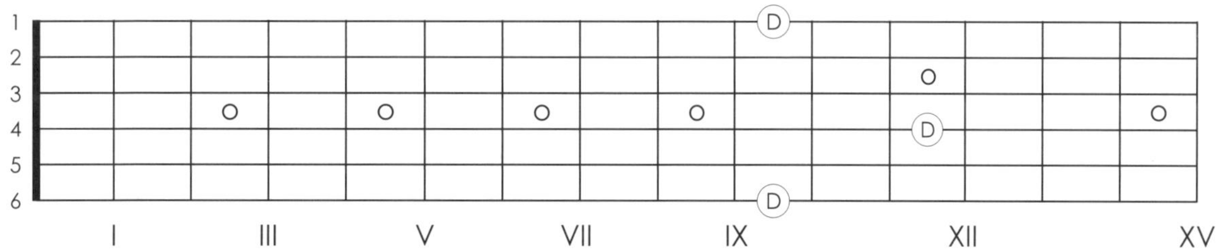

Minor Pentatonic Scale Pattern #1 in the Key of D

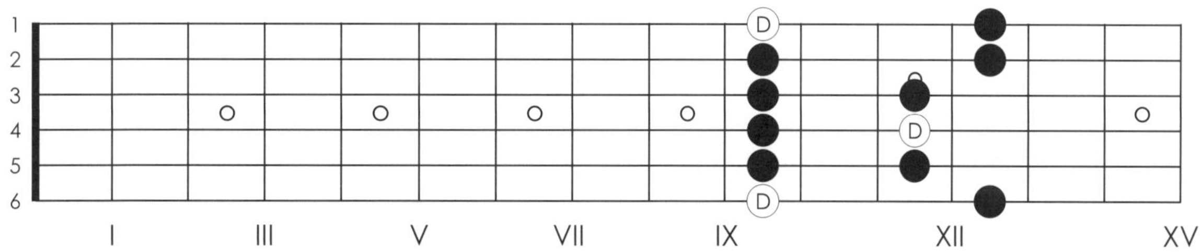

Here is the drill to use for getting all five pattens down solid.

Transposition Drill #1

- Pick a pattern
- Pick a key
- Play that pattern in that key, one time, ascending and descending

Important!

Do four to five different keys with a pattern and then do the same with the next pattern and so on. That way you are working with just one pattern for a while and letting your brain get used to transposing that one pattern. This will do a lot to develop the fluency of your scale vocabulary.

Here are some examples of transposing pattern #2:

Tonic Shape #2 in the Key of E

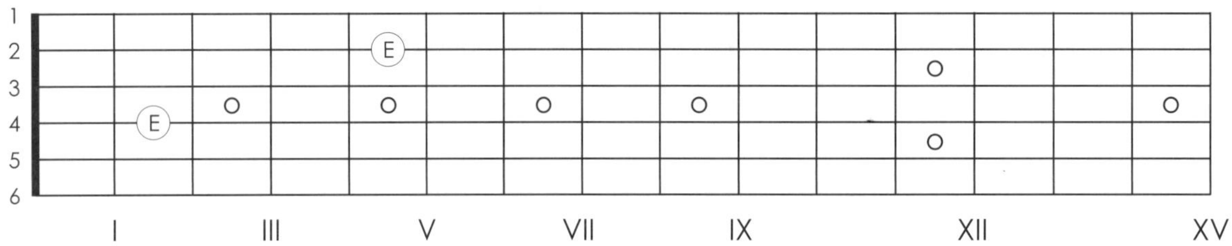

Minor Pentatonic Scale Pattern #2 in the Key of E

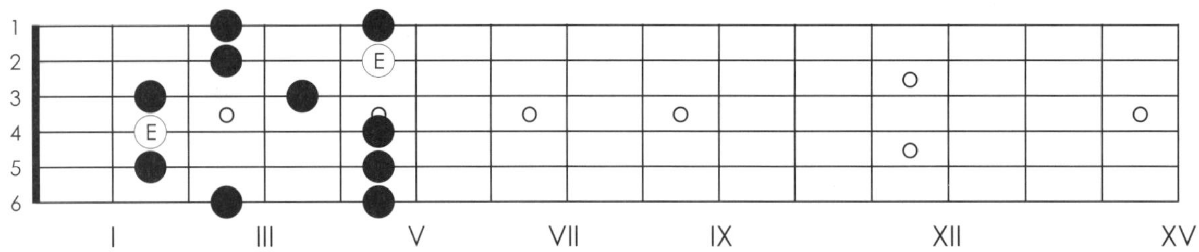

Tonic Shape #2 in the Key of B♭

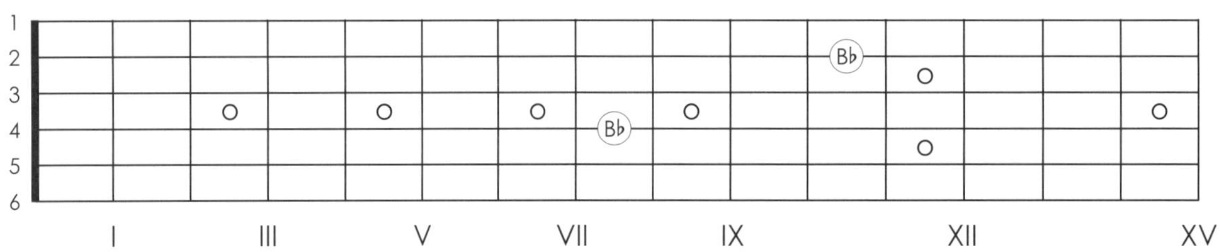

Minor Pentatonic Scale Pattern #2 in the Key of B♭

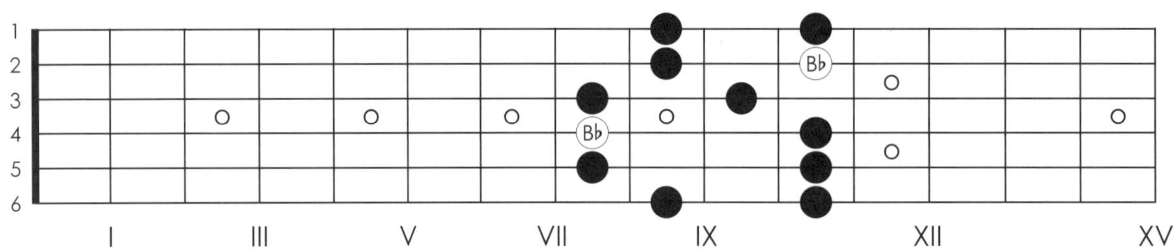

Part Two

Sometimes, depending on the pattern and the key, you will find yourself in **open position**, which means your hand is down by the nut.

Important!

When in open position, use 1st position fingering. That means that your 1st finger is at the 1st fret, your 2nd finger is at the 2nd fret, your 3rd finger is at the 3rd fret and your 4th finger is at the 4th fret. Sometimes you will be playing the scale pattern with a whole new fingering, so go slowly!

Here's an example of transposing a pattern to open position:

Tonic Shape #1 in the Key of E

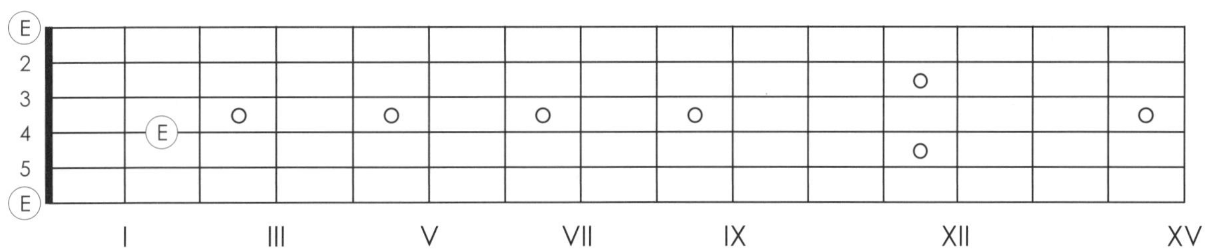

Minor Pentatonic Scale Pattern #1 in the Key of E

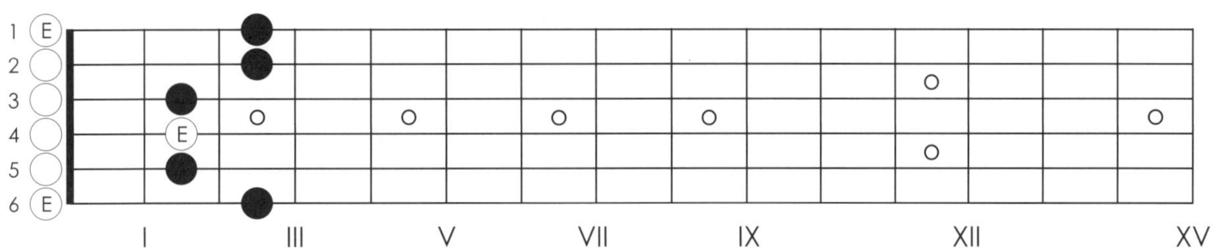

And with the new fingering...

Minor Pentatonic Scale Pattern #1 in the Key of E

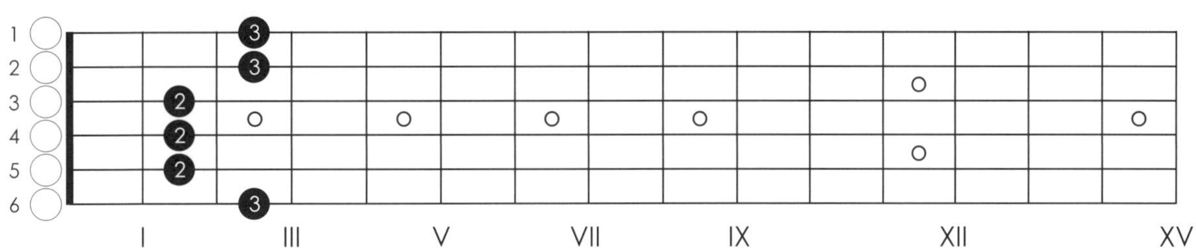

Part Three

After you have been doing this drill for a while and you feel comfortable with transposing the patterns around the fretboard, you can start expanding the exercise to include the entire fretboard.

The guitar fretboard has a range of almost two octaves along the strings. This means that the notes at the 12th fret are the same as the notes at the nut, only they are an octave higher. A lot of people say that the guitar "repeats itself" at the 12th fret. So *all* the notes from the 12th fret on up are an octave higher than all the notes from the nut on up. The reality is, twelve frets up from *any* fret on *any* string is an octave higher (and vice versa). This results in you being able to play some of the scale patterns in two places on the fretboard, an octave apart.

So when you are transposing a pattern, play it in both octaves, if possible. For example, pattern #1 in the key of B can be played in VII position and then an octave higher in XIX position. And in the key of F, you can play that same pattern in I position and again in XIII position. Notice that each position is twelve frets apart: VII and XIX, and I and XIII.

How high you can go also depends on the range of the fretboard of the guitar you are playing. Acoustic guitars usually have shorter fretboards (thus fewer frets) than electric guitars. Most electric guitars have 22 frets—some more, some less.

Sometimes, depending on the pattern and the key you choose, there will only be one possible position to play it in. As with pattern #1 in the key of D, you will only be able to play it in X position.

By working with your minor pentatonic scales patterns doing Transposition Drill #1, you will develop your fluency of the scales in a way that will enable you to play music at a higher level—meaning that you can create freely and easily. That is what makes music so much fun!

Learn about vibrato

Lesson

80

Vibrato adds a lot of expression to your guitar playing. It is just like the vibrato that singers use with their voice. This lesson will be just an introduction to vibrato so that you can get acquainted with the techniques and subtleties involved.

What you're doing here is creating a consistent and steady fluctuation in pitch. It can vary from a slight fluctuation to a more extreme fluctuation. It can be fast or slow or anywhere in between. The important thing is to be aware of it and how you use it.

The mechanics of how to vibrato are very similar to how you do string bends. Use the leverage between the side of your hand and the neck of the guitar. You can also push up or pull down on the string, the results are the same. Experiment with both.

When you are doing a full bend on a string, you can add vibrato to it by dropping the pitch down using the finger that you're bending with, and then pushing up and returning it to the original bent pitch.

Have fun exploring this new technique. Practice adding vibrato to various notes on different strings with various fingers, all around the fretboard. Remember to listen for it and watch for it when you hear/see guitar players playing solos. You can also observe singers and how they do it with their voice. Strive to emulate that sound and you are guaranteed to develop a musical vibrato that will add depth and beauty to your own guitar playing.

Lesson 81

Learn to play a blues rhythm riff

This blues rhythm riff is the most common riff you hear a blues guitarist play. It is very simple but sounds really cool.

It is based on these three barre chords:

They're more of a visual reference because you aren't actually playing the whole chord. You will only be playing the bottom two strings of the chord and your 4th finger will be in motion.

Here is the riff for G7. Spend some time getting comfortable with it. The C7 and D7 riffs are very similar.

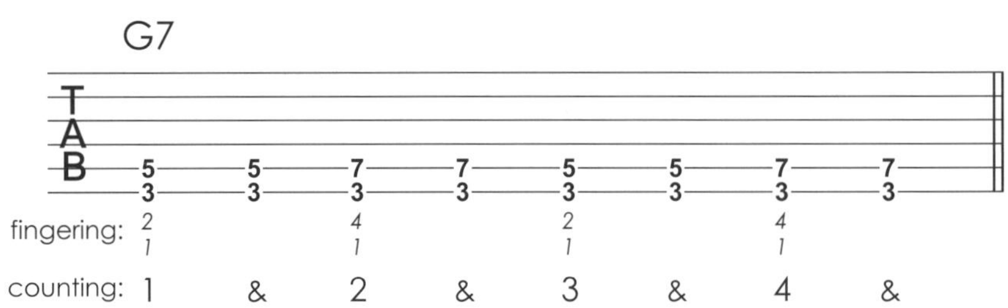

Mute the strings with the side of your right hand near the bridge when you play and it will sound "lighter."

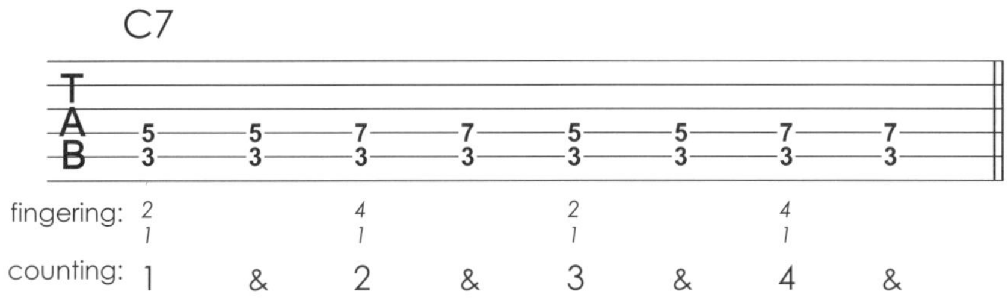

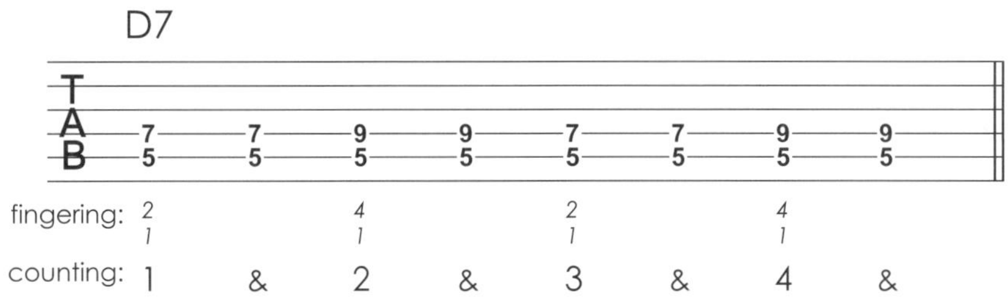

This chord progression is called a 12-bar blues and it is the foundation for this style of music. Guess what? It's twelve bars long!

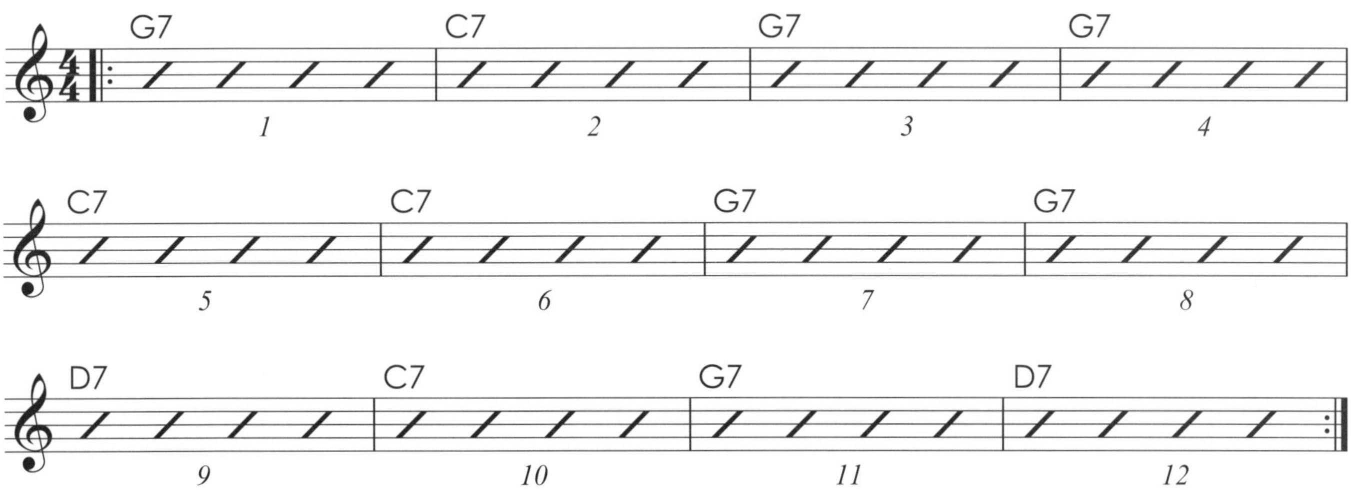

The last two bars of a blues progression, bars 11 and 12, are referred to as the **turnaround**.

Now take each of the riffs, G7, C7 and D7, and put them in the order of the progression.

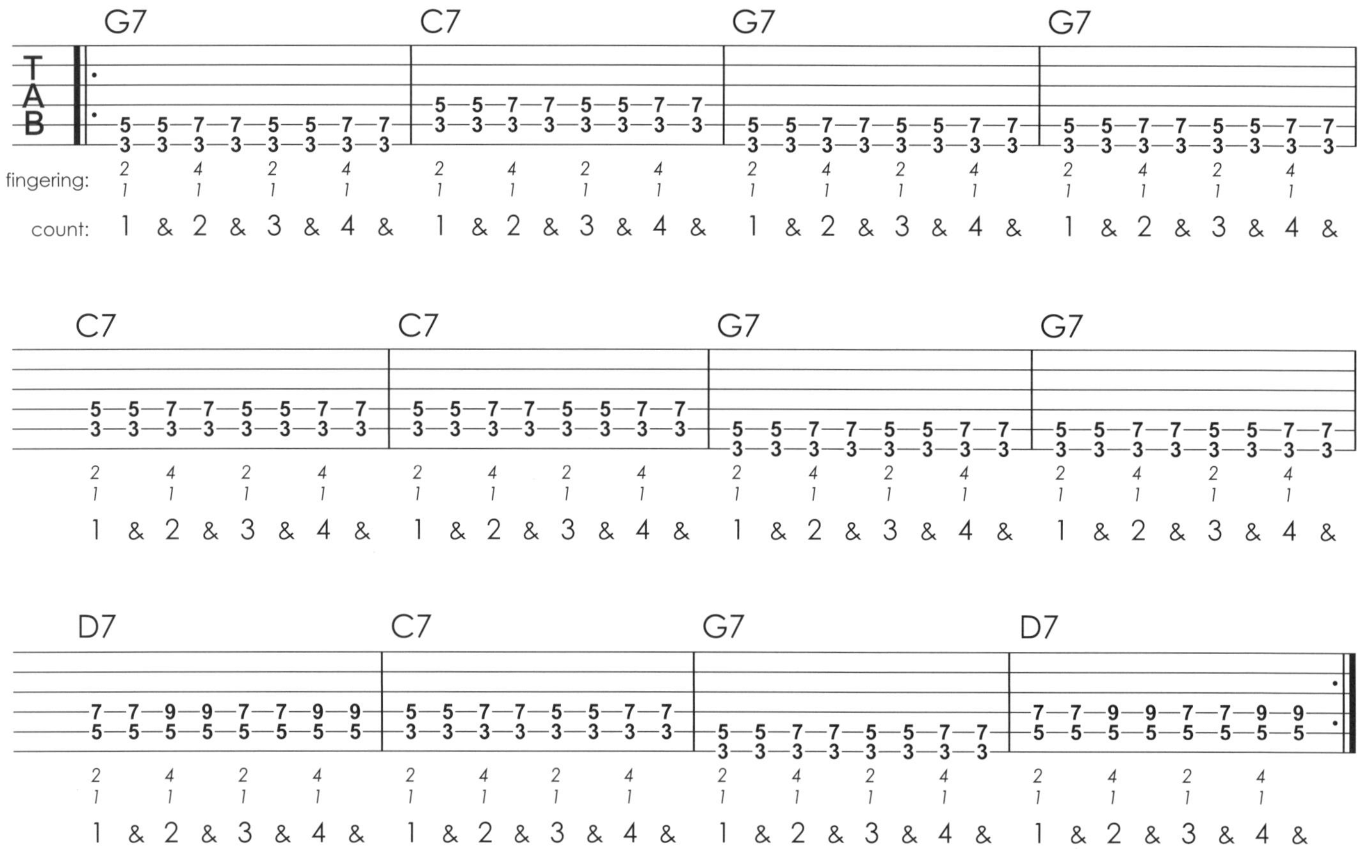

The chord symbols say G7, C7 and D7, but you're not really playing a chord, per se—it's more like the dominant 7th sound is *implied*. Dominant 7th chords are what blues music is based on.

Also, listen to the **shuffle** feel I use in the video. This is another important aspect of the blues style. For now, just let your body emulate this rhythm as you play the riff and you can explore the music theory involved later. In actuality, playing blues music is more about the *feel* of the music. Listen to a lot of blues recordings and you will start to hear what I am talking about.

Learn to play a riff based on Minor Pentatonic Scale Pattern #1

Lesson 82

Now it is time to start using the scale patterns to play music, so let's take a look at some riffs. A riff is a musical "sentence". It is also called a **lick**, **phrase**, or a **motif**. Playing lead guitar involves using riffs to create a guitar solo. You eventually want to learn many of these riffs so that you can *improvise*—create your own melodies in the moment.

Learning to improvise is a lot like learning to speak a language, in that you put together sentences to make a conversation that has a point to it. We'll get more into all of what is involved with that later. This lesson is just an introduction. Now we will use all the techniques and vocabulary we've learned so far to play riffs based off of the minor pentatonic scale patterns.

Learn the left hand fingering and articulation first. Then, focus on the right hand picking.

G Minor Pentatonic Scale Pattern #1

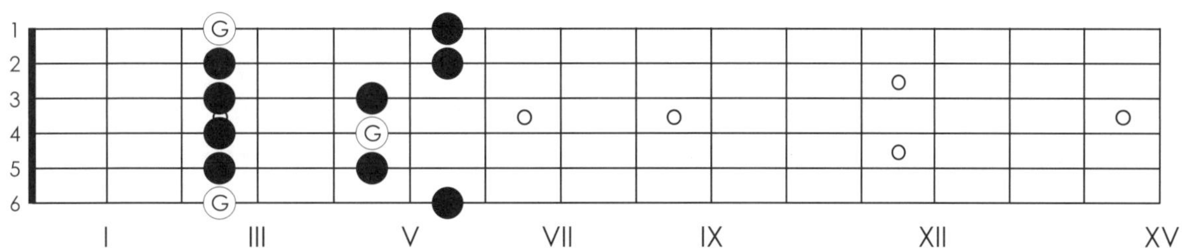

Riff #1 in the Key of G Minor

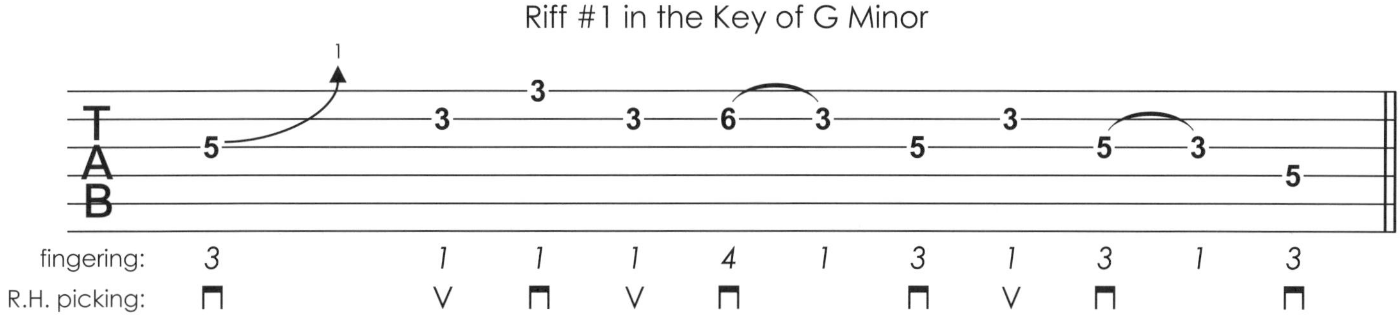

Pay attention to the 1st finger as you play the notes on the 2nd and 1st strings. Make sure the notes don't ring together or sound disconnected. You can achieve this by dropping the finger down onto the 1st string and then popping it back up again to play the note on the 2nd string.

For now, play the notes evenly spaced. The riffs you will be learning are designed to sound good with a variety of rhythmic approaches. Wait until you've got the riff down playing the notes evenly before you experiment with variations with the rhythm of the notes.

Once you've gotten everything down so you can accurately and consistently play the riff, you can explore transposing the riff to other keys. Use the tonic shape to transpose the scale pattern and then the riff lays right on top of the pattern.

Here is the riff transposed to the key of C:

C Minor Pentatonic Scale Pattern #1

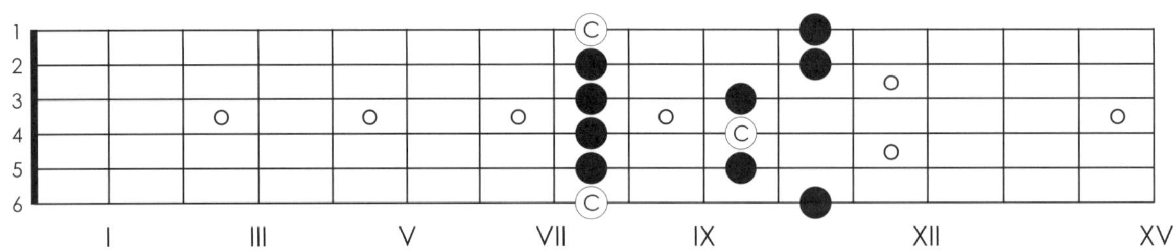

Riff #1 in the Key of C Minor

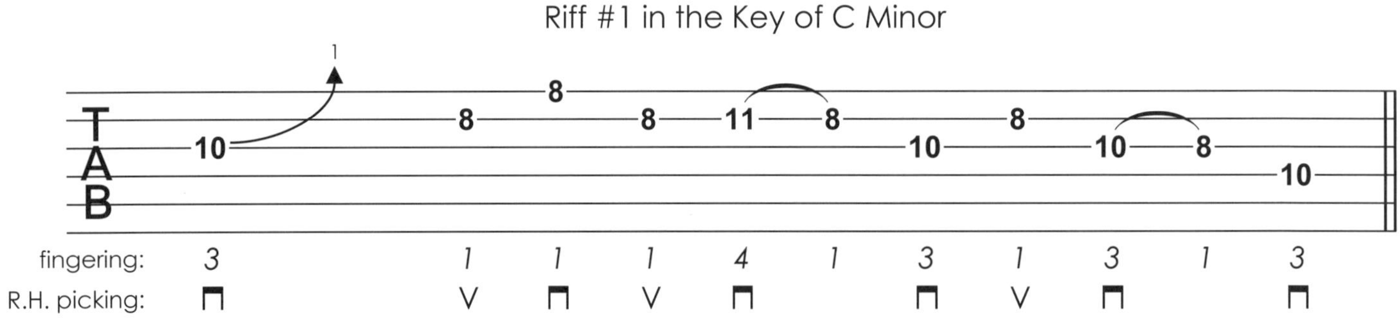

Learn to play a riff based on Minor Pentatonic Scale Pattern #2

This riff is based on pattern #2 and starts with a bend and release. Here you pick the first note, bend up a whole step, then keep the pressure on the string as you release the bend back down to the starting pitch, which is then followed by a pull-off.

G Minor Pentatonic Scale Pattern #2

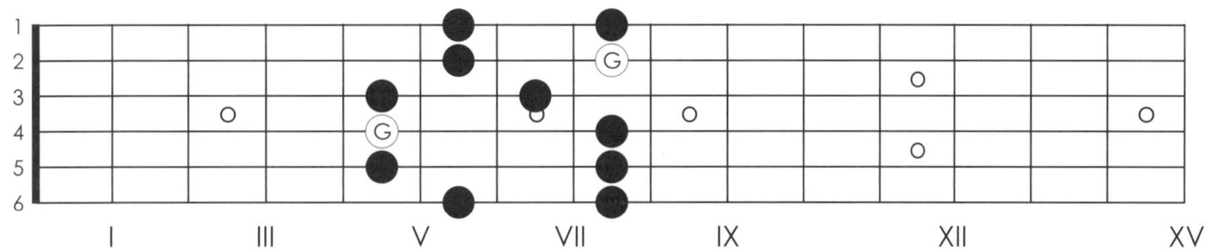

Riff #2 in the Key of G Minor

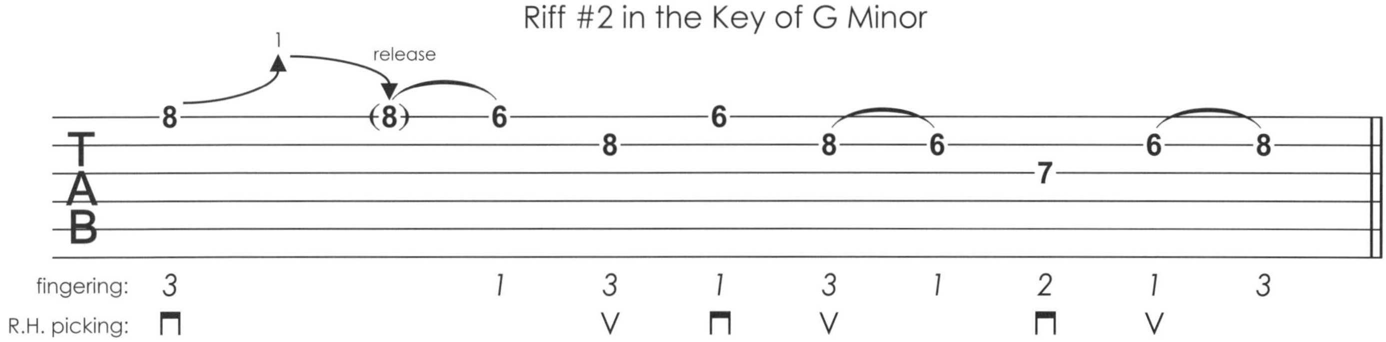

Notice that the fingering in this riff is different than the fingering of the scale pattern it is derived from. This is very common. When you use a scale to make music, fingering becomes more about what works best for what you are striving to achieve. In this case, with the bending, hammer-ons and pulls, using your 1st and 3rd fingers feels the best. Then the 2nd finger on the 3rd string is right there ready to go.

Lesson

84 Learn to play a riff based on Minor Pentatonic Scale Pattern #3

This riff utilizes a lot of **legato** technique, which means hammer-ons and pull-offs. This term is somewhat of a misnomer in guitar studies because its *real* meaning is "smooth and connected". It is a word used by *all* musicians to describe going from one note to another in a smooth and connected manner. Guitarists often use the term to refer to hammer-ons and pull-offs.

G Minor Pentatonic Scale Pattern #3

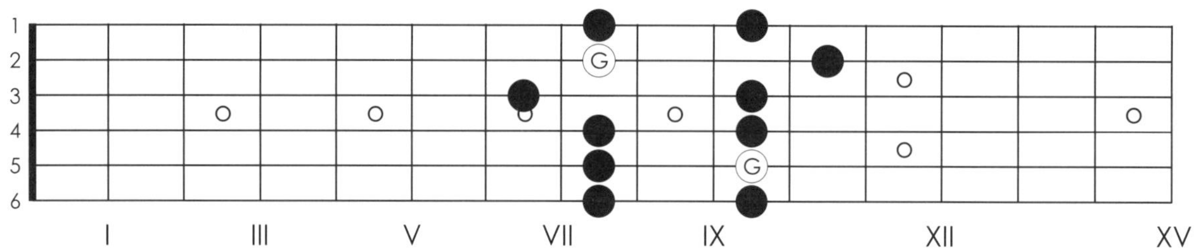

Riff #3 in the Key of G Minor

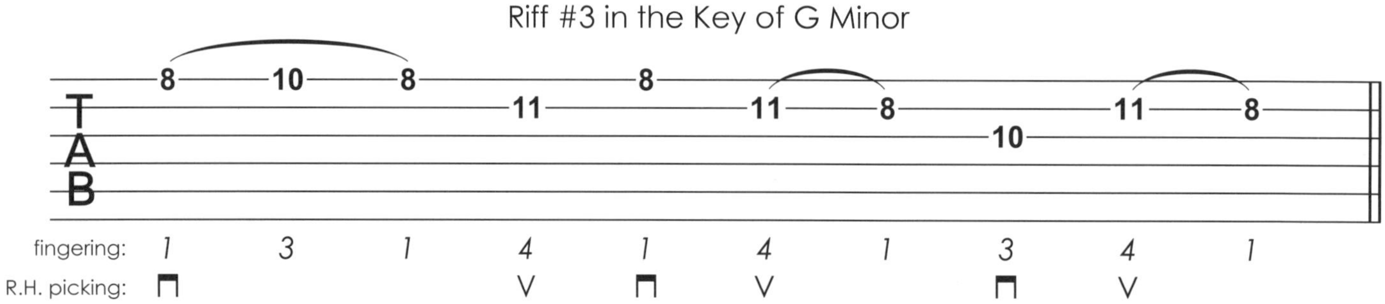

It is always a good idea to get the riff down really well at first before you start to transpose it to other keys. Give your brain and your fingers enough time to get a solid grasp of the phrase in G. Then, when you start to move it around the fretboard, it will all go smoother.

Here is the same riff in the key of E:

E Minor Pentatonic Scale Pattern #3

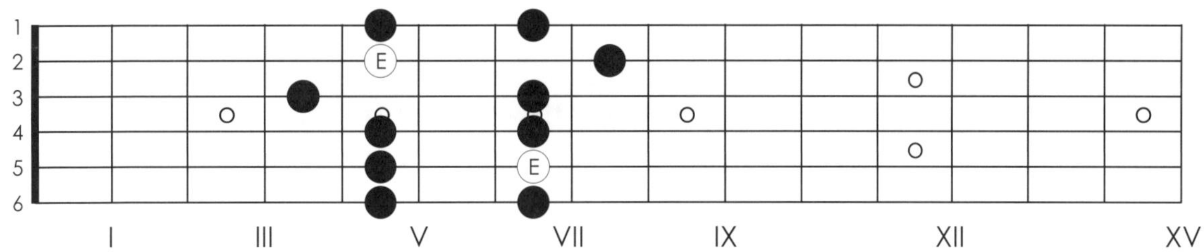

Riff #3 in the Key of E Minor

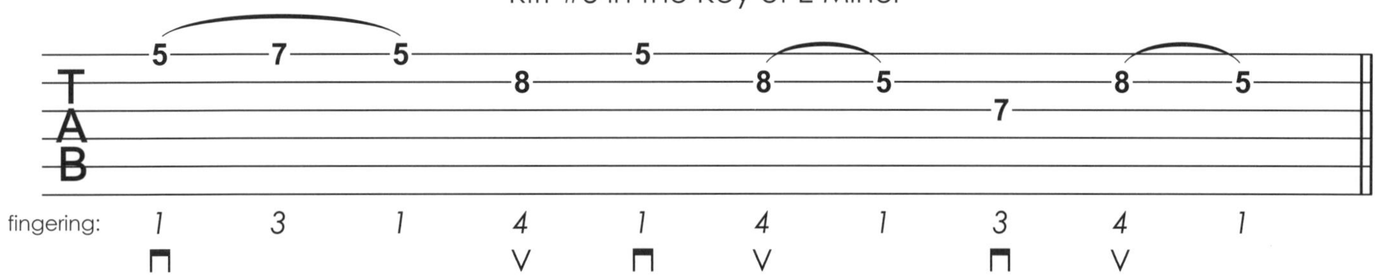

Lesson 85

Learn to play a riff based on Minor Pentatonic Scale Pattern #4

Here is riff #4. It is in the X position. This means that your 1st finger is at the X fret and then all the remaining fingers line up on the subsequent frets.

G Minor Pentatonic Scale Pattern #4

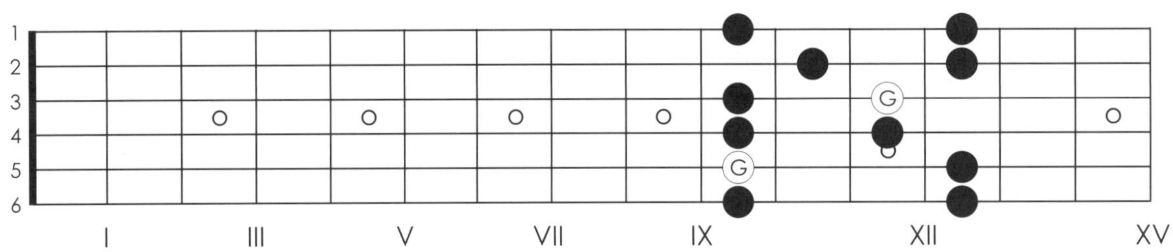

Riff #4 in the Key of G Minor

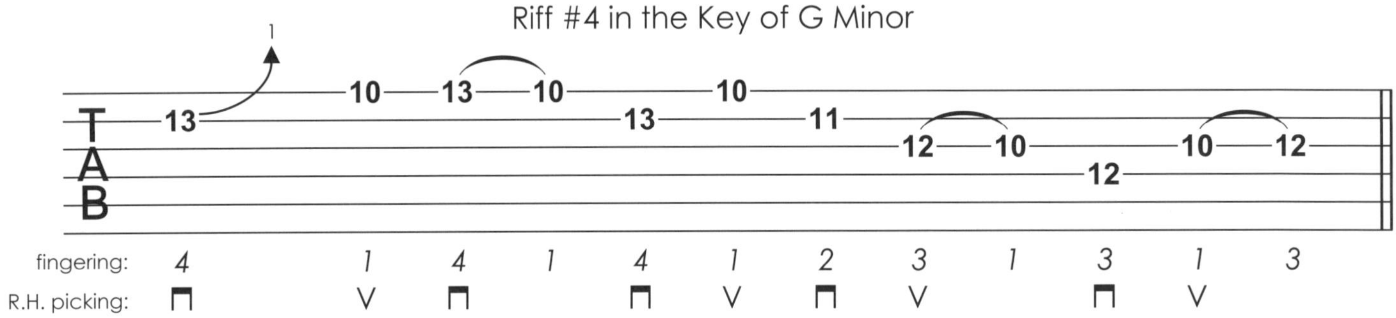

It is interesting to point out that the pitch you are bending up to at the beginning of the riff is the note D. The next note in the riff on the 1st string is also a D. You are basically just hitting two D's for the first two notes of this phrase, but using a bend to play the first D sounds cooler!

Lesson 86

Learn to play a riff based on Minor Pentatonic Scale Pattern #5

The fingering for this riff is completely different from the fingering for the scale pattern it's based on. It all starts with a slide into the XV fret with the 3rd finger.

G Minor Pentatonic Scale Pattern #5

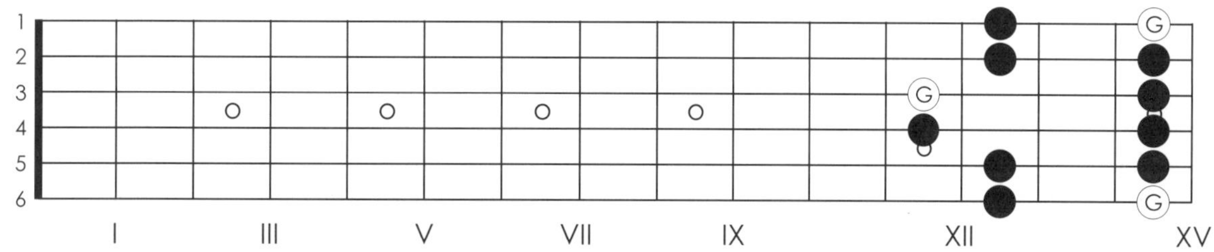

Riff #5 in the Key of G Minor

It is good to end a phrase with some vibrato. Just remember that you don't always have to put vibrato on the last note of a riff.

Here is the riff transposed to the key of A:

A Minor Pentatonic Scale Pattern #5

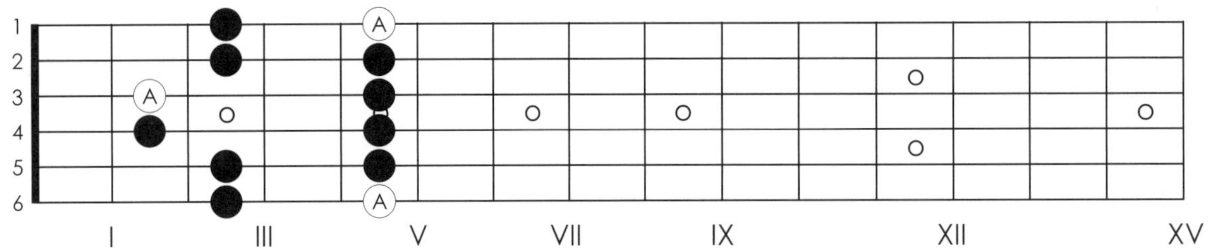

Riff #5 in the Key of A Minor

These five riffs we've looked at are good examples of common phrases you will find guitarists playing in a variety of musical styles. This is a good start towards building your own personal riff vocabulary. It is something most accomplished players do to some extent and it is a proven way to grow as a musician.

Learn to play a jazz chord progression

Lesson 87

Here are some common guitar chords that are found in jazz music. This will give your fingers and your ears something new to play with. Get acquainted with each chord individually at first.

Cmaj7

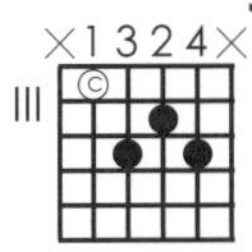

Am7

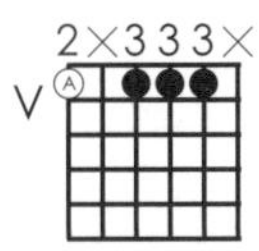

Dm7

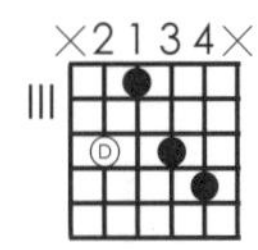

G13

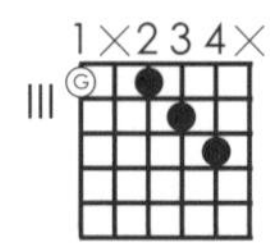

Now put them into this chord progression. As usual, start with doing just one strum per beat to get used to the chord transitions. Then work on playing through the chord progression in tempo.

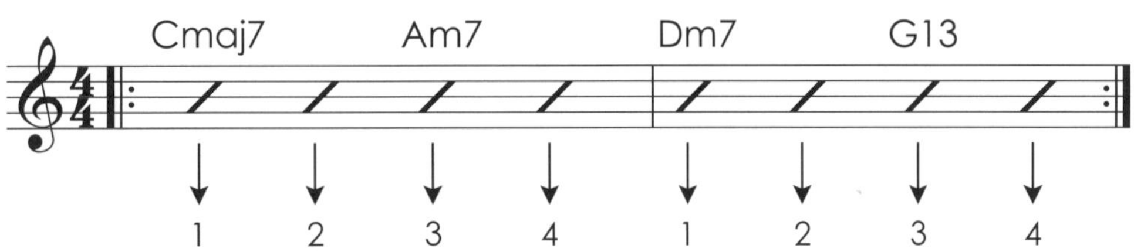

Important!

There is a guide finger in this progression which connects the Dm7, G13 and Cmaj7 chords. The 4th finger stays on the 2nd string as you go between these chords.

Do all down strums while cutting the chord short by relaxing the left hand on the strings after you strum. This will create a jazz feel that is simple but effective. Also, notice that these chords have their **roots** on the 5th or 6th string so use that to guide you to the correct fret.

Lesson

88 Learn to play a jazz-blues chord progression

The 12-bar blues progression is used a lot in jazz, but with additional chords to make it more interesting. The chords in this lesson have some names that might be intimidating, but that doesn't mean they are hard to play!

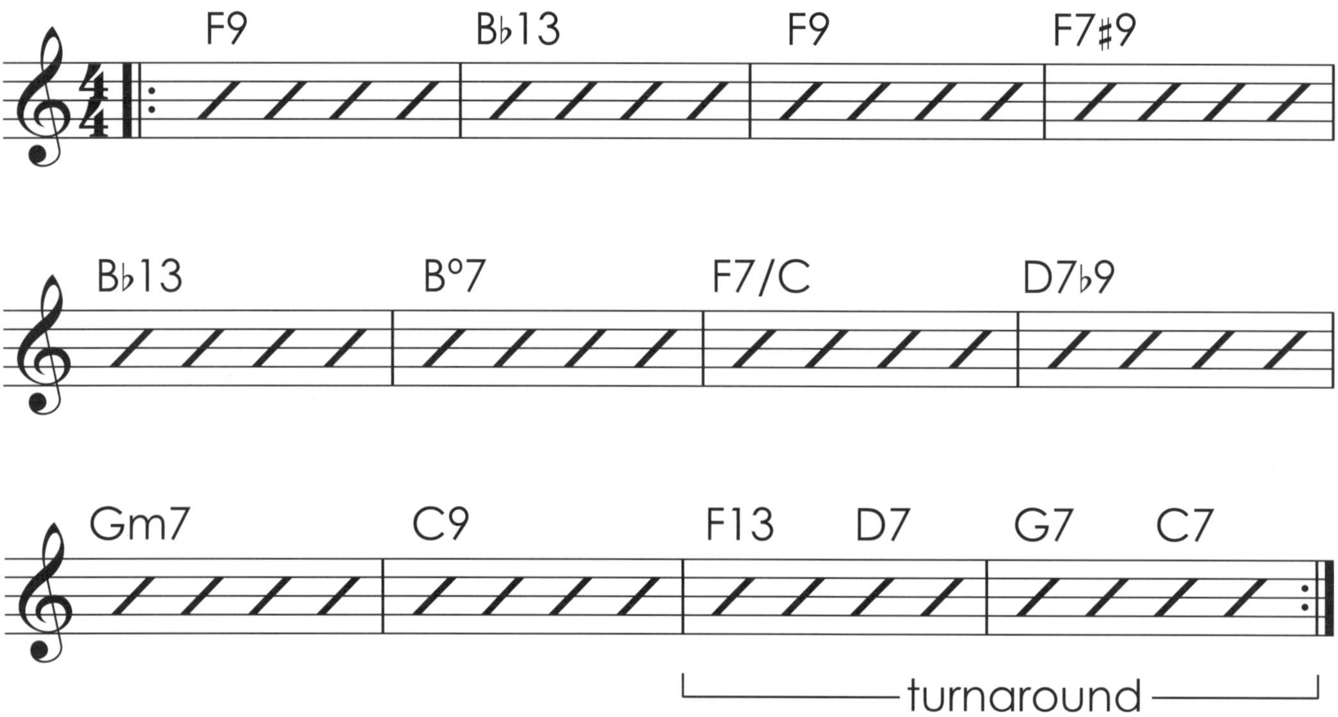

The last two bars of a blues progression are referred to as the **turnaround**.

Important!

Remember to look for **common fingers**, **guide fingers** and **similar shapes** as you work through these chords.

Again, you can do all down strums while cutting the chord short by relaxing the right hand after you strum. This is sometimes called **choking** the chord. Another rhythm is called the **Charleston rhythm**. It is easier for you to pick it up by listening to me play it in the video than for me to try and explain it to you. In jazz, we often use the word **swing**, instead of **shuffle**.

Remember, this is just an introduction to jazz, so you can get started with these basic examples. The jazz genre of music is broad and deep.

Here are the chords used in this lesson. Spend time with each and get familiar with these new fingerings.

The F7/C has a C in the bass, giving it a slightly different sound. This kind of variation is common in jazz chord usage.

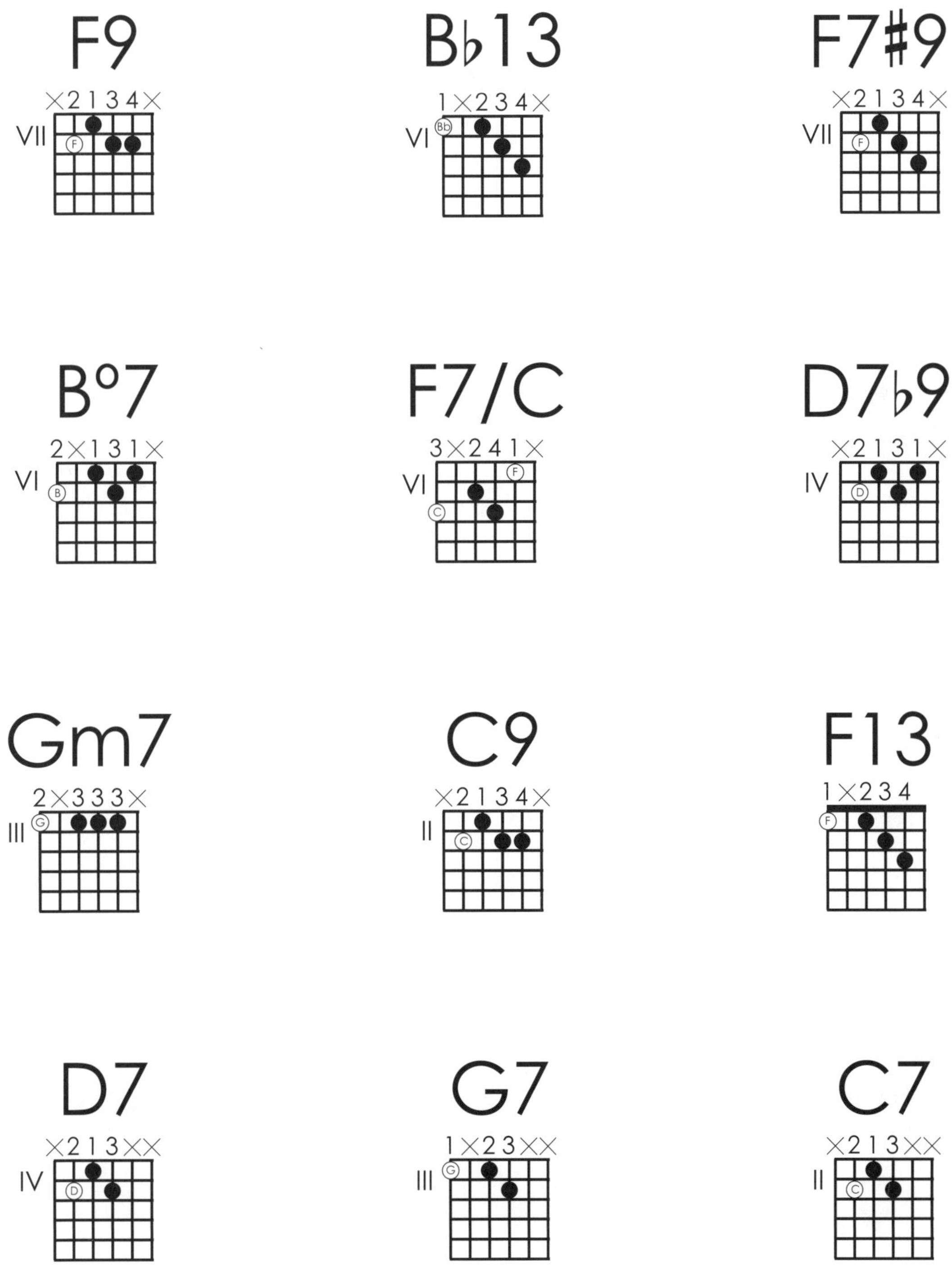

Lesson 89

Learn Major Scale Pattern #1

The major scale is the most important scale in music. The whole planet uses it to make music and define music theory. These next few lessons will show you how to play this scale on the guitar in a way that is very similar to how you played the minor pentatonic scale patterns.

Here is the first of five patterns for the major scale:

G Major Scale Pattern #1

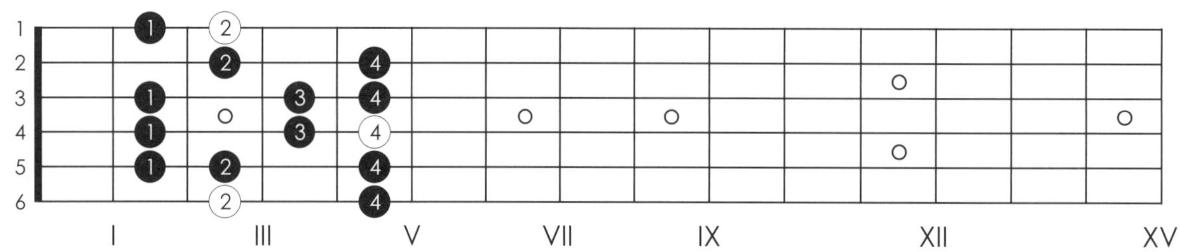

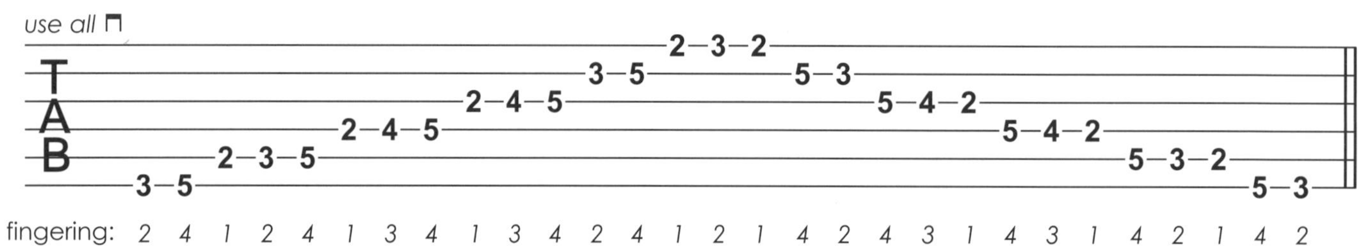

The major scale has seven different notes:

G major scale = **G A B C D E F♯**

This first pattern covers two octaves worth of the G major scale notes, starting on G and going up to G (two octaves higher).

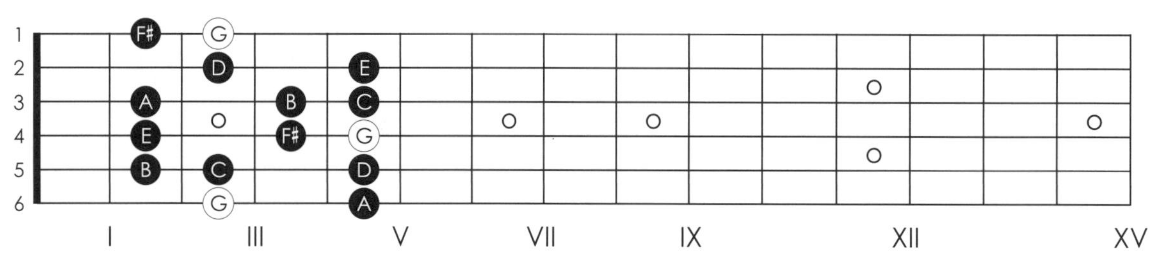

Our brains are "wired" in a way where we like to hear this scale played from the tonic up to a tonic and back down again. That is how scales have been practiced for centuries. However, as a guitarist, it is more practical to know your scales in a different way: you want to be able to locate all the notes of any particular scale that occur in the position that the hand is in at the moment. That is how these following patterns have been organized.

So for pattern #1, let's add the F♯ that occurs on the 6th string, 2nd fret and the A that occurs on the 1st string, 5th fret. This way, when you use this pattern to make music, you will have *all* the notes of the major scale right under your fingertips.

And of course, the tonic shapes tell you what key the pattern is in.

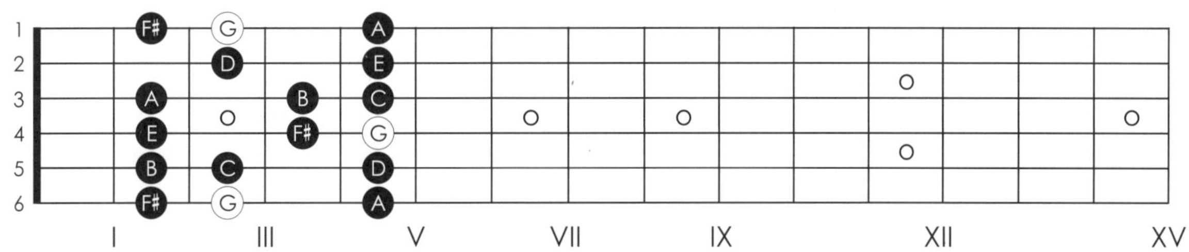

Here's the fingering for the complete pattern:

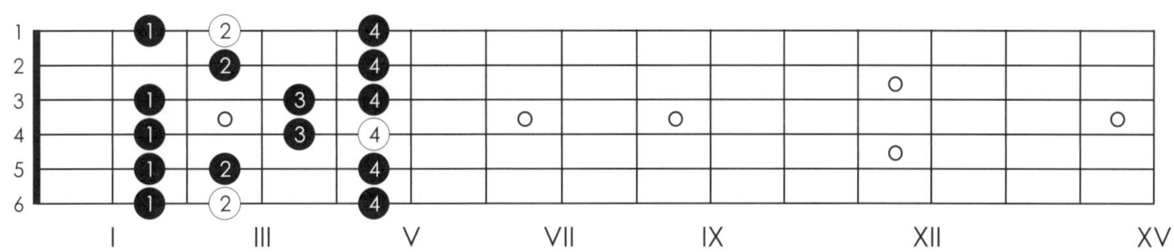

So spend some time getting to know this new scale. As always, when learning new material you want to take it very slowly. Use the same approach you did when you learned the minor pentatonic scale patterns:

- Go slowly! No tempo, just one note at a time
- Multiple passes, ascending and descending
- Strive for ten or more accurate repetitions
- Focus on fingering for now—note names will come later

Lesson 90

Learn Major Scale Pattern #2

Here is the second of the five patterns for the major scale. It starts on the note A and goes up to the note C. The tonics are on the 2nd and 4th strings.

G Major Scale Pattern #2

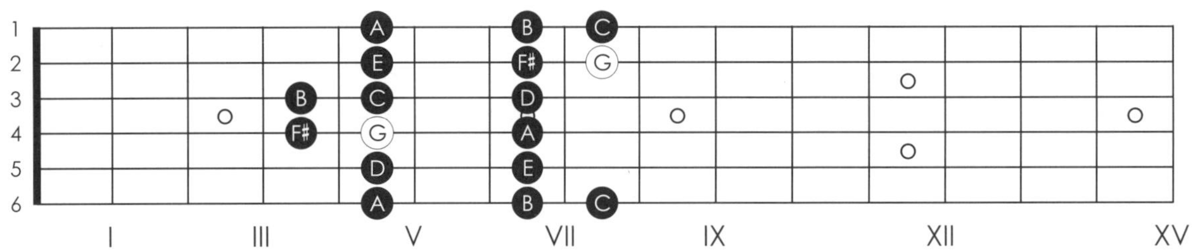

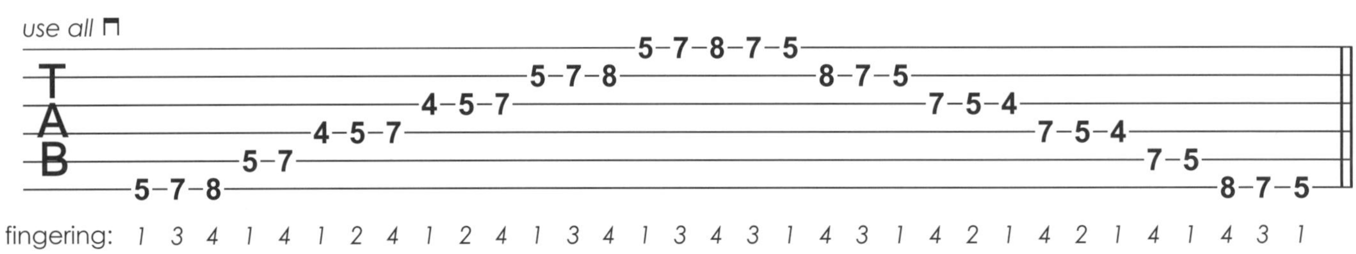

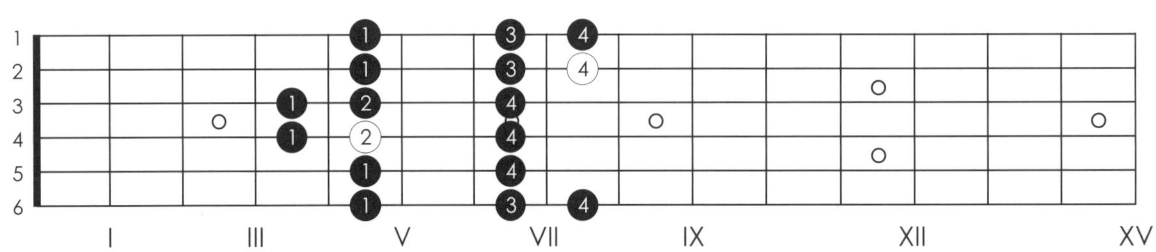

Notice the fingering on the 5th string. Using your 4th finger on the VII fret facilitates a smooth transition from V position to IV position.

Lesson 91

Learn Major Scale Pattern #3

Here is the third of the five patterns for the major scale. It starts on the note B and goes up to the note D. The tonics are on the 2nd and 5th strings.

G Major Scale Pattern #3

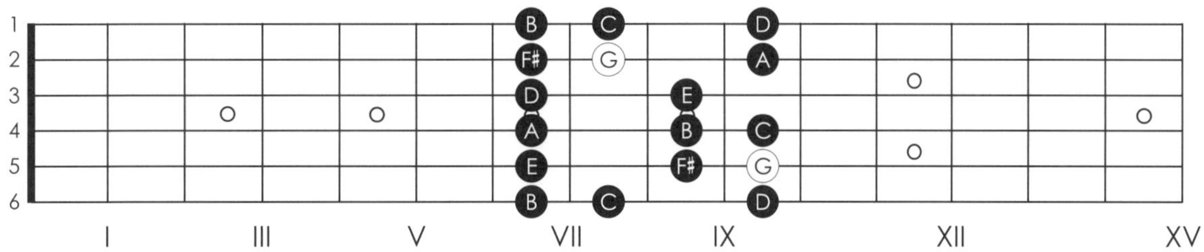

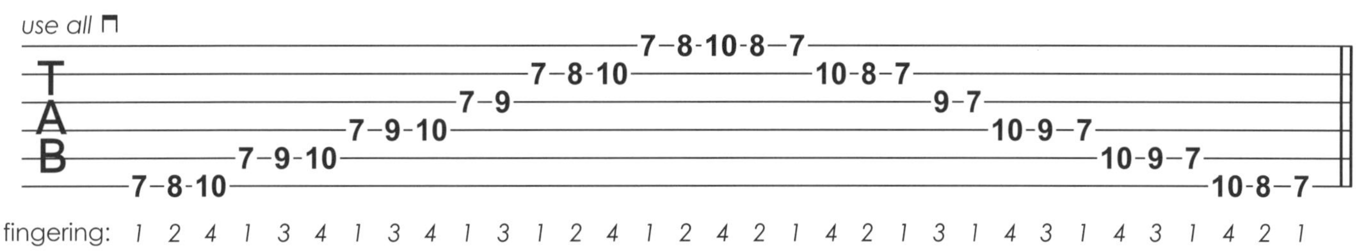

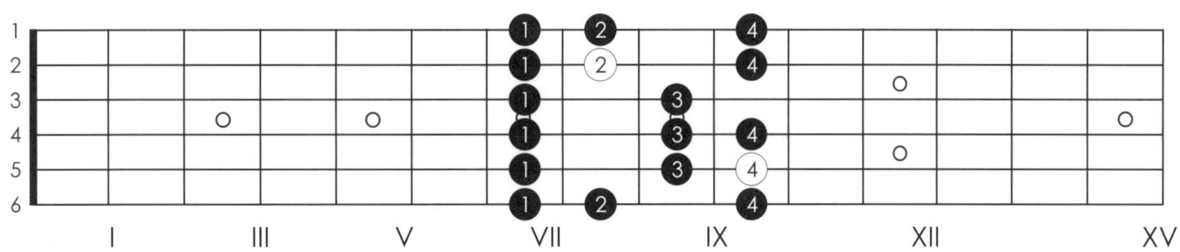

Lesson

92 Learn Major Scale Pattern #4

Here is the fourth of the five patterns for the major scale. It starts on the note D and goes up to the note E. The tonics are on the 3rd and 5th strings.

G Major Scale Pattern #4

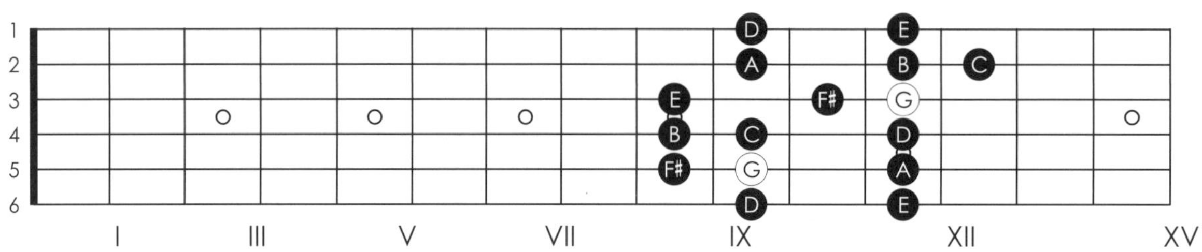

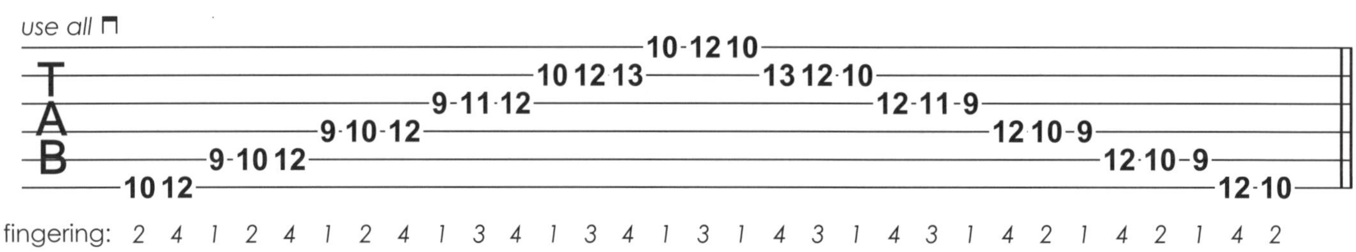

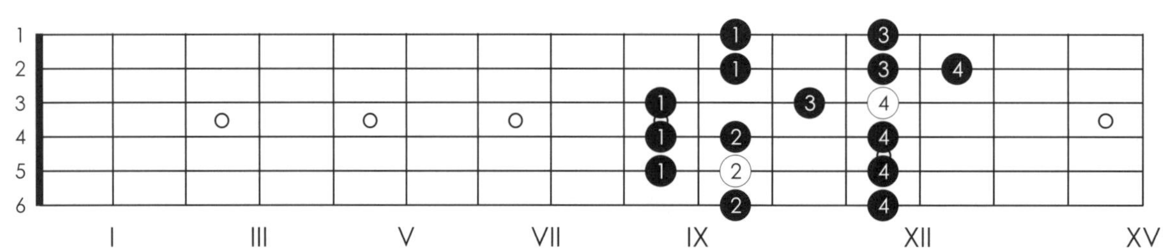

Lesson 93

Learn Major Scale Pattern #5

Here is the fifth of the five patterns for the major scale. It starts on an E and goes up to the note G. The tonics are on the 1st, 3rd and 6th strings.

G Major Scale Pattern #5

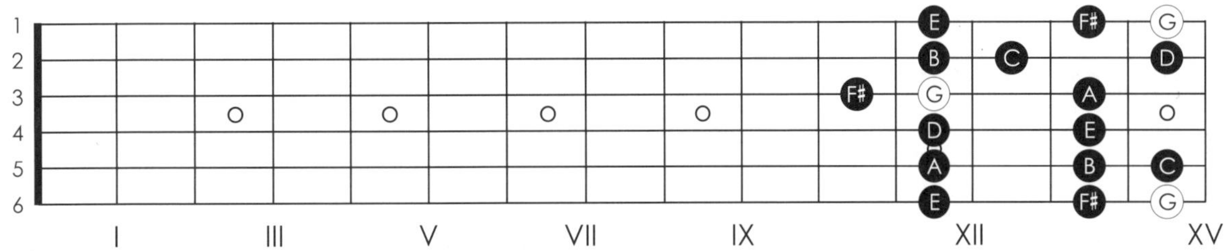

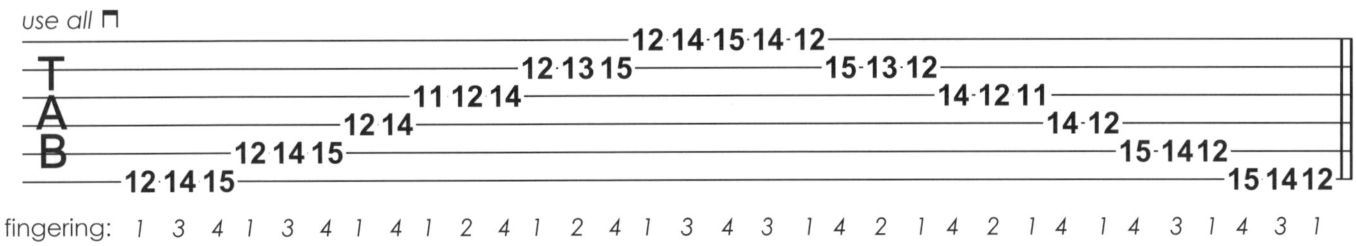

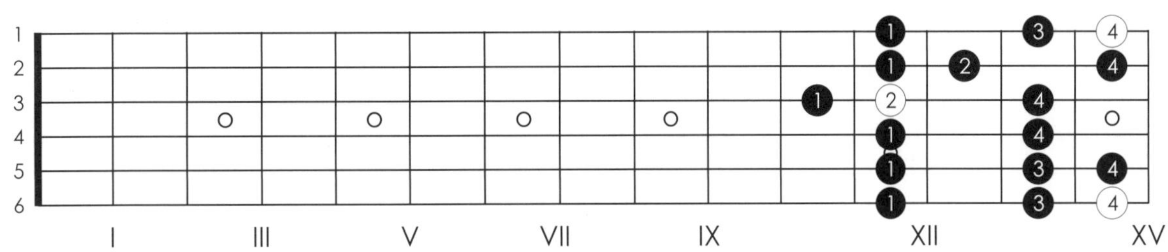

Notice the fingering on the 4th string. This helps with the position shift.

Important!

Once you've become comfortable with all five patterns, use Transposition Drill #1 to get accustomed to moving the major scale patterns around the fretboard to different keys.

Lesson 94

Learn Transposition Drill #2

Ultimately, when you are working on a project with a clearly defined goal, it is invaluable to be able to see the "big picture."

This second transposition drill will help you see the whole fretboard all in one key. Whether you are playing someone else's songs, or creating your own music, this musicianship skill will prove to be invaluable.

Transposition Drill #2

- Choose a scale type
- Choose a key
- Play that scale in that key over the entire fretboard, starting with the lowest possible pattern
- Play each pattern just one time ascending and descending

Remember to use the tonic shapes to navigate the fretboard. Start with the *lowest* tonic shape (you can be sure it's the lowest by trying to play the *next* lowest tonic shape). In this example in the key of C, the third tonic shape in I position is the lowest possible shape.

Tonic Shape #3 in the Key of C

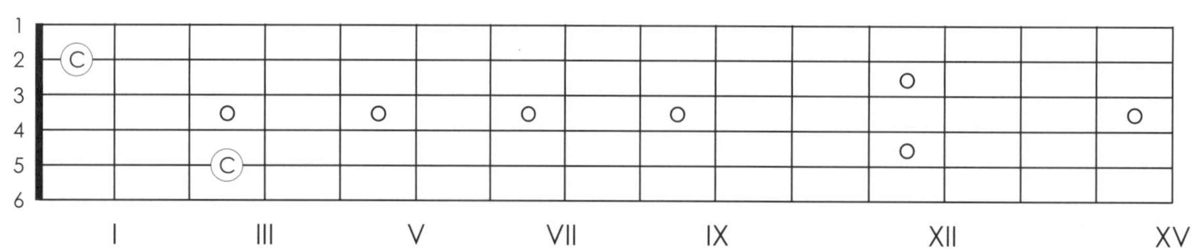

So pattern #3 fits over this tonic shape.

Minor Pentatonic Scale Pattern #3 in the Key of C

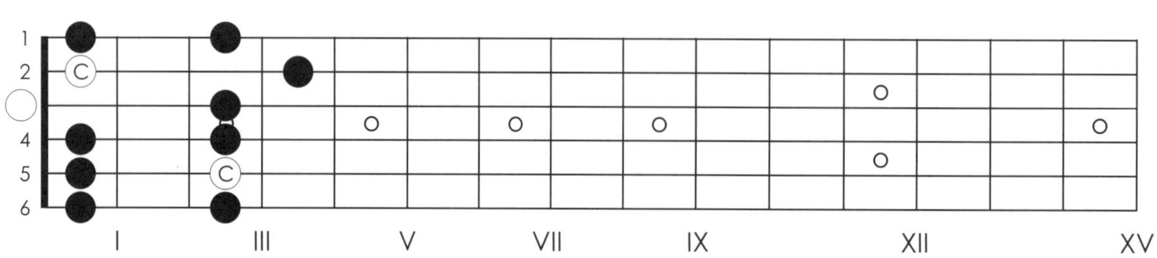

But this puts us in **open position**, so you will use I position fingering to play the pattern:

Minor Pentatonic Scale Pattern #3 in the Key of C:
Open Position with First Position Fingering

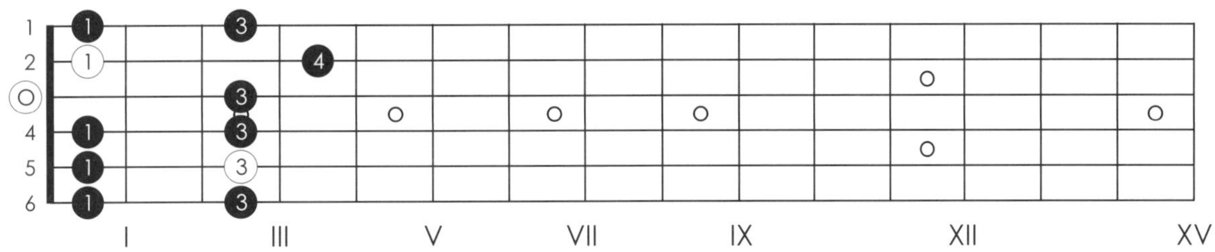

Here are the rest of the patterns in the key of C:

Minor Pentatonic Scale Pattern #4 in the Key of C

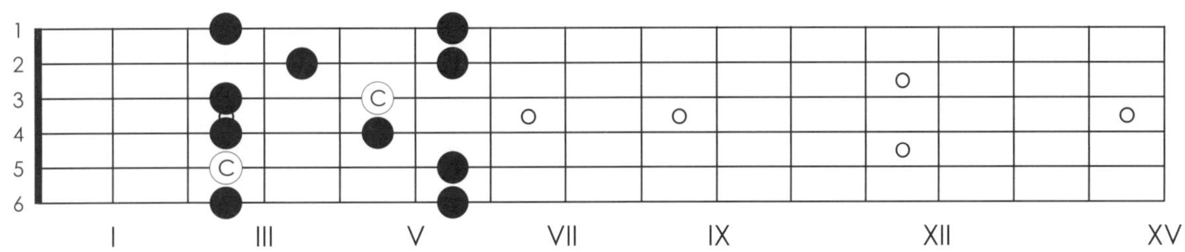

Minor Pentatonic Scale Pattern #5 in the Key of C

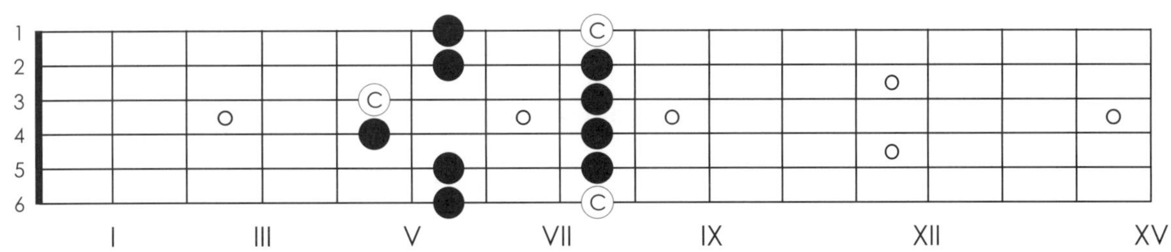

Minor Pentatonic Scale Pattern #1 in the Key of C

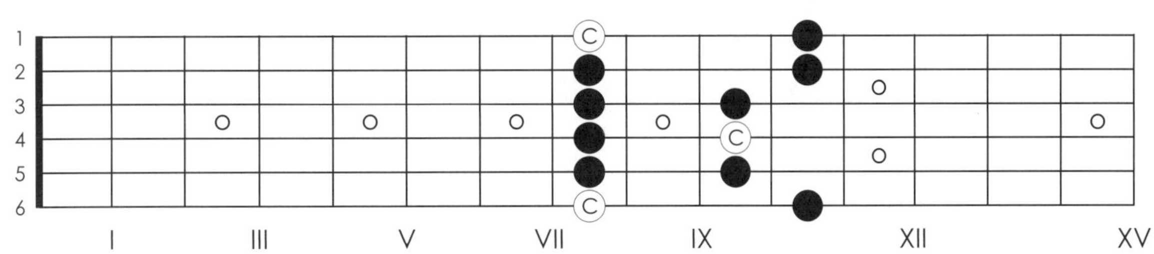

Minor Pentatonic Scale Pattern #2 in the Key of C

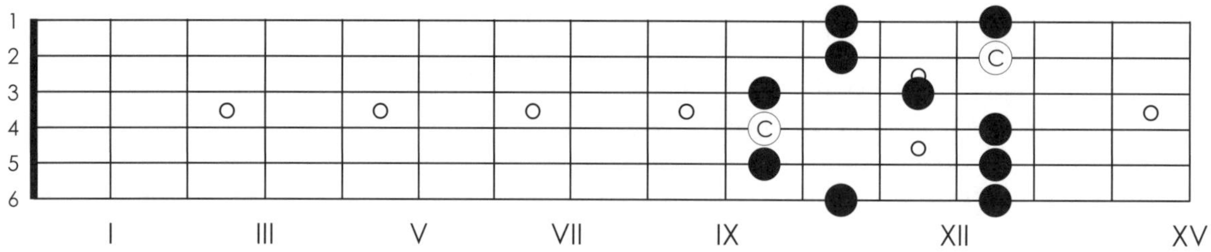

Minor Pentatonic Scale Pattern #3 in the Key of C

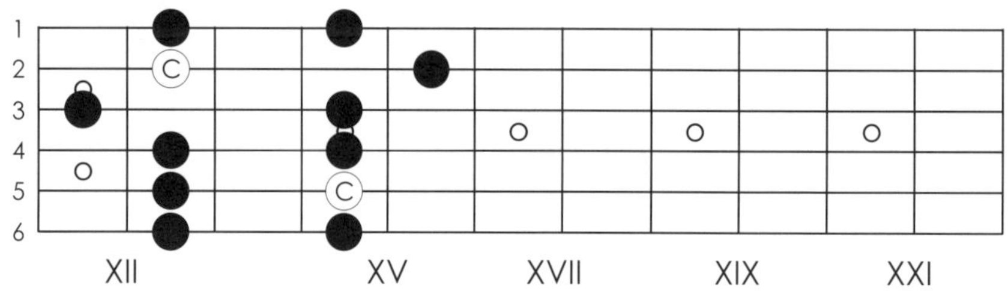

Minor Pentatonic Scale Pattern #4 in the Key of C

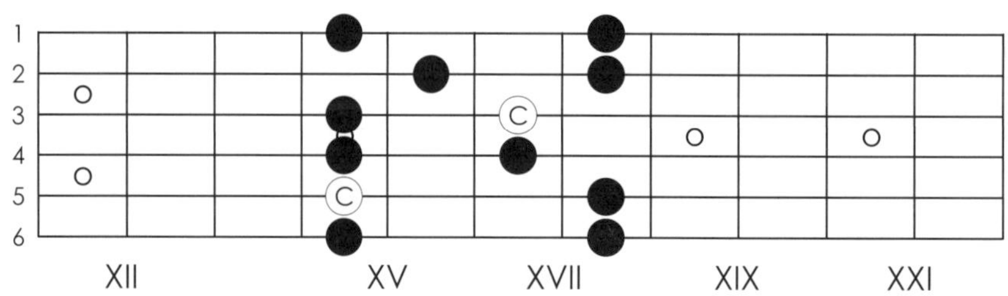

Minor Pentatonic Scale Pattern #5 in the Key of C

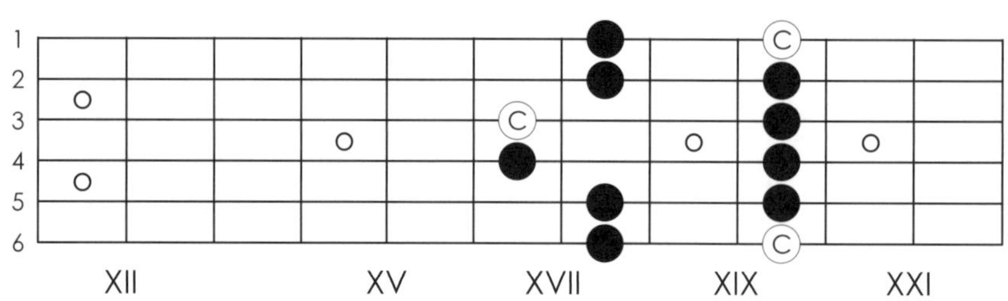

Notice that tonic shape #1 fits at the top of the fretboard, but there are not enough frets to actually play the pattern, at least not on this electric guitar (most electric guitar fretboards end at the 22nd fret—some less, some more).

Tonic Shape #1 in the Key of C

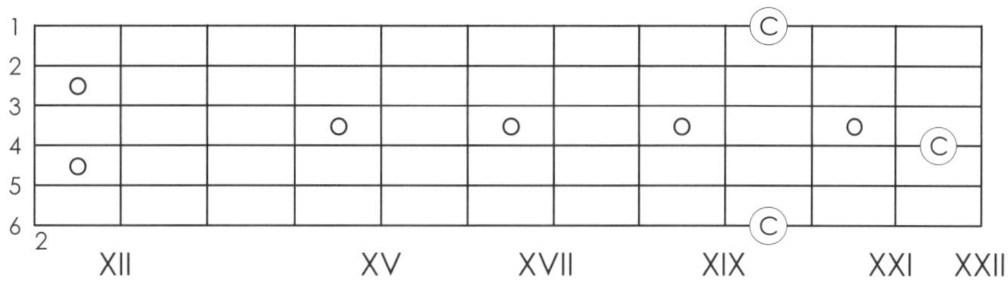

Here are all of the notes of C minor pentatonic on the entire fretboard:

All the Notes of the C Minor Pentatonic Scale

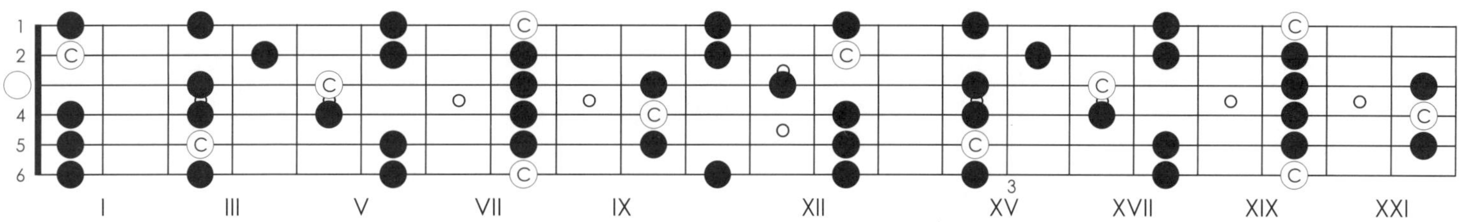

All the Tonics Shapes in the Key of C

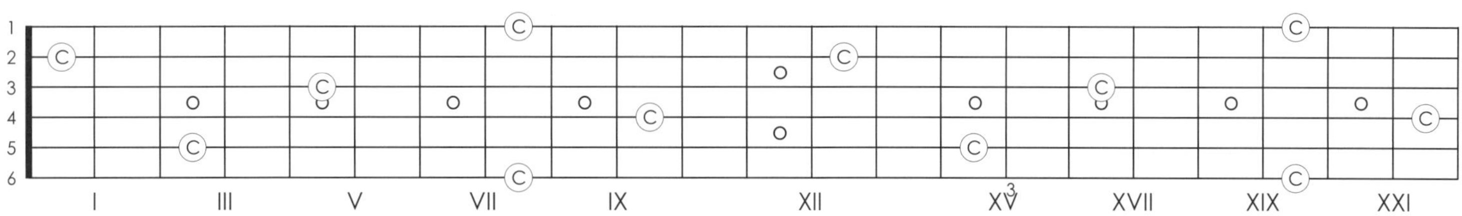

Getting to the point where you can see the entire fretboard in any scale type in any particular key is one of the ultimate goals for the "thinking guitarist." Spending time on this drill with both the minor pentatonic and the major scales is well worth the effort.

Lesson 95

Learn to play a riff based on Major Scale Pattern #1

Now we are going to look at some riffs that are based on the major scale. You will be able to use these riffs over almost any chord progression that is in the key of G major.

These riffs utilize the various techniques we've been studying in the course, like hammer-ons and pull-offs, slides, vibrato, and they also give you a chance to experience a practical application of the skills you learned in the transposition drills.

So you see, we've been breaking things down into smaller goals and now we are putting it all back together to create music!

This first riff is based on pattern #1:

G Major Scale Pattern #1

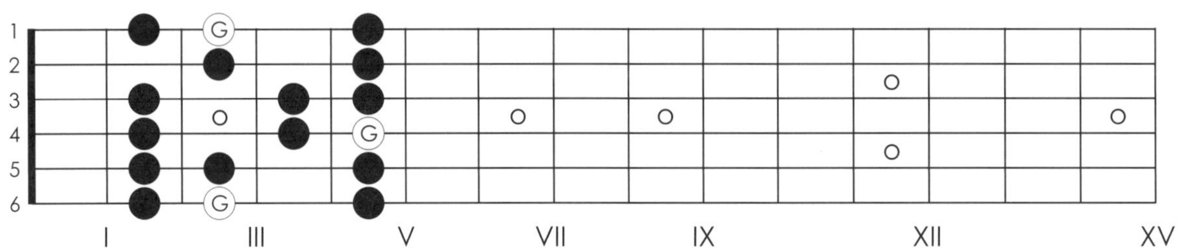

Riff #1 in the Key of G Major

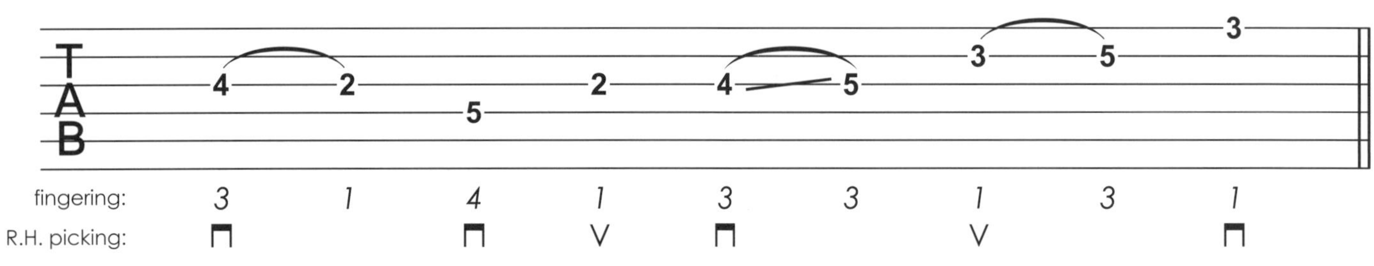

While you are playing the riff, visualize the tonic shape it "lays over". See it in your mind as you play the notes of the phrase. The tonic shapes are your point of reference. This will enable you to transpose more easily.

G Tonic Shape #1

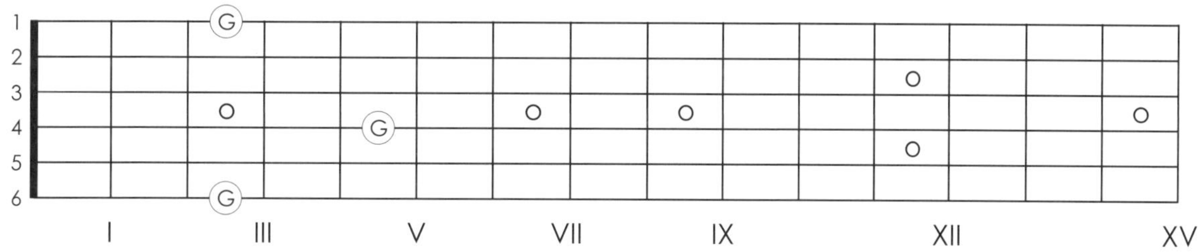

Here is the riff in a few different keys:

Riff #1 in the Key of D Major

Riff #1 in the Key of B♭ Major

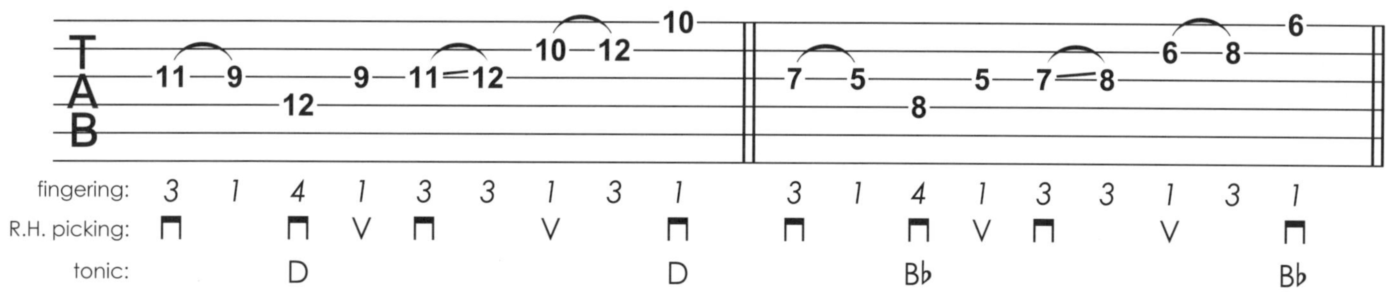

Riff #1 in the Key of A Major

Riff #1 in the Key of E Major

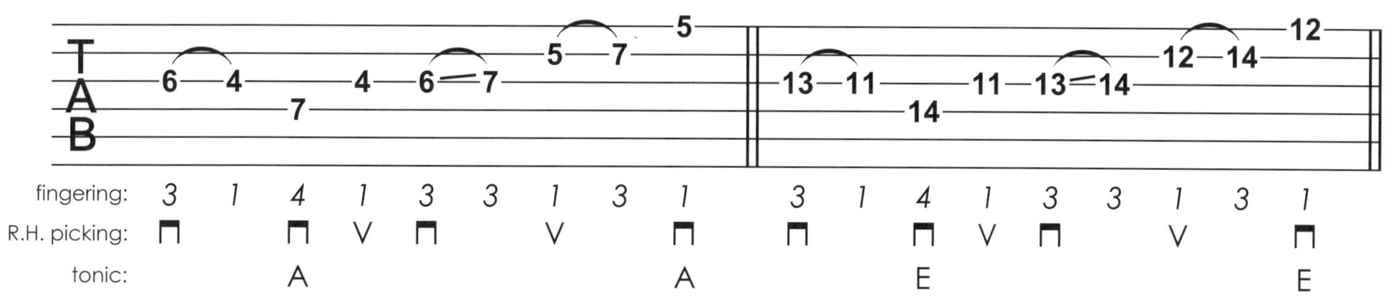

Lesson

96 Learn to play a riff based on Major Scale Pattern #2

This riff is based on pattern #2:

G Major Scale Pattern #2

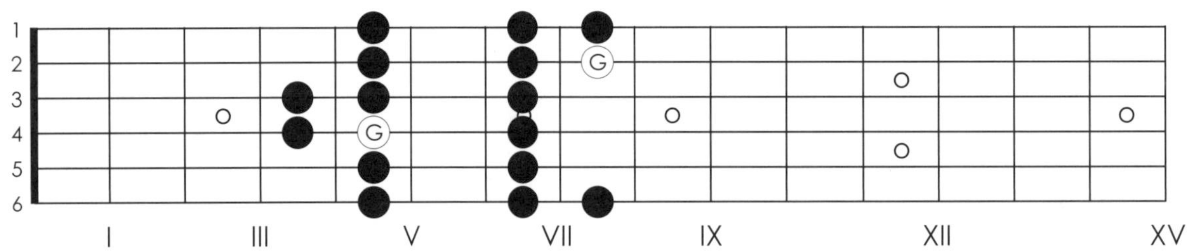

Riff #1 in the Key of G Major

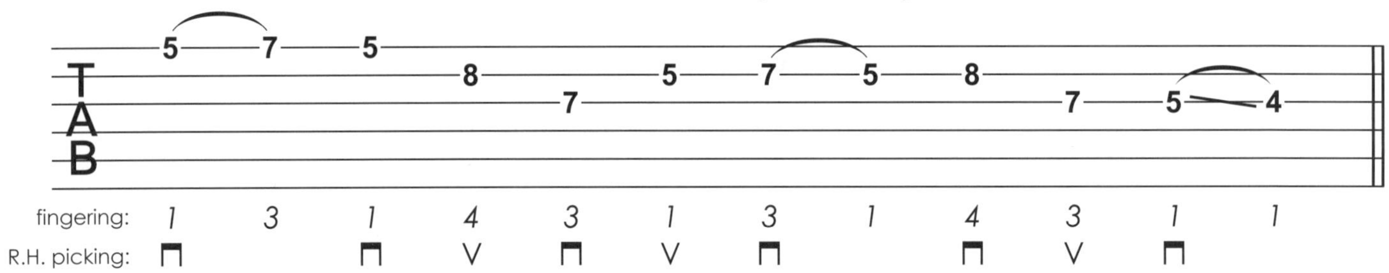

Learn to play a riff based on Major Scale Pattern #3

This riff is based on pattern #3:

G Major Scale Pattern #3

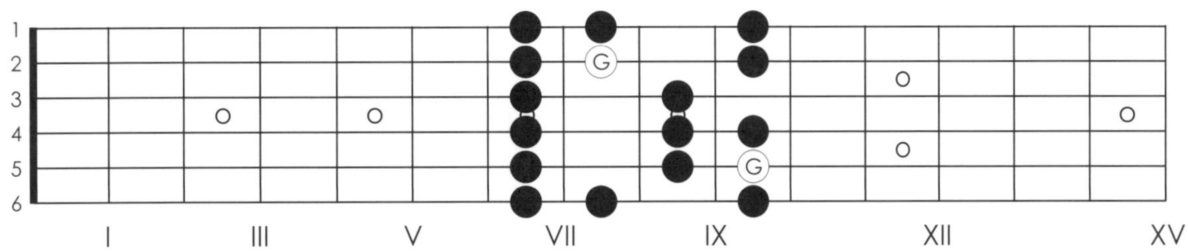

Riff #3 in the Key of G Major

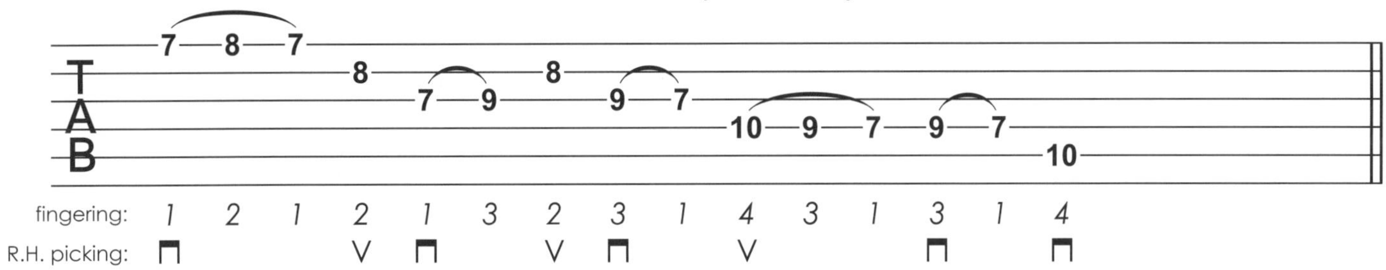

You could experiment with the picking strategy on this one. Just be consistent with whatever you choose to do with your right hand.

Lesson 98

Learn to play a riff based on Major Scale Pattern #4

This riff is based on pattern #4:

G Major Scale Pattern #4

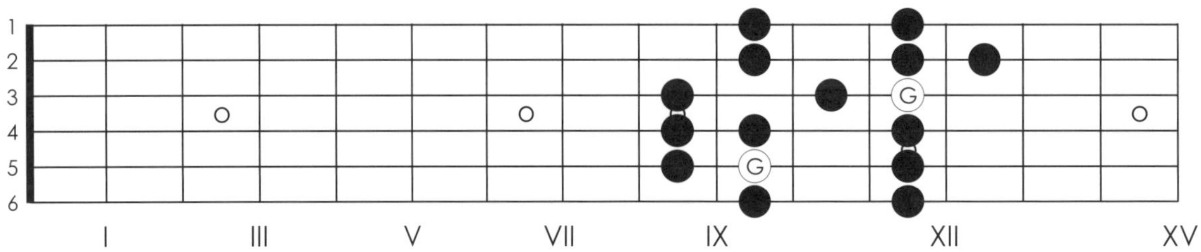

Riff #4 in the Key of G Major

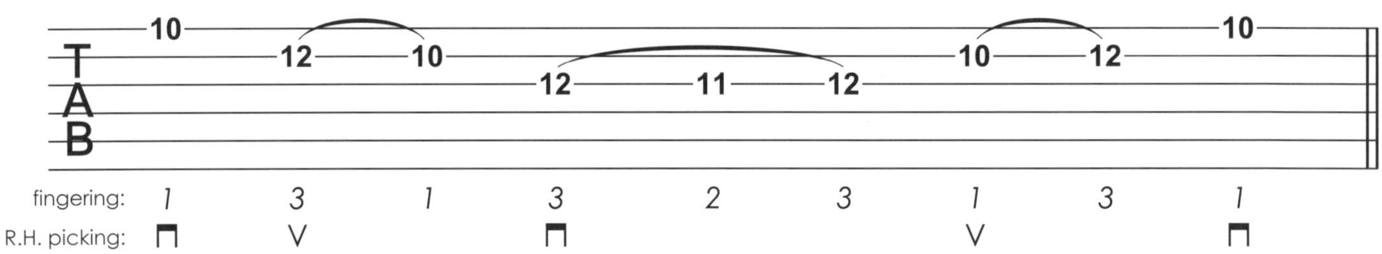

Lesson

99

Learn to play a riff based on Major Scale Pattern #5

This riff is based on pattern #5:

G Major Scale Pattern #5

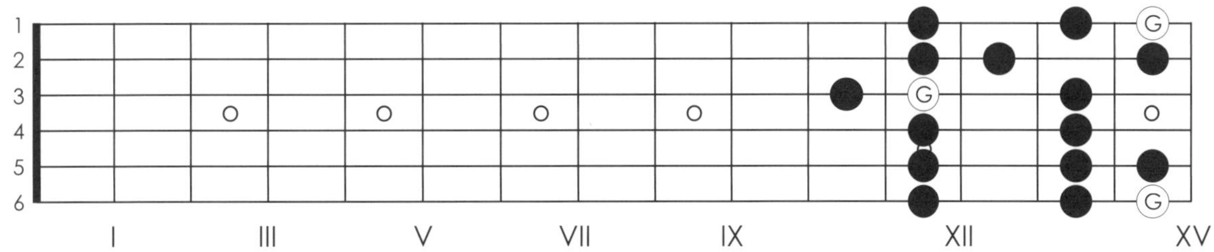

Riff #5 in the Key of G Major

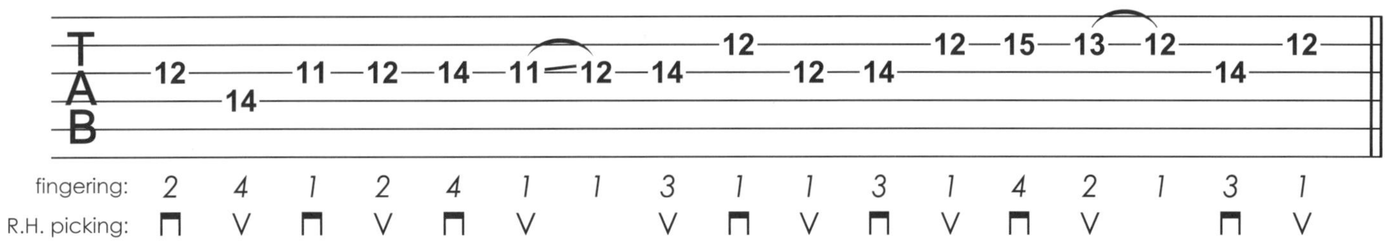

These riffs will get you started on building a vocabulary of phrases you can use when improvising. You can play these along with live or recorded music in the key of G major. If the song you're playing is in a key other than G major, transpose the riff so that the tonic shapes match the key of the music.

Appendix

The Basic Chord Vocabulary

Major:

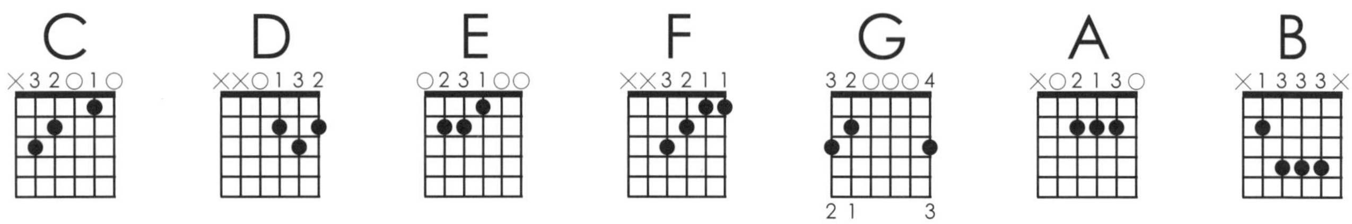

Minor:

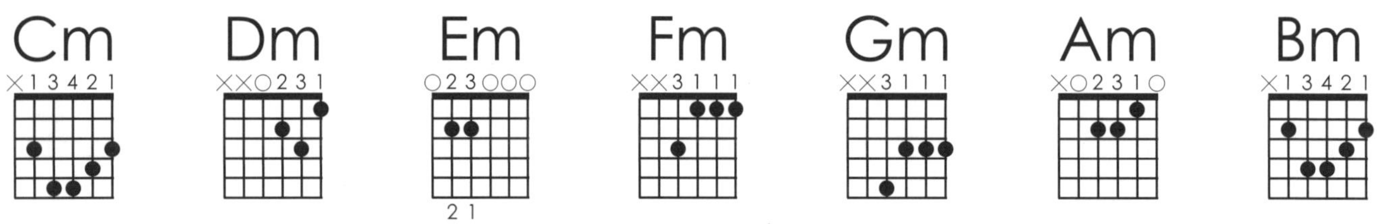

Dominant Seventh:

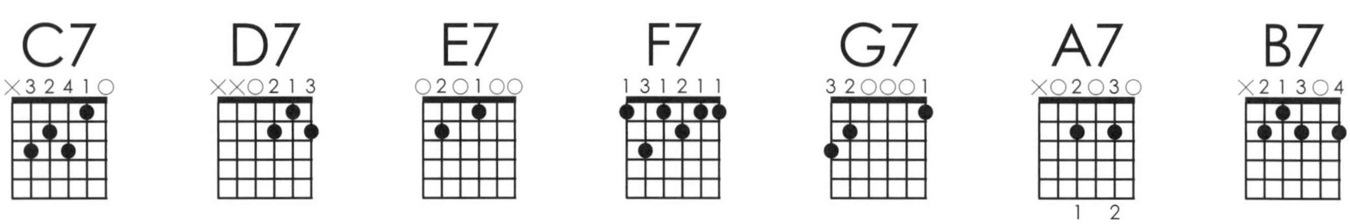

Barre chords—root on the 6th string:

Major

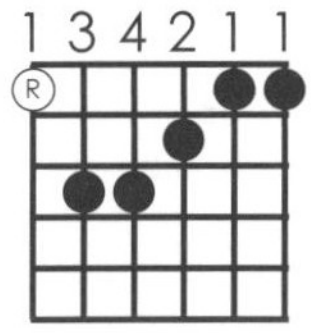

Minor

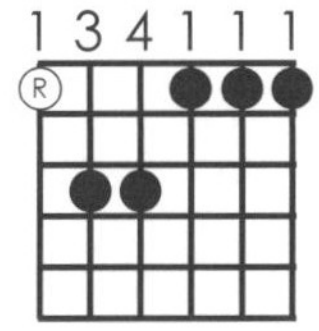

Dominant 7th

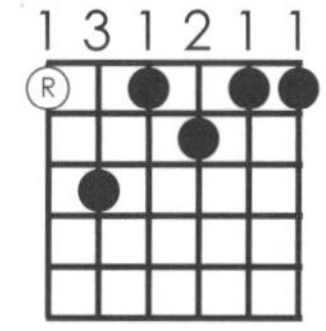

Barre chords—root on the 5th string:

Major

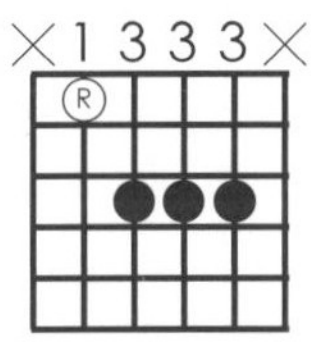

Minor

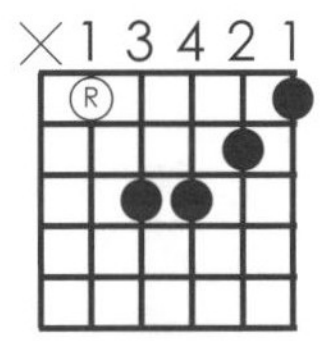

Dominant 7th

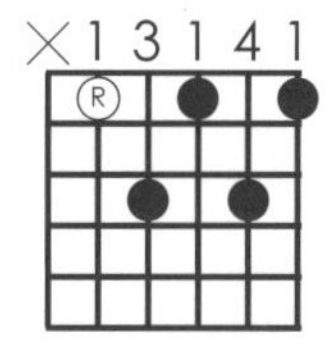

Power chord—root on the 6th string:

5

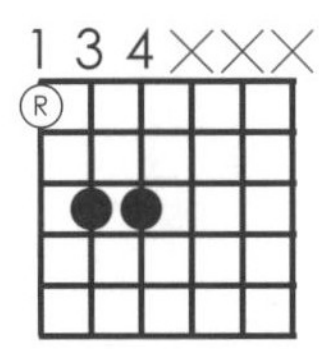

Power chord—root on the 5th string:

5

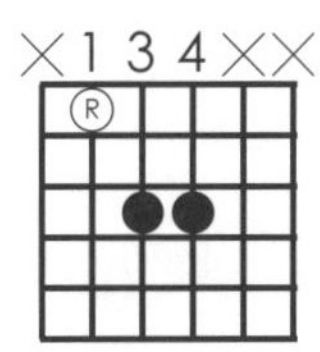

(power chords are neither inherently major, minor, nor dominant 7th and their chord symbol is the root plus a "5")

Scale Vocabulary

The Minor Pentatonic Scale

(T) = Tonic

Pattern #1

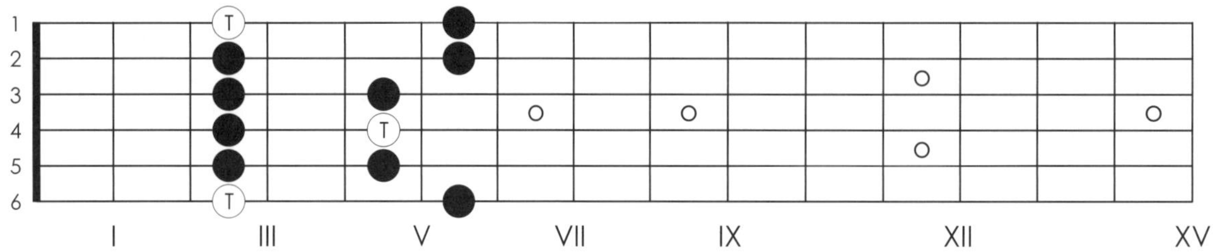

Pattern #2

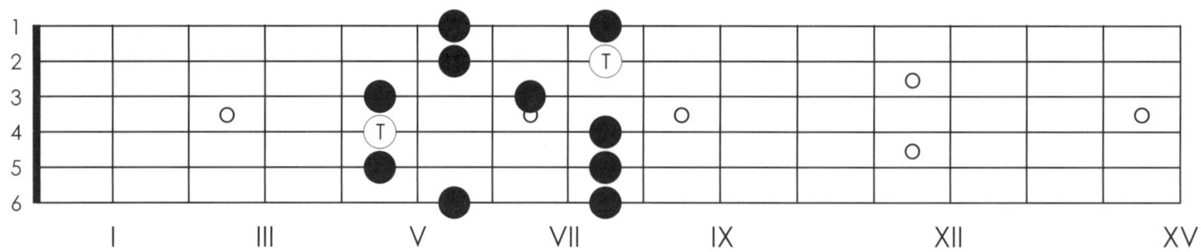

Pattern #3

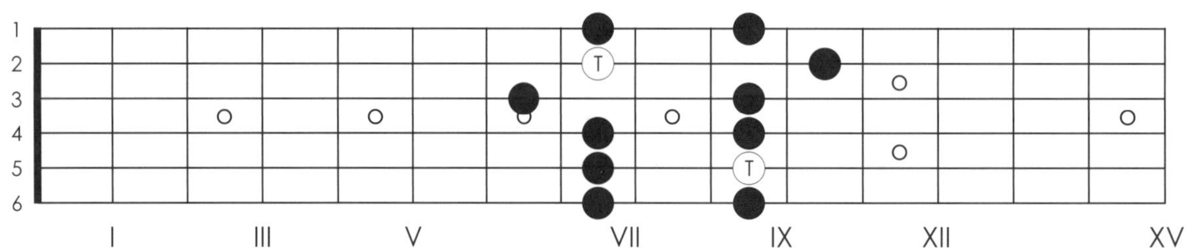

Pattern #4

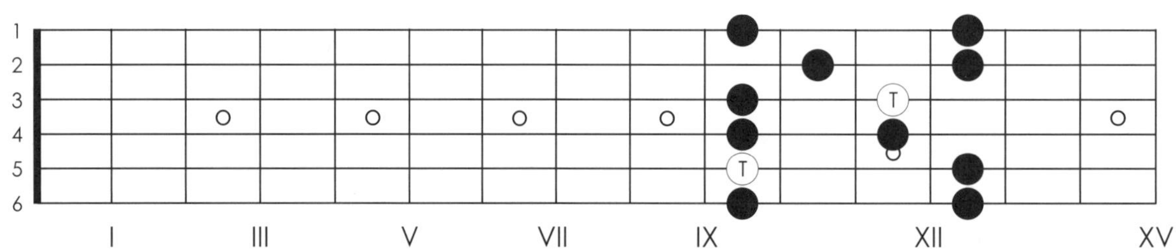

Pattern #5

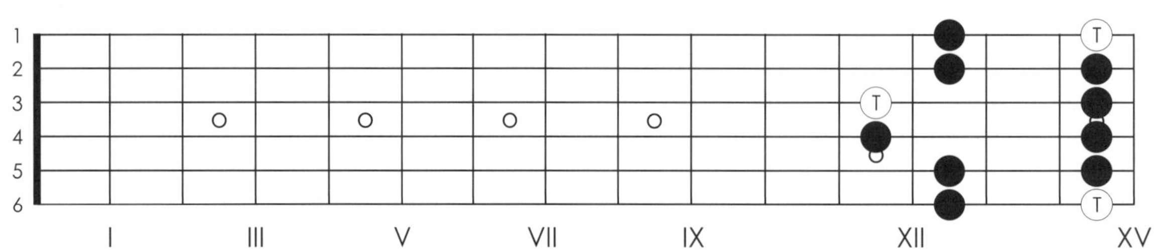

(Refer to Lessons 67-71 and 78 for fingering options.)

The Major Scale

(T) = Tonic

Pattern #1

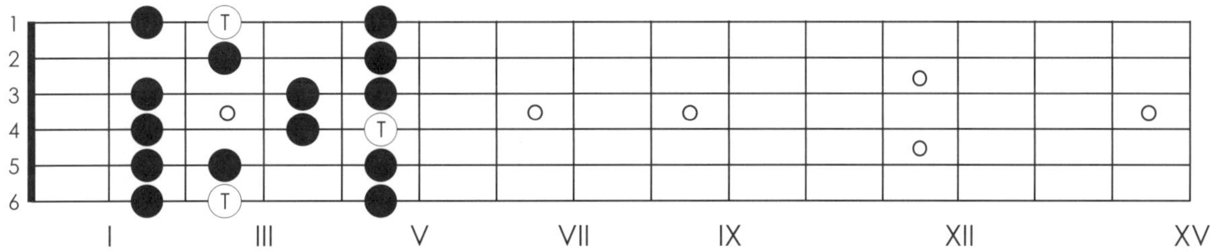

Pattern #2

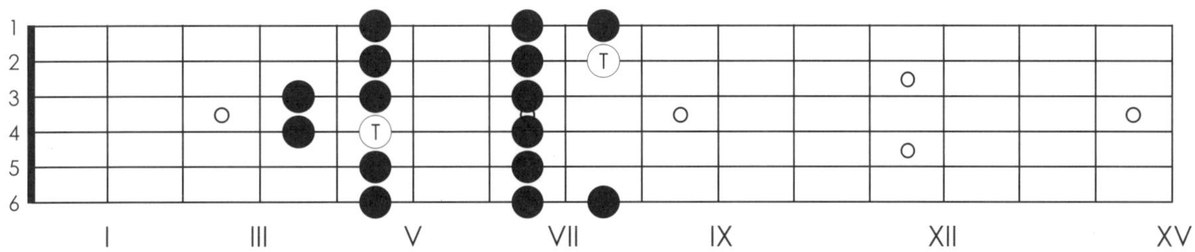

Pattern #3

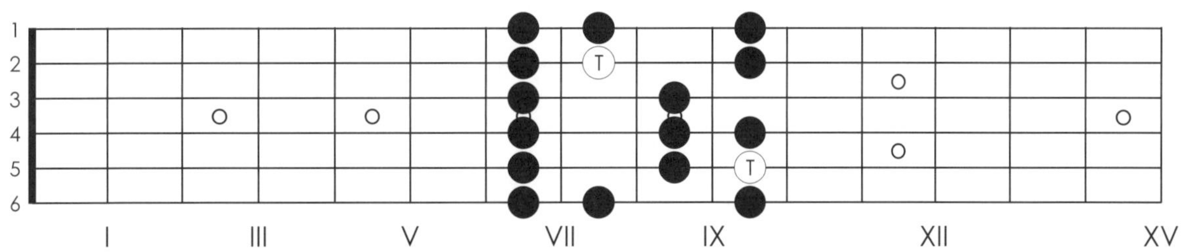

Pattern #4

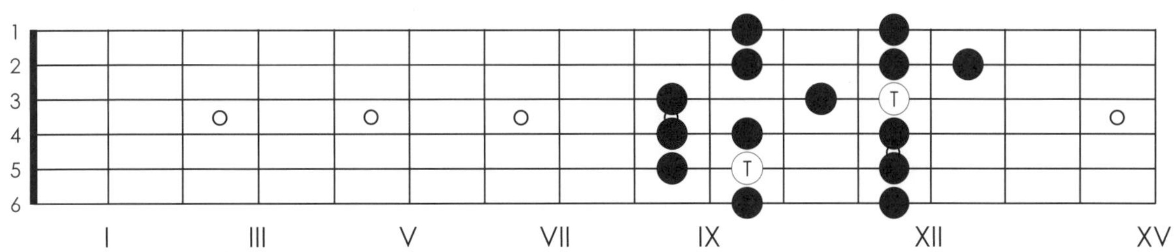

Pattern #5

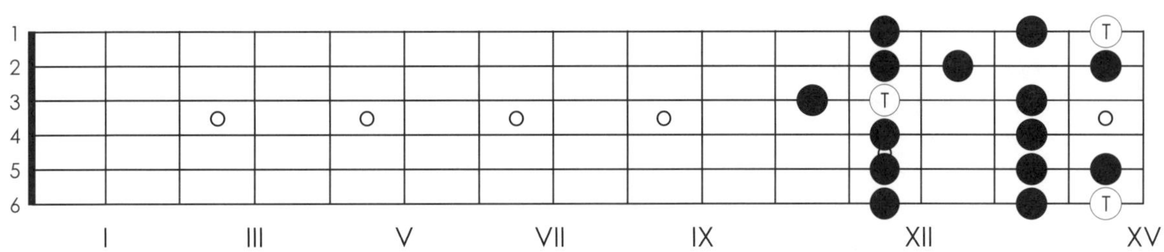

(Refer to Lessons 89-93 for fingering options.)

The Tonic Shapes

Ⓣ = Tonic

Tonic Shape #1

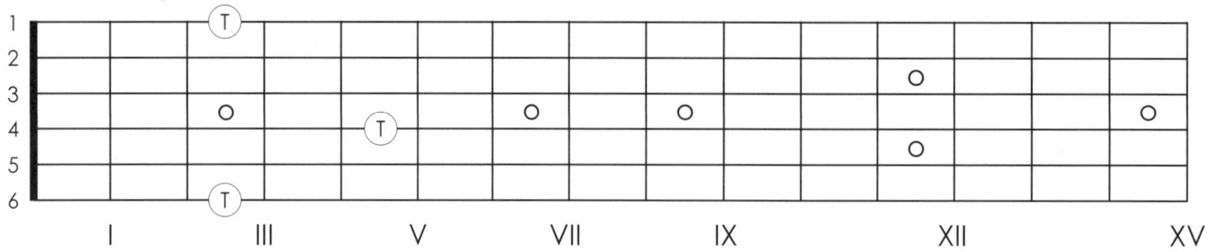

Tonic Shape #2

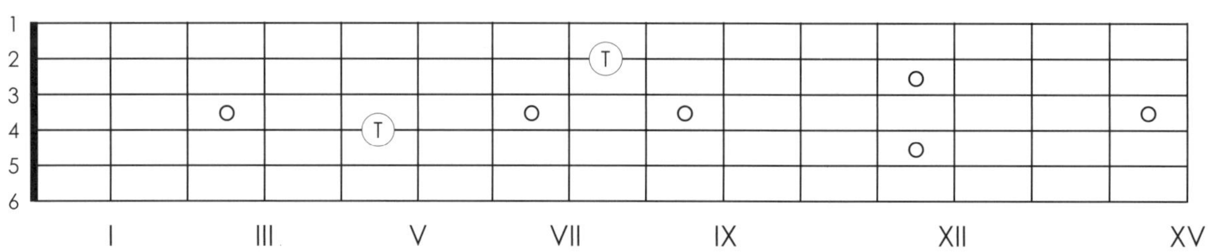

Tonic Shape #3

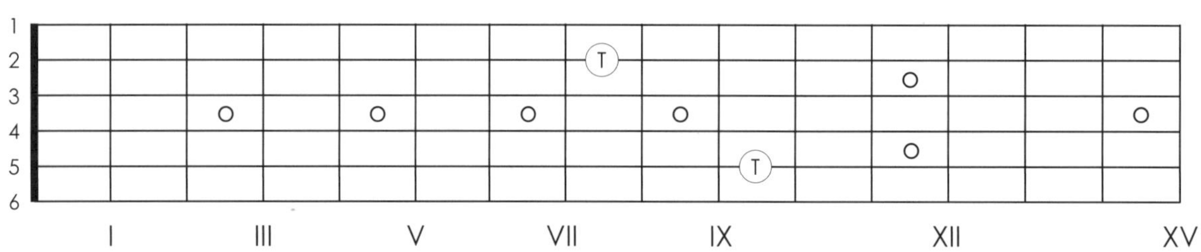

Tonic Shape #4

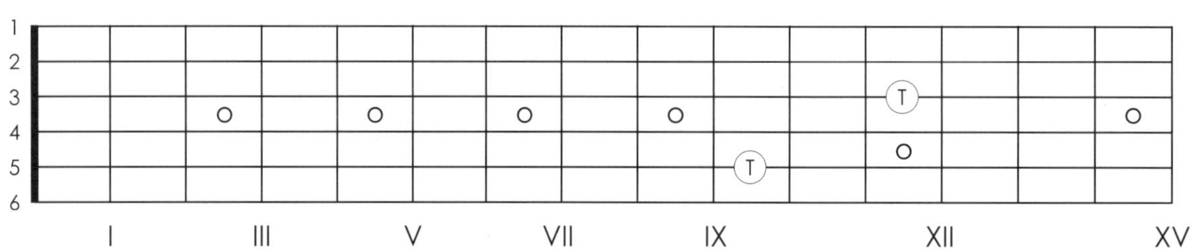

Tonic Shape #5

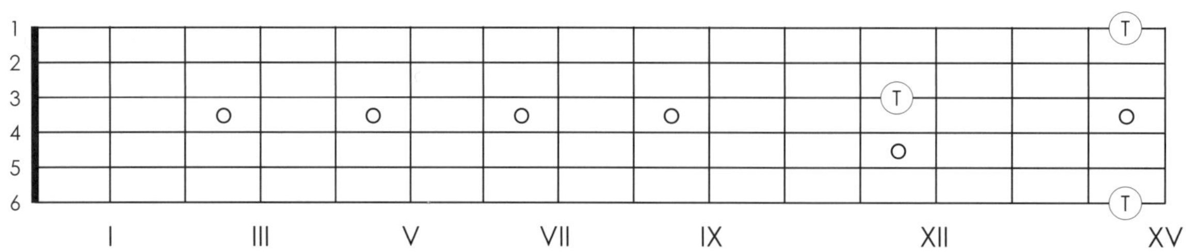

All the Notes of the Minor Pentatonic Scale (in the key of G)

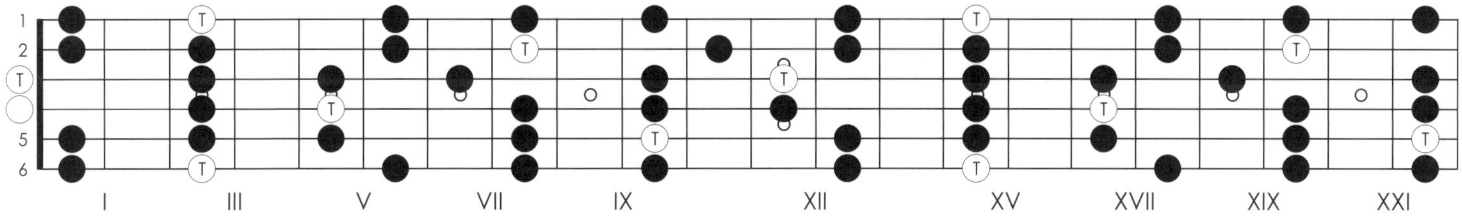

All the Notes of the Major Scale (in the key of G)

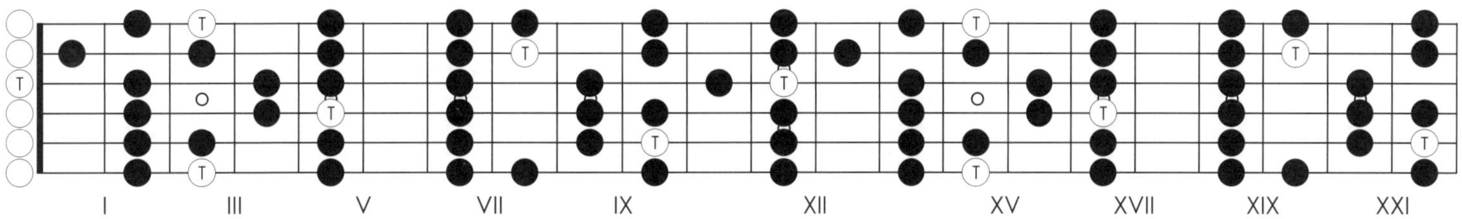

All the Tonic Shapes (in the key of G)

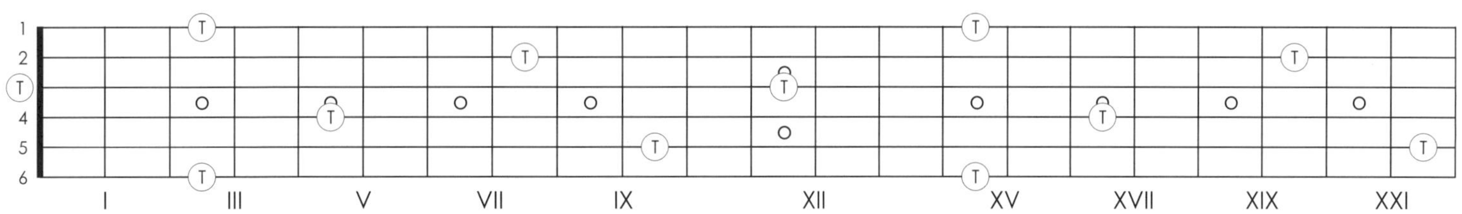

Note Names on the Fretboard

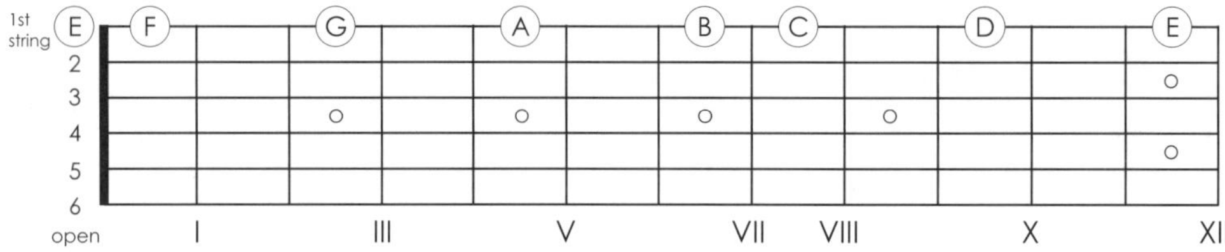

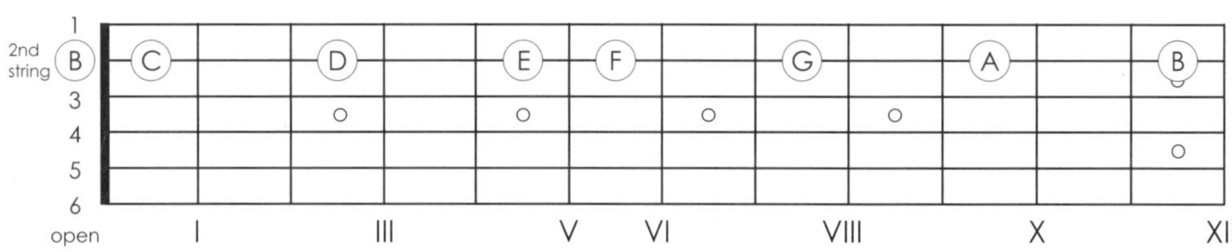

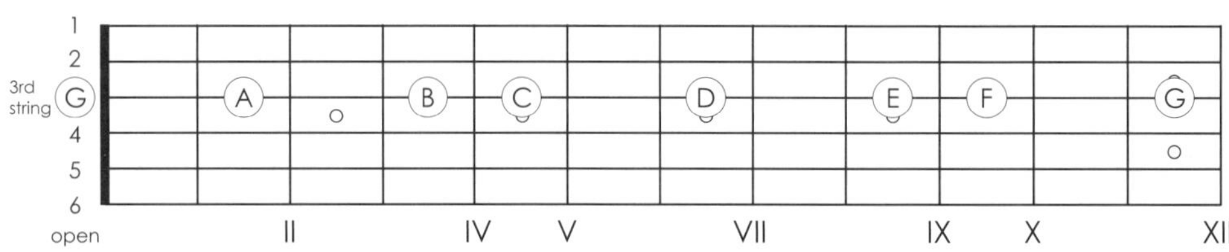

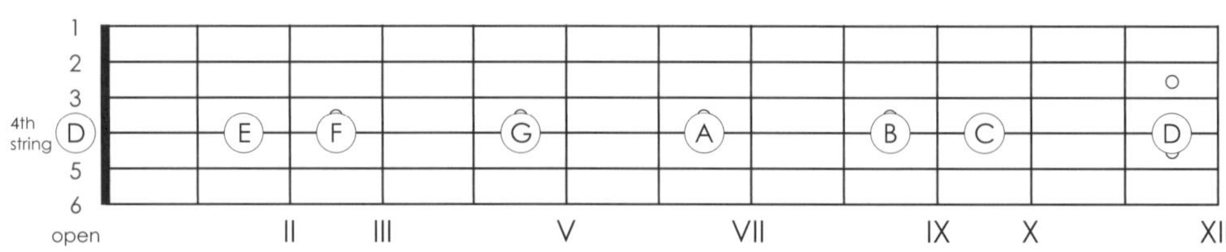

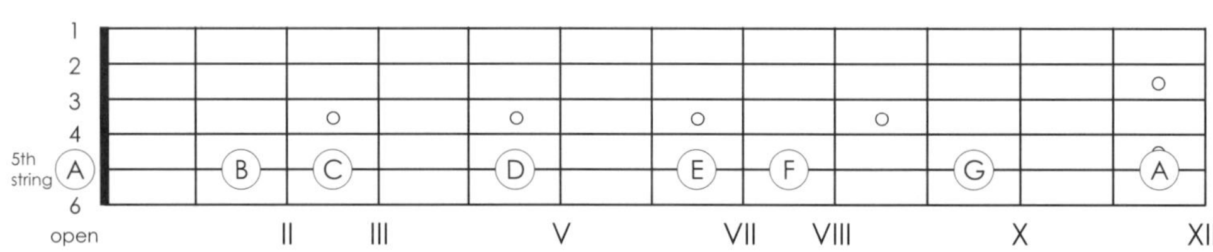

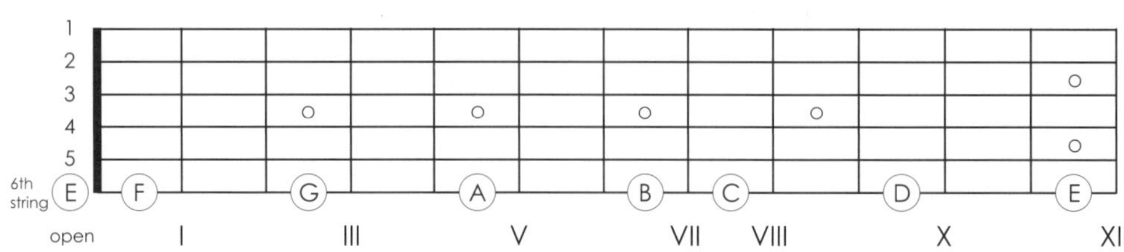

Concordance

Chord vocabulary:

L4 L5 L6 L8 L10 L15 L16 L49 L51 L52 L55 L56 L58 L66 L74 L87 L88

Chord transitions (moving from chord to chord):

L11 L12 L13 L17 L18

Chord progressions:

L19 L20 L21 L22 L23 L33 L34 L39 L40 L50 L59 L74 L81 L87 L88

Strumming:

L7 L14 L24 L25 L26 L27 L28 L29 L30 L31 L32 L33 L34 L36 L37 L38 L39 L40 L54 L87 L88

Fingerpicking:

L42 L43 L44 L45 L46 L47 L59

Building technique:

L7 L9 L14 L24 L25 L26 L31 L54 L60 L61 L62 L64 L65 L73 L75 L76 L77 L78 L80

Barre and power chords:

L15 L51 L52 L55 L56 L58 L59 L74

Slash chords:

L66 L88

Jazz chords:

L87 L88

Minor pentatonic scales:

L67 L68 L69 L70 L71 L72 L78 L79 L82 L83 L84 L85 L86 L94

Major scales:

L89 L90 L91 L92 L93 L94 L95 L96 L97 L98 L99 (L79—doesn't mention major scales yet, but this drill is designed to be applied to all scale vocabulary)

Riffs and Licks:

L81 L82 L83 L84 L85 L86 L95 L96 L97 L98 L99

Transposing scales (changing keys):

L72 L79 L82 L84 L86 L94 L95

Navigating the fretboard:

L1 L2 L35 L41 L48 L58 L62 L63 L72 L79 L94

Music theory:

L19 L24 L25 L26 L35 L36 L41 L54 L57 L58 L63 L66 L67 L72 L77 L79 L81 L89 L94

Rhythm guitar: L4 to L41 L48 L49 L50 L51 L52 L54 L55 L56 L57 L58 L59 L66 L74 L81 L87 L88

Lead guitar:

L35 L41 L53 L57 L60 L61 L62 L63 L64 L65 L67 L68 L69 L70 L71 L72 L73 L75 L76 L77 L78 L79 L80 L82–L86 L89–L99

Index

accent L26 L27 L28 L32 L36 L50

alternate picking L61 L62 L78

backbeat L54

bar L19 L20 L27 L36 L46 L50 L54 L81 L88

bar lines L19 L27

barre chord L15 L35 L51 L52 L55 L56 L58 L59 L74 L81

beat L19 L20 L22 L26 L36 L50 L54 L74

bend L77 L80 L82 L83 L85

blues L49 L77 L81 L88

body L1

bridge L1 L74 L81

Charleston rhythm L88

choking L88

chord L4 L5 L6 L8–L24 L26 L28 L31 L33 L34 L35 L39 L40 L44–47 L49–L52 L54 L55 L56 L58 L59 L66 L72 L74 L81 L87 L88

chord diagram L4 L58

chord families L8

chord progression L19–L23 L33 L34 L39 L40 L45 L46 L47 L50 L59 L66 L74 L81 L87 L88 L95

chord transition L11 L12 L13 L17 L18 L21 L33 L87

common finger L11 L13 L17 L23 L79 L88

country L40 L49 L77

downstroke L53 L59 L60 L62 L64 L65 L76 L78

dynamics L25 L26

eighth note L36 L50 L54 L59

enharmonic L57 L58

fingerpicking L42 L43 L44 L45 L46 L47 L53 L59

fingerstyle L42

flat L57 L77

fret L1 L2 L4 L5 L6 L8 L10 L11 L12 L15 L17 L35 L41 L48 L49 L51 L52 L55–L58 L62 L63 L68 L72 L75 L77 L79 L85 L86 L87 L89 L90 L94

fretboard L1 L2 L9 L35 L41 L48 L52 L55 L56 L57 L62 L67 L71 L72 L75 L77 L79 L80 L84 L93 L94

fretboard range L79

funk L54

guide finger L12 L13 L87 L88
half step L41 L57
hammer-on L64 L65 L73 L75 L76 L78 L84 L95
headstock L1
jazz L87 L88
key L67 L72 L79 L82 L84 L86 L89 L93 L94 L95 L99
lead guitar L82
legato L84
lick L82
major scale L89 L90 L91 L92 L93 L94 L95 L96 L97 L98 L99
measure L19 L36
minor pentatonic scale L67–L71 L75 L77 L78 L79 L82–L86 L89 L94
motif L82
neck L1 L4–L7 L10 L31 L48 L49 L51 L52 L56 L57 L62 L77 L80
note name L35 L41 L57 L58 L63 L67–72 L79 L89 L94
nut L1 L2 L3 L35 L51 L52 L58 L79
octave L63 L72 L79 L89
octave shape L72
open position L51 L79 L94
open string L2 L3 L4 L33 L44 L45 L47 L54
percussive muted strum L54
phrase L75 L82 L84 L85 L86 L95 L99
pitch L41 L63 L77 L80 L83 L85
pop L4 L23 L40 L44 L54
position L51 L55 L62 L64 L65 L67 L68 L69 L70 L73 L76 L78 L79 L85 L89 L90 L93 L94
pseudo-chromatic exercise L62
pull-off L65 L73 L75 L76 L78 L83 L84 L95
repeat signs L19 L27
rhythm L18 L19 L21 L24 L26 L30 L32 L36 L37 L50 L54 L56 L59 L81 L82 L88
rhythm guitar L30 L54 L56
riff L81 L82 L83 L84 L85 L86 L95 L96 L97 L98 L99
reggae L54
rock L23 L40 L49 L54 L59 L74 L77
root L58 L72 L87
saddle L1 L3 L74
sharp L57 L77
shuffle L81 L88

similar shape L11 L12 L13 L23 L88
sixteenth note L36 L37 L38 L39 L54
slash chord L66
slide L12 L75 L86 L95 L96 L99
string bend L77 L80 L82 L83 L85
string set L12 L43 L44 L45 L46 L47
string L2–L15 L17 L23 L24 L27 L28 L31 L34 L35 L41–L49 L51–L55 L57–L65 L68 L69 L72 L73 L74 L76–L83 L85 L88–L93
strumming L4–L7 L10 L11 L14 L18–L34 L36–L40 L45 L47 L49 L50 L54 L55 L59 L87 L88
swing L88
tempo L18 L24 L25 L27 L33 L44 L62 L67–71 L87 L89
time signature L19
tonic L58 L72 L79 L82 L89 L94 L95 L99
tonic shape L72 L79 L82 L89 L94 L95 L99
transpose, transposition L79 L82 L84 L86 L93 L94 L95
treble clef L19
tuner L3
tuning machines L1
turnaround L81 L88
upstroke L53 L60 L61 L78
vibrato L80 L86 L95
whole step L41 L77 L83

Biography

As a composer, performer, and educator, Matthew Von Doran has a passion for using his vast experience to show others how to develop the skills necessary to play music... the music with which they feel most connected. Every day, he looks for the better way to explain the fundamental concepts of music and guitar playing.

With over three decades experience teaching the guitar, he has discovered all of the essential elements involved in laying down a solid foundation for the player. The Guitar Advantage instruction course represents his effective approach to learning these skills in a streamlined, comprehensive manner.

After spending most of his life enjoying a successful music career in Los Angeles, California, Matthew currently calls St. Louis, Missouri his base of operations as he continues to travel the world playing, recording, and teaching music of any and all styles. His mission is to use his unique perspective of music and learning to help people find their own way on the path of musical fulfillment.

Career Highlights:

- Released the acclaimed modern jazz album of original compositions, *In This Present Moment*, featuring Jimmy Haslip, Peter Erskine, Larry Goldings, Bob Sheppard, James Genus, Terri Lyne Carrington, and more
- A world tour with La Quinta Estacion, winner of the 2010 GRAMMY for Best Latin Pop Album
- Over 15 years playing with the Don Miller Big Band, on-set band for television shows *Seinfeld* and *The Nanny*
- Ten years teaching on the faculty at the GRAMMY Foundation's Summer Music Career Camp in Los Angeles, California
- Teaching residencies for the Center of Creative Arts (COCA), the Sheldon Theater, and the Ex'treme Institute in St. Louis, Missouri
- Extensive recording session work for numerous artists in studios around the world